Pedagogical Translation for Language Teaching

Bloomsbury Guidebooks for Language Teachers

This series brings together books that enhance language educators' teaching practice. The books provide practical advice and applications, suitable for use in a range of contexts and for different learning styles, which are evidence-based and research-informed. The series appeals to practitioners looking to develop their skills and practice and is also suitable for use on a variety of language teacher education courses. The books feature a range of topics and themes, from critical pedagogy, to using drama, poetry or literature in the language classroom, to supporting language learners who have anxiety.

Also available in the series:
Teaching English to Young Learners, edited by Janice Bland
Critical Pedagogies for Modern Languages Education, edited by Derek Hird
A Poetry Pedagogy for Teachers, Maya Pindyck, Ruth Vinz, Diana Liu and Ashlynn Wittchow
Using Literature in English Language Education, edited by Janice Bland
Designing World Language Curriculum for Intercultural Communicative Competence, Jennifer Eddy
Performative Language Teaching in Early Education, Joe Winston
Using Theories for Second Language Teaching and Learning, Dale T. Griffee and Greta Gorsuch
Researching Language Learning Motivation, edited by Ali H. Al-Hoorie and Fruzsina Szabó
Language Learner Strategies, Michael James Grenfell and Vee Harris
Compelling Stories for English Language Learners, Janice Bland
Process Drama for Second Language Teaching and Learning, Patrice Baldwin and Alicja Galazka
Psychology-Based Activities for Supporting Anxious Language Learners, Neil Curry and Kate Maher
Teachers as Curriculum Designers for Transcultural Communicative Competence, Jennifer Eddy

Forthcoming in the series:
Teaching Beginner Level English Language Learners, Lesley Painter-Farrell and Gabriel Díaz-Maggioli

Pedagogical Translation for Language Teaching

Literacy-Based Strategies for Emergent Bilingual, Bilingual, and World Language Learners

SARAH ALBRECHT

BLOOMSBURY ACADEMIC
LONDON • NEW YORK • OXFORD • NEW DELHI • SYDNEY

BLOOMSBURY ACADEMIC
Bloomsbury Publishing Plc, 50 Bedford Square, London, WC1B 3DP, UK
Bloomsbury Publishing Inc, 1359 Broadway, New York, NY 10018, USA
Bloomsbury Publishing Ireland, 29 Earlsfort Terrace, Dublin 2, D02 AY28, Ireland

BLOOMSBURY, BLOOMSBURY ACADEMIC and the Diana logo are trademarks of
Bloomsbury Publishing Plc

First published in Great Britain 2026

Copyright © Sarah Albrecht, 2026

Sarah Albrecht has asserted her right under the Copyright, Designs and Patents Act, 1988, to be identified as Author of this work.

Series design: Grace Ridge
Cover image © melita / Alamy Stock Vector

All rights reserved. No part of this publication may be: i) reproduced or transmitted in any form, electronic or mechanical, including photocopying, recording or by means of any information storage or retrieval system without prior permission in writing from the publishers; or ii) used or reproduced in any way for the training, development or operation of artificial intelligence (AI) technologies, including generative AI technologies. The rights holders expressly reserve this publication from the text and data mining exception as per Article 4(3) of the Digital Single Market Directive (EU) 2019/790.

Bloomsbury Publishing Plc does not have any control over, or responsibility for, any third-party websites referred to or in this book. All internet addresses given in this book were correct at the time of going to press. The author and publisher regret any inconvenience caused if addresses have changed or sites have ceased to exist, but can accept no responsibility for any such changes.

A catalogue record for this book is available from the British Library.

A catalog record for this book is available from the Library of Congress.

ISBN: HB: 978-1-3504-1275-0
PB: 978-1-3504-1274-3
ePDF: 978-1-3504-1276-7
eBook: 978-1-3504-1277-4

Series: Bloomsbury Guidebooks for Language Teachers

Typeset by Newgen KnowledgeWorks Pvt. Ltd., Chennai, India
Printed and bound in Great Britain

For product safety related questions contact productsafety@bloomsbury.com.

To find out more about our authors and books visit www.bloomsbury.com and sign up for our newsletters.

CONTENTS

List of Tables vi

Introduction 1

Part I Translation and Literacy

1 Translation in Language Learning Reborn 15
2 Language Learning and Literacy 33
3 Translation and Second Language Acquisition 51
4 Approaches to Pedagogical Translation 63

Part II Translation for Linguistic and Cultural Learning

5 Literacy, Translation, and Linguistic Learning 77
6 Literacy, Translation, and Cultural Learning 93
7 The Potential of Authentic Texts 113
8 Changing Modalities 133

Part III Considerations in Teaching Translation

9 The Benefits of Collaboration 153
10 Literacy Objectives and Measuring Learning 171
11 Considerations for Literacy-Based Language Teacher Preparation 193

Conclusion: Moving Toward Equitable Outcomes in Language Learning 211

References 215
Index 237

TABLES

5.1 Translation Spotlight: Guided Writing Activity 90
6.1 Translation Spotlight: Translation of Proverbs Activity 107
6.2 Translation Spotlight: Translation of an Advertisement 111
7.1 Translation Spotlight: Translation of Bilingual/Dual-Edition Children's Books 129
8.1 Translation Spotlight: Video Subtitling 148
9.1 Translation Spotlight: Family Story Writing 166
10.1 Sample Alignment of Translation Quality Assessment and ACTFL Proficiency Standards, Translation of Proverbs Activity 181
10.2 Sample Differentiated World and Heritage Language Objectives 185
10.3 Rubric: I Can Write a Narrative in My Additional Language 190
11.1 Translation Spotlight: Sample Thematic Unit 207

Introduction

As a novice teacher of Spanish to secondary students in the United States, I approached instruction from a foreign language perspective. Over time, I arrived at the uncomfortable conclusion that my pedagogy was all wrong, as about one-third of my learners were, to some degree, bilingual speakers of Spanish. How could I be teaching these students a "foreign" language when it was not foreign to them? Approaching instruction this way seemed unfair as I was not recognizing or drawing upon these students' linguistic and cultural backgrounds. However, a solution seemed complicated, as the rest of the students in my classes were, in fact, world language learners.

So, I started on a journey to learn how to equitably teach these types of complex groups. Along the way, I met Dr. Sonia Colina at the University of Arizona, and, at her invitation, joined with her on her pedagogical translation grant funded by the Center for Educational Resources in Culture, Language and Literacy (CERCLL). Through the framework of Dr. Colina's grant, I began incorporating pedagogical translation into my secondary courses. I soon recognized it as an extremely versatile pedagogy that could be implemented across language-learning environments.

The journey also led to an additional master's degree in Spanish, followed by a PhD in Language, Reading and Culture, focusing on bilingual and heritage language instruction. I researched pedagogical translation in additional mixed secondary Spanish classes and taught post-secondary Spanish for heritage language learners (HLLs), piloting translation activities and offering professional development on translation to other instructors. Currently, as an assistant professor of bilingual education, I prepare heritage speakers of Spanish to teach in bilingual classrooms and am piloting pedagogical translation activities in my own and other colleagues' courses, working in an overall monolingually oriented environment.

Given this background, I approach this work from an equity-focused, bilingual lens, with the teaching of Spanish in the United States as my background. Throughout the book, I therefore share many examples from this theoretical and practical perspective, although I do my best to point out when other theoretical and practical approaches might be applied and to draw in additional global contexts. However, I acknowledge the diversity of knowledge and experience that readers will employ as they engage with the text, and encourage all to apply their own contexts and experiences in order to develop the adaptations that are most suitable for this flexible, research-based strategy.

As my own experience has shown, in ever-globalizing, diverse educational environments, literacy pedagogies which function across and within languages and cultures are critically important to equitably meet the learning needs of all students. Hence, the main argument of this book is that socially situated literacy should be a primary goal in language-learning environments and pedagogical translation, or the use of translation as a teaching tool for explicit objectives (Floros, 2021), is a specific, achievable, and relevant way of accomplishing this goal. However, pedagogical translation is still generally not included in teacher preparation or development programs (Fois, 2020). This book is therefore designed to offer both theoretical underpinnings and practical guidance for incorporating translation as a pedagogical tool for teaching literacy in language-learning environments. This rationale requires an interdisciplinary unpacking of what the language-learning environments and who the language learners are, what socially situated literacy is and why its acquisition matters, the influence of Translation Studies (TS), and what pedagogical translation looks like. This introduction briefly presents these components and the subsequent structure of the book, which addresses these issues more fully.

Given the previously mentioned interdisciplinarity of pedagogical translation, Pintado-Gutiérrez (2021) points out that it "tends to borrow terminology from other fields in order to establish its theoretical and pragmatic frameworks" (p. 220), as becomes immediately apparent in this introduction and throughout the book. Some terminology, such as *bilingual, multilingual,* and *plurilingual,* indexes approaches which may also connect to historical or political contexts, making it difficult to select and use one term for a broad audience. I have done my best to define and, where needed, provide a rationale for selecting a particular term, but, as Pintado-Gutiérrez (2021) also points out, the goal is not "questioning the *status quo* of terms that are well established" (p. 220, emphasis in original) across multiple fields, but instead to provide consistency in both approach and terminology to the degree possible.

Returning to interdisciplinary unpacking, we start with a consideration of language-learning environments. A language-learning environment may be one in which language is being explicitly taught and/or learned, as opposed to a socially immersive environment in which a second language is implicitly acquired (Krashen, 1981; Lichtman & VanPatten, 2021), although acquisition may be a goal in language classrooms (Lichtman &

VanPatten, 2021). An important consideration is whether the language-learning environment is monolingual or multilingual, as this will affect the linguistic and cultural approach to language teaching, including texts selected for translation. While monolingual classrooms may still be common, according to Wilson and González-Davies (2017), "Increased migration and the economic situation in recent years has made the chances of finding a monolingual community minimal" (p. 208), with multilingual speakers possessing linguistic and cultural multicompetence (Cook, 1992). With this consideration in mind, this book will largely approach language-learning environments as bilingual, although activities and recommendations may always be modified according to context.

While there are many definitions of persons who are considered *bilingual*, this book draws upon Grosjean (1989), who defined bilingual persons as "those people who use more than one language in their everyday lives" (p. 4). This book will follow Grosjean and use *bilingual* to refer to speakers of two or more languages. This book will also follow an expanded conception of language learners and language learning, in general considering language learners as emergent bilinguals (EB) and language learning to be a process of bilingualization (Turnbull, 2018; Widdowson, 2003), particularly in consideration of today's globalizing society and the growing number of bi- or multilingual speakers worldwide.

García and Flores (2013) have chosen to use the term *bilingual* to describe learners who are *plurilingual* in the European Union or *multilingual* in the United States as *bilingual* indexes past and current campaigns in the United States to silence the civil rights struggle. While *plurilingual* admirably indexes the development of additional languages and cultures, García et al. (2020) argued that these are generally dominant and that the experiences, languages and cultures of minoritized peoples tend to be bypassed. Additionally, *multilingual* may reflect a monolingual perspective in which languages are seen to reside next to each other in the speaker's mind rather than as a single linguistic repertoire (García & Flores, 2014). While this book is intended for a global audience with many different linguistic and educational contexts, the minoritization of non-dominant languages and cultures, played out in educational environments, is common among many of them. Hence, the term *bilingual* will be used as the general term to place translation as an equity-focused pedagogy.

Language-learning environments may involve second, world, or heritage language learners, or mixed groups; at primary, secondary, and post-secondary levels. All will be addressed in this book given the versatility of pedagogical translation. Second language learning occurs in cases where the second language is spoken and there is access to speakers of the language outside the classroom, while world language learning occurs where one's native language is spoken (Block, 2003). The term *world* will be used as opposed to *foreign* as foreign languages are often no longer foreign but are living within our local or internet communities (Phipps & González, 2004).

Finally, heritage language learning involves the study of a home language in which learners have some degree of receptive to productive bilingualism which is different from the dominant societal language (Valdés, 2001; Zapata, 2018). García and Flores (2013) point out that bilingual speakers use one unified repertoire from which they select features "that have been socially assigned to different languages" (p. 148). It is with this underlying structure in mind that language will be addressed throughout the book, although it is often necessary to refer to socially identified languages.

Similarly, some scholars advocate for consolidating rather than dichotomizing types of language learning or language learners. For example, Mitchell and Miles (1998) defined second languages as "any languages other than the learner's 'native language' or 'mother tongue'" (as cited in Block, 2003, p. 32) and proposed that foreign or world languages should be included within the umbrella of second languages as "the underlying learning processes are essentially the same for more local and for more remote target languages, despite differing learning purposes and circumstances" (p. 32). Extending this move toward a consolidated approach, terms such as "other," "additional," or "new" (Block, 2003; Cook, 2010) may be used instead of "second," "foreign," or "world" terms which dichotomize languages and which imply "a unitary and singular L1 [first language]" (Block, 2003, p. 56), make assumptions about the learner's prior language experience and subordinate the new language in its "second" place. For these reasons, the use of *additional* or *new* in terms of new language learning will largely be used in this book rather than *second* or *L2*. Similarly, *home language* will largely be used rather than *first* or *L1*. Nevertheless, because unique sociocultural contexts do affect approaches to language teaching, world, second, heritage, and official language-learning environments may at times need to be identified, although some direct quotations make use of varying terminology. Hartmann and Hélot (2020) cited literature across language-learning fields to generalize that pedagogical translation "plays an essential role in additional language learning and teaching" (p. 95). This broader approach is useful as translation is applied to the process of any additional language learning.

Regarding differentiation of terms used to describe language learners, García (2009) proposed applying the term EB to students in the United States who speak languages other than English in order to recognize their bilingualism and to create asset rather than deficit based–learning environments and policies as reflected in terms such as *English language learners*. This term has since become widely accepted and used. Subsequently, Turnbull (2018) advocated for expanding EB to "any person who is actively in the process of acquiring knowledge of a second language and developing bilingual languaging skills for use in a given situation relevant to their individual needs to learn the target language" (p. 1043), thereby including world or foreign language learners and recognizing language learning as a process of bilingualization rather than the acquisition of two (or more) monolingual entities. Regarding primary-grade language instruction, García (2009) definitively stated that bilingual education is the *only way* to educate children in the 21st century (p. 5, emphasis in original) and asserted that in today's world, "monolingual schooling seems utterly inappropriate" (p. 16).

Beyond the language teaching approach, language may be learned for a variety of personal and social reasons. Language learning is often considered utilitarian, based upon skill acquisition (Phipps & González, 2004). While pedagogical translation might be used in language for specific purposes, courses or programs, the focus of this book is on language instruction more generally. For example, utilitarian views would posit that recently arrived second language learners benefit academically from learning the dominant language and that world language learners benefit in the workplace or in travel abroad if they can speak more than one language. Similarly, schools benefit if recently arrived students score well on standardized tests and workplaces benefit from multilingual workers.

However, language learning can also be a social justice issue, as utilitarian approaches are not necessarily aligned with the reality of social interactions. According to Phipps and González (2004), "the 'other' is no longer 'out there' in the colonies and in 'exotic' far-flung places" (p. 18); crucially, interaction with texts from or members of other cultural groups or speakers of other languages can happen within one's home community, and as this happens, a sense of community belonging among groups can increase. Language learning therefore becomes *languaging,* or becoming part of a new "network of relations" by "engaging with another language and the life of the people who live it and use it" (Phipps & González, 2004, p. 93), with the goal of human connection and meaning making which exceeds utilitarian purposes (Halliday, 1978). García and Flores (2013) argued that for bilinguals, the goal of *languaging* is not enough; instead, they must have the opportunity to *translanguage,* using their entire linguistic repertoires in order to "respond to the different cultural contexts and social backgrounds that shape their language practices" (p. 153). While utilitarian goals clearly cannot be ignored, it is toward the larger goals of languaging and translanguaging that this book is addressed. Indeed, as Pym (2018) noted, encouraging successful movement between languages by language learners demonstrates "a sophisticated, humanist understanding of what language learning is all about" (p. 213).

The "network of relations" brings up the critical question of who the language learners are in our classrooms. Language teaching may initially be perceived as taking place in a world language classroom in which students learn another language for business or travel. However, given the fact of global migration, many language learners are learning an additional language in order to be able to function in a new linguistic and cultural environment. For example, migrant students in Germany study German for half of a school day for one year before being placed in mainstream classes so that they can "catch up" with their German-speaking peers (Marx et al., 2021).

Teachers are often untrained, and students are often exited early due to lack of institutional support. Similarly, in the United States, immigrant students often receive inadequate language support before being mainstreamed, again in an often unsuccessful effort to help them catch up academically (Sikes & Villanueva, 2021). Additionally, some children of immigrants or heritage language learners may study their home language—which is not the dominant language in society—in order to connect with family and their culture (García, 2009). Many language learners, then, end up in mainstream, content-area classes, or in "foreign" language classes to learn their home language, where bilingual teaching strategies like pedagogical translation will be critical for equitable instruction.

Although pedagogical translation can be used between any languages, the role of English language learning in counterpoint to other world languages cannot be ignored (Phipps & González, 2004). Globally, English is the most-studied second language, and other languages are typically translated into English, demonstrating its social, economic, and linguistic capital, and cycling back to a utilitarian focus on performativity (Lee, 2013; wa Thiong'o, 2023). Addressing the potential for perpetuating power imbalance through translation, Baker (2018b) cautions that "Far from a disinterested practice that merely 'transfers' different types of knowledge between cultural groupings with equal power and resources ... translation creates traditions and narratives that actively shape the world for us" (n.p.). Indeed, it is between dominant languages and cultures that translation may be typified by two-way flow, while one-way translation into English represents movement from the marginalized to the dominant language. This in turn may lead toward abandonment of the home language (wa Thiong'o, 2023) or perception of the non-dominant language as sub-par and worthy only of "an orality insufficiently refined to bear the weight of communal representation" (Phipps & González, 2004, p. 16).

On the other hand, drawing from TS, translation from English to other languages or translation between languages other than English serves as a form of resistance and as a means of socially empowering other languages (Lee, 2013; wa Thiong'o, 2023; Tymoczko, 2007). Translation may thereby extend beyond utilitarianism to human connection, serving as a mediator between "monolithic cultural and linguistic blocks" (Cook, 2010, p. 78), a dissolver of borders (Phipps & González, 2004) and as "the common language of languages" (wa Thiong'o, 2023, p. 11). As wa Thiong'o (2023) noted, "In translation, there are no indigenous, vernacular, native, local, ethnic and tribal literatures, while English and French produce world and global literature. There are only languages and literatures" (p. 94). From this perspective, translation is "a highly complex activity that requires both reflexivity and criticality toward the languages in play, the power in play, the cultures in contact" (Phipps & González, 2004, p. 161). Translation is here referred to in non-educational environments. However, the potential of translation for facilitating equal cultural and linguistic exchange, and therefore for cultivating and developing a biliteracy capable of bearing the weight of communal representation, extends to pedagogical translation (Cook, 2010; Manyak, 2004; Pacheco et al., 2015).

Through this development of biliteracy for communal representation, we circle around to socially situated, literacy-based language teaching. This view of literacy departs from the autonomous view of literacy, which is skills-based, focusing on the ability to read and write and in which texts are interpreted as autonomous units outside of social contexts (Kramsch, 2008; Street, 1984). Instead, socially situated literacy is based upon the ideological view of literacy. Through the ideological view of literacy, the literacy skills of reading and writing are socially contextualized, culturally embedded, and connected to political and institutional power, thereby affecting participant meaning making (Street, 1984). Texts, within these social contexts, become Discourse, or the link between language, who people are in a given social situation and what they are doing in that situation (Gee, 2012). Following the ideological perspective, this book defines literacy as "engaging in the ever-developing process of using reading and writing as tools for thinking and learning in order to expand one's understanding of oneself and the world" (Kern, 2000, p.40), with this literacy as a process rather than an end product.

However, with the incorporation of literacy-based language teaching, care must be taken to make sure that text-centered talk, particularly around literature, be student- rather than instructor-centered (Warner & Dupuy, 2018). These dual components of literacy connect to Freire's assertion that reading the word and the world are inseparable (Freire, 1970; Gee, 2012). In a socially situated, literacy-based approach to language teaching, then, learners are prepared through use of texts to be multilingually, multiculturally, and multi-textually competent (Kern, 2000). Professionally, written translation and oral interpretation are considered separate modalities, but within pedagogical translation both are encompassed within linguistic mediation (Gasca Jiménez, 2022). For the purpose of this volume, then, texts may be oral or written, with literacy involving an understanding of the connection between oral and written language, as well as of the contexts of language use (Gee, 2012). Similarly, this book follows Colina and Lafford (2017) in including oral interpretation within the broader definition of translation of texts. Additionally, in today's digital world, multimodal and/or multimedia texts are often the gateway for second language learners' exposure to new language or culture and will also be considered in the selection of texts for translation (Warner & Dupuy, 2018).

Within the umbrella of socially situated literacy, the concepts of biliteracy and multiliteracies must also be considered. Viewing additional language learning as a process of bilingualization leads to a similar perspective that additional language learning is a process of becoming biliterate. Theoretically, biliteracy appears in the overlap between literacy and bilingualism, as biliteracy has to do with reading and/or writing in two languages (Hornberger, 1989). Edwards (2015) expanded this definition to include the social component of "cultural knowledge to interpret texts; a sensitivity to how, when, where, why and with whom a written language should be used; and the ability to communicate across a range of contexts, both socially and academically, in two or more languages" (p. 77). According to Escamilla et al. (2009), acquisition of literacy in a second language may be viewed as "a single trajectory to biliteracy, rather than ... as two separate and distinct processes" (p. 144). Biliteracy is key particularly to home language maintenance and development in second language environments.

The pedagogy of multiliteracies was conceived when the New London Group met in 1994 to discuss needed changes in literacy pedagogy to reflect the skills students would need in a globalizing society. As part of the rationale for their pedagogy of multiliteracies, the New London Group reflected on the changed nature of language learning in diverse, globalizing societies: "When the proximity of cultural and linguistic diversity is one of the key facts of our time, the very nature of language learning has changed" (New London Group, 1996, p. 64), with global need being reflected in local practices. As a result, the underpinnings of literacy pedagogy must change to provide students with the abilities they need to function in this culturally and linguistically diverse world. In language-learning environments, literacy-based pedagogy entails a shift in focus from communication to meaning (Warner & Dupuy, 2018). A multiliteracies approach, therefore, deals with textual multiplicity, with texts being visual, aural, spatial, and behavioral, or, in other words, multimodal, and assumes the active participation of literacy educators and their students in social change. According to Kern (2000), pedagogical translation fits neatly within a multiliteracies approach to literacy-based language teaching.

Translation can range from the natural translation that occurs within contexts of language use to professional, product-oriented translation, and to translation used within educational contexts (Block, 2003; Cook, 2010; Welch, 2015). Within educational contexts, translation may be used in multiple ways. First, it is a natural language–learning strategy often used covertly by learners regardless of its frequent prohibition in the classroom (González-Davies, 2017). Instructors may use it concurrently, to clarify meaning for second language learners; however, concurrent translation tends to be discouraged as students may tune out of the second language and focus only on what is already understandable (Escamilla et al., 2009). It has been used for language teaching in the past, under the grammar translation method, which has largely been discredited yet lingers on as a conflation of classroom translation: If translation is used in the classroom, then it must be grammar translation; therefore, translation in the classroom must be avoided (Cook, 2010).

However, pedagogical translation is none of the above. Instead, pedagogical translation, also referred to as translation for other learning contexts (TOLC) (González-Davies & Soler Ortínez, 2021) and translation in language teaching (TILT) (Cook, 2010), entails the goal of transferring meaning or cross-linguistic mediation used to teach and learn languages through negotiating language, culture, and register (Council of Europe, 2020; Gasca Jiménez, 2022; Laviosa, 2022; McLaughlin et al., 2022). This broad perspective encompasses oral communication or interpretation (Colina & Lafford, 2017). Considered from a sociocultural theory (SCT) lens, "human activities take place in cultural contexts and are mediated by language and other symbol systems" (Huong, 2003, p. 33; Vygotsky, 1978). In fact, "individuals have no choice but to create or construct meanings and knowledge through participation in ... interpersonal, intersubjective interaction" (Kiraly, 2000, p. 4). These contexts often include geographical areas of languages in contact (Gasca-Jiménez, 2022). Because translation, and in our case pedagogical translation, involves human activity in two languages, mediation is a key underlying concept. According to the Common European Framework of Reference for Languages: Learning, Teaching, Assessment (CEFR) (Council of Europe, 2020), mediation "make(s) communication possible between persons who are unable, for whatever reason, to communicate directly" (p. 34) through oral or written means, in this case, translation.

Laviosa (2022) noted a shift from "translation *for* language teaching toward the emerging view of translation *in* language teaching" (p. 20, emphasis in original), or translation based more upon interpretation of texts. The distinction seems to focus on a differentiation between content in language learning and context of language use. Considering pedagogical translation as bilingual teaching provides a context. Cook (2010), for example, argued that bilingual teaching and translation "cannot be considered separately" (p. xix) as translation "is part of everyday bilingual language use ... needed by all learners" (p. xx) and can improve both bilingual and monolingual communication, while Escamilla et al. (2009) argued for the need to create space for "students to be deliberately and strategically bilingual" (p. 153). Conceptualizing the context of language learning as bilingual rather than monolingual, therefore, clarifies the move toward translation *in* language teaching.

Pedagogical translation might be interlingual or between languages, or intralingual or within variants of a single language (Floros, 2021). Because pedagogical translation is a tool for teaching additional languages, interlingual translation is generally assumed as the approach. However, intralingual translation might be considered for certain purposes. In mixed monolingual–bi/multilingual learning environments, translation could be differentiated, with bilingual students translating interlingually and monolingual students translating intralingually. Mixed classrooms should be assumed to be the rule rather than the exception in today's world characterized by migration and globalization (Floros, 2021), highlighting the need for pedagogical strategies like translation which can accommodate all learners (González-Davies, 2017). Intralingual translation could also be used in a second or world language class to familiarize students with dialects.

Some distinction has been made between the focus of pedagogical translation versus professional translation, with the former focused on translation as a means toward language learning and the latter focused on translation for the production of a professional end product. While pedagogical translation is used incontrovertibly as a language-learning tool, arguments have been made for its use as an end in itself as well. For example, the CEFR (Council of Europe, 2020) presents translation as a mediation skill to be acquired in language learning and used in "informal, everyday situations" (p. 107). González-Davies and Soler Ortínez (2021) noted the need for translation as an end in itself because "Rather than relying on intuition and goodwill to succeed in managing the languages and cultures that now coexist on an everyday basis, specific skills are deemed necessary to prepare competent plurilingual speakers" (p. 434), namely, mediation skills such as translation. Similarly, Colina and Lafford (2017) argued that pedagogical translation should be incorporated as a "fifth skill" in language teaching along with listening, speaking, reading, and writing.

Although translation and multimodality are considered in Chapter 8, for the purpose of this book translation activity will involve some form of movement between written and/or oral texts, including those with differing written sign systems. Intersemiotic translation that involves movement between language and sign systems other than written, such as sign language or other visual modes, is beyond the scope of this book, with the exception of the inclusion of multiple modes in otherwise language-based translation activities.

As an explicit strategy, pedagogical translation will involve the development of language and/or content objectives which a translation activity will serve to meet. When developing translation activities to meet specific objectives, it might be helpful to keep in mind that pedagogical translation can make implicit language processes explicit and provide students with a top-down or inductive opportunity to explore a new language, requiring critical thinking (Pavan, 2013). The development of aligned objectives and translation activities will be further addressed in Chapter 10.

This book consists of three parts. The first is primarily theoretical, focusing on translation and literacy, with Chapter 1 outlining the historical trajectory of translation in language learning, Chapter 2 expanding upon the theoretical frameworks of literacy as a social practice used in this book and connecting them to language learning and Chapter 3 exploring and connecting relevant theoretical frameworks from TS and second language acquisition (SLA). Chapter 4 addresses different approaches to pedagogical translation. The second part combines theory and practice, expanding conceptions of literacy and translation to linguistic (Chapter 5) and cultural learning (Chapter 6) and applying them to authentic (Chapter 7) and multimodal texts (Chapter 8). This part also includes sample literacy-based translation activities called Translation Spotlights at the end of each chapter which can be modified by grade and objective. While pedagogical translation has been supported by the literature for several decades, its implementation has lagged (Linares, 2022). The last part of the book, therefore, focuses on considerations in teaching, including the benefits of collaborative structures (Chapter 9), the creation and evaluation of translation-based literacy objectives and assessments (Chapter 10); and teacher preparation (Chapter 11). This part also includes sample literacy-based translation activities at the end of each chapter. It is anticipated that primary and secondary pre- and in-service language teachers and language program directors, bilingual and world language teacher preparation programs, after-school home language programs, and post-secondary world language programs may all benefit from the literacy-based pedagogical translation strategies presented in this book.

Part I: Translation and Literacy

1

Translation in Language Learning Reborn

This chapter explores the evolution of translation in language teaching throughout the twentieth and into the twenty-first century and justifies its pedagogical use. Through the latter half of the twentieth century, translation was shunned in language teaching due to the fall from favor of the Grammar Translation Method. It was replaced by the Direct Method, which focuses on communicative competence in various iterations (Cook, 2010). These iterations have tended to focus on oral language use and staying in the second language, denying the value of home language use as a language-learning tool (Cook, 2001). However, with the turn of the twenty-first century, the field of SLA began a multilingual turn, reopening the way for use of the first language in SLA and hence the use of translation as a pedagogical tool. Although this path is well established (Kramsch, 2012; May, 2013, 2019; Ortega, 2013), barriers remain to the implementation of pedagogical translation, including societal, institutional, and personal monolingual language ideologies (Cook, 2001; Conteh & Meier, 2014), standard language ideology, and disciplinary silos (Colina, 2002), which will all be addressed. The chapter ends with an examination of how language ideologies affect classroom use of translation (Woolard & Schieffelin, 1994; Kroskrity, 2004, 2015), together with recent literature on the impact and implementation of pedagogical translation in the language classroom.

The Evolution of Translation in Language Teaching

Grammar Translation

Grammar Translation began developing in Europe in the late eighteenth century and coalesced as a method by the mid-nineteenth century, becoming the primary method of foreign language teaching in European schools for the next one hundred years (Richards & Rodgers, 2001). Developed for secondary students in Prussia as a means of simplifying more complex language-teaching methods designed for adults, it was later "grossly distorted in the collision of interests between the classicists and their modern language rivals" (Howatt & Widdowson, 2004, p. 156). Initially, Grammar Translation lessons included 1–2 grammar rules, some vocabulary and some lessons to translate. Richards and Rodgers (2001) outline seven major characteristics of Grammar Translation, as follows:

1. The primary purpose of foreign language study is to prepare students to read literature in the second language and to foster intellectual development.
2. Reading and writing are the main focus, while speaking is used for repetition of translated sentences rather than communication.
3. Vocabulary is selected based upon the texts being used and is taught through memorizing word lists.
4. Discrete grammar rules are taught at the sentence level.
5. Accurate reproduction is a primary focus of teaching and evaluation.
6. Grammar is the focus and is taught deductively and sequentially.
7. The students' first language is used to explain new material in the second language (additional language) and for comparison between the two.

These characteristics eventually morphed into "a jungle of obscure rules, endless lists of gender classes and gender-class exceptions, self-conscious 'literary' archaisms, snippets of philology, and a total loss of genuine feeling for living language" (Howatt & Widdowson, 2004, p. 156).

On the heels of these excesses, Grammar Translation largely fell from favor in language teaching by the mid-twentieth century, and the focus of language teaching and learning shifted. This shift set the stage for the fields of SLA and TS to develop during the second half of the twentieth century as separate fields which did not draw upon each other. Both concluded without empirical evidence that translation was not communicative and therefore not beneficial for SLA, and that while language learning was needed in translator training, the way translators learned language should be different than other language learning (Cook, 2010; Pym, 2018). Meanwhile, the Communicative Approach, a variation of the Direct Method discussed in what follows, became the most popular language teaching method across ten countries, and Grammar Translation, the least (Pym & Ayvazyan, 2013). However, Grammar Translation is still used, including when reading literature is the primary purpose of language study or in conjunction with other methods (Richards & Rodgers, 2001; Cook, 2010) and in combination with other methodologies on popular language-learning sites such as Duolingo (How Does Duolingo work? n.d.). In sum, Grammar Translation "has stood the test of time and proved to be remarkably resilient to the innovations that have been introduced in language teaching" (Richards & Rodgers, 2001, p. 6), continuing to be supported in practice although unsupported empirically.

The Direct Method

Despite the tenacity of Grammar Translation, it was largely replaced by the mid-twentieth century by various iterations of the Direct Method. The Direct Method appeared on the opposite side of the translation spectrum as a language teaching approach when emphasis on the purpose of language learning changed from additional language literacy to communication. Direct Method iterations are therefore communicative and include approaches such as audiolingualism (in the United States) and situational teaching (in Great Britain), total physical response (TPR), and task-based and communicative language instruction (CLI) (Cook, 2010). Of key importance for considering the use of translation in language teaching, the Direct Method moved away from Grammar Translation's cross-language teaching that focused on grammatical form and permitted both home and additional language use to intralingual teaching with a focus on meaning through communication, excluding students' home language and permitting only additional language use (Cook, 2010). It therefore largely eschewed the seven previously mentioned components of Grammar Translation as well as translation itself, moving from a focus on reading and writing in Grammar Translation to communicative approaches.

The Direct Method rests on four pillars: monolingualism, naturalism, native-speakerism, and absolutism (Cook, 2010). The first, monolingualism, supports the belief that most language users are monolingual or speakers who know one language and speak in monolingual environments and that second or additional languages are learned the same way as the first language (González-Davies, 2017; Skutnabb-Kangas, 1988). Additionally, the home language may permanently interfere with additional language learning, so it must be excluded. Skutnabb-Kangas (1988) pointed out that very few nations, like Iceland, are truly monolingual and that monolingualism is "not so much a linguistic phenomenon (even though it has to do with language). It is rather a question of a psychological state, backed up by political power" (p. 13) or an ideology. The Direct Method pillar of monolingualism has therefore rested on ideology.

Based upon these monolingual assumptions, Direct Method language teaching prepares the learner to function and teachers to teach in a monolingual environment (Cook, 2010). Naturalism is based upon the supposition that classrooms can replicate the process of acquiring language in an immersion environment and replicate monolingual first language acquisition. According to the third pillar of the Direct Method, native speakers are the ideal model for additional language learners, and therefore native speakers are the best teachers. However, among other issues, it is unclear how *native speaker* is to be defined, particularly when speakers may have more than one language learned during childhood, either simultaneously or sequentially; when speakers may experience loss of the first language learned; and when it is difficult to determine at what point "native-like" speech can no longer be acquired (Cook, 2010; Escamilla et al., 2014). Finally, the fourth pillar, absolutism, supports the belief that the Direct Method is the one, absolute way to language learning success. According to Cook (2010), "The notions that monolingual instruction is better and more natural than bilingual instruction, that inductive learning is better than deductive teaching, and that the adult learner should follow the path of the native-speaker infant, ran through the communicative language teaching revolution of the 1970s, and continue in many of the supposedly cutting-edge movements of the 2000s" (p. 18).

However, these foci of the Direct Method have been criticized for various reasons. Cook (2010) maintained that the pillars themselves are more indicative of commercial claims of unequivocal product superiority, evident in the development and marketing of language curricula, rather than by questioning through empirical study. García's (2014) identification of commercial interests in promoting certain varieties of Spanish seems to support Cook's claim. González-Davies (2014) identifies the need for "linguistically prepared citizens, preferably with good mediation skills such as translation, interpreting, [and] intercultural competence" (p. 3), while Phipps and González (2004) point to the limiting factors of a hyperfocus on speech in communicative language teaching as detrimental to cultural learning, metalinguistic awareness, and literacy acquisition, all of which are much more difficult to address in an environment which forbids home language use.

Time to Turn

The Direct Method pillars of monolingualism, naturalism, native-speakerism, and absolutism coincide with the traditional SLA perspective of SLA as multiple monolingualisms (Gurney & Demuro, 2022) and cognitive processes devoid of social context. However, around the turn of the twenty-first century, some scholars began arguing against this approach and for multilingual and social turns in SLA. A vanguard of German translation and linguistics scholars began debating about a return to translation in language teaching during the 1970s–1980s (see Pym, 2018, for a summary), and calls in its favor were picked up by additional scholars in education and applied linguistics (see e.g., Widdowson, 1978; Howatt, 1984; and, for continuing calls from Spain, de Arriba Gracia, 1996; Hernández, 1998). However these initial calls were neither recognized nor acted upon until the multilingual and social turns in SLA (Cook, 2010). The following sections focus on these turns and their effects on the re-entry of translation into language teaching.

The Multilingual Turn

Despite the fact that most of the world's 200-plus nations are officially monolingual, the number of languages is in the thousands, pointing to the de facto number of multilingual speakers in the world (Skutnabb-Kangas, 1988). Multilingualism, defined as the "ability to use several linguistic systems in everyday life and to draw on several cultural contexts of experience in order to put forth several identities" (Kramsch, 2012, p. 116), is central to the language experience of most people. This ability is often born of necessity when individuals speak a home language which has no official rights, and it speaks to a power imbalance between the group of speakers required to learn additional languages and the dominant societal language. While linguistically all languages could share equal rights, politically and culturally this is generally not the case (Skutnabb-Kangas, 1988). As wa Thiong'o (2023) noted, "There is beauty, power, and glory in many languages, but monolingualism has blinded nations into having a mono-view of reality" (43).

This mono-view of reality has translated into SLA theory and classroom practice. From its inception in the 1950s, the field of SLA has had a monolingual bias rather than recognition of the multilingual reality of the majority of the world's population or of bilingual first language acquisition (Block, 2003; Ortega, 2013). This bias assumes that monolingualism is the launching place from which additional language acquisition occurs as well as that additional languages reside in compartmentalized spaces in the brain, rather than as a unitary system. The multilingual turn in the field of SLA arose as a response to this monolingual bias (Ortega, 2013) and the "monolingual habitus" (Goltsev et al., 2022, p. 438) of Direct Method teaching in which monolingualism is made to appear as the normal or natural state of affairs. With the availability of varying linguistic systems and cultural contexts, the focus in the multilingual turn therefore shifted from individual, acontextual cognitive development and native-speaker authority to the potential for varying language structures appearing at varying times

(Kramsch, 2012). Scholars in TS have also advocated for a plurilingual rather than monolingual approach in language learning, challenging the basic assumptions of the Direct Method and highlighting the multilingual character of translators and translation (see e.g., González-Davies, 2017; Pym, 2010, 2023).

This shift also facilitates a shift in traditional power weighting favoring the dominant societal language (Hornberger & Skilton-Sylvester, 2000). In doing so, the multilingual turn reverses deficit perspectives of multilinguals which have arisen from the traditional SLA goal of speaking the second language like a native speaker or native-speakerism (Goltsev et al, 2022; Ortega, 2013). Instead, the multilingual turn "aims at a positive perception of linguistic diversity as a resource and its productive use" (Goltsev et al., 2022, p. 138). This positive perception of linguistic diversity can be linked to approaching all language teaching as bilingualization and a recognition that students will be relying on their home language as they learn an additional language (Gasca Jiménez, 2022; Turnbull, 2018; Widdowson, 2003). A multilingual perspective therefore recognizes students' bilingual or multilingual identities, including experiences of migration and oppression (Ortega, 2013).

From a bilingual education perspective, translanguaging similarly positions language as a process, rather than a product limited by institutional or political moves and recognizes learners' bilingual or multilingual identities and practices (García et al., 2017; Gasca Jiménez, 2022; Gurney & Demuro, 2022). As the fluid use of all languages in a speaker's repertoire, translanguaging challenges linguistic boundaries (García, 2009). MacSwan (2017) defines a repertoire as "a catalog of the ways we each can talk in different social contexts" (p. 188), including the small component of grammar, a key distinction which becomes relevant particularly in designing translation objectives, activities, and assessments which work toward bilingualization. In examining the role of translanguaging within the multilingual turn, Sembiante (2016) notes, "As a social and political act, translanguaging has the potential to be transformative for bi/multilinguals because it destabilizes language hierarchies by expanding and extending norm-driven practices that eventually create spaces for more hybrid language use in otherwise monolingual education systems" (pp. 54–55). Through a translanguaging stance, the instructor creates space for students to utilize their full linguistic resources, with language functioning as a continuum rather than as a distinct monolingual entity.

In the field of English as a Second Language (ESL), Liu and Fang (2022) have also examined the role of translanguaging as part of the multilingual turn. Referring to May (2013, 2019), they proposed that "English learning should be approached from a more flexible and multilingual perspective, as teachers should incorporate bilingual or multilingual education into their classroom to embrace a multilingual turn" (p. 396). To do so, both teachers and students need to recognize the importance of home language use in language teaching, which cycles back to the importance of resistance to monolingual bias and the need for acceptance of home language use and bilingual teaching strategies in order for translation as a pedagogy to be more fully established.

Challenges to a full multilingual turn remain. Reflecting on the progress of the multilingual turn, May (2019) notes a dichotomy in the multilingual turn between monolingual bias, focusing on "elite language learners and sequential language learning" and "a related reluctance to address seriously the normalcy of multilingual language use" (p. 123). Continued monolingualism in SLA has been attributed to social norms, political nationalism and "public monolingualism" (p. 122) as the norm in the modern nation state. According to Ortega (2013), monolingual bias and rejection of multilingual repertoires equate with rejection of the language and culture of the speakers. Through a raciolinguistic lens, it is sociolinguistic inequity, rather than language itself that determines whether or not multilingual practices are supported (Ortega, 2013). Also addressing sociolinguistic inequity, Mendoza (2020) posits that the struggle is due to the hegemony of the global north and the emergence of "turns" to reflect change in these social and cultural contexts rather than historical and actual global realities. Whatever the case, "suppression of home languages, at best, is internalized due to the persistent belief that 'forgetting' one's mother tongue and speaking the dominant language is the only way to achieve economic and social success. At worst, it is a manifestation of contemporary colonialism. In all cases, it is a form of discrimination" (Hurwitz & Kambel, 2020, p. 6).

Monolingual ideologies have persisted across global contexts. Voevoda (2020), for example, chronicled the minoritization of ethnic and migrant languages across Europe and into Siberia, as reflected by standardized testing in dominant languages and by economic opportunities. Lin (2015) noted the lasting prevalence of monolingual immersion ideologies in Asia. Within Lin's context, this included government and official policies. Lin posited that these monolingual immersion approaches have been difficult to dislodge in part due to the persistent view of multilingualism as parallel monolingualisms, resulting in official discourses that "have hampered the conceptualization, research and exploration of innovative pedagogical methods to enhance students' bilingual and multilingual development" (Lin, 2015, p. 76).

Similarly, in many primary and secondary dual-language programs in the United States, institutional policies continue to require strict separation of languages, causing teachers to go "underground" in order to be able to capitalize on students' bilingual strategies through translanguaging (Babino & Stewart, 2018). In the author's own bilingual teaching methods courses, after observing policies of strict language separation in primary schools, pre-service teachers have commented that the only way they anticipate being able to use translanguaging would be through specialized "charter" schools. These schools have greater autonomy than traditional public schools, illustrating the influence of institutions and the state on language practice and the need for policy change, institutional change, and critically conscious teachers who have developed a clear multilingual stance (García, 2014; Sikes & Villanueva, 2021).

The Social Turn

As the field of SLA developed through the 1950s–1960s, it moved from a focus on linguistic knowledge to the input–interaction–output (IIO) model (Block, 2003), which harkens to Krashen's (1981) input hypothesis and is largely centered on exchanging information. However, it was not until around the turn of the twenty-first century that Firth and Wagner (1997) and Block (2003) led the call for a social turn, arguing that cognitive models of language acquisition in SLA were missing an essential social component:

> Language is not just linguistic competence or linguistic competence + conversation skills put to use to exchange information ... What is needed is ... a move to the view that (1) language is about social problems and language use in addition to the formal features of language; (2) its study is based on data collected from existing speech communities; and (3) any discussion of it either begins with or highlights social functions before moving to explore how formal features are organized to serve them. (Block, 2003, p. 89)

In other words, the field of SLA needed to focus on how social contexts such as identity and culture influence language use beyond information exchange. During this same time period, when the CEFR (Council of Europe, 2001) was first published, in addition to listing reception, production, and interaction as language activities which contribute to communicative competence, mediation was included, with proficiency descriptors first being added in the revised 2018 edition (Council of Europe, 2018). Mediation functions in tandem with reception, production, and interaction and involves "co-construction of meaning in interaction and constant movement between the individual and social level in language learning" (Council of Europe, 2020, p. 36), thereby linking to social contexts. However, challenges to the social turn have also remained and will be addressed in the following section.

Barriers to Pedagogical Translation

Despite movement away from monolingual teaching norms through the multilingual and social turns, multiple barriers remain to established, widespread implementation of pedagogical translation. These barriers include language ideologies, which link talk and social structures (Woolard & Schieffelin, 1994). Ideologies in general "serve particular interests which they tend to present as universal interests" (Bourdieu, 1991, p. 167). Language ideologies in specific are "beliefs, or feelings, about languages as used in their social worlds" (Kroskrity, 2004, p. 498) and are linked to political and economic power and cultural identity (Lee, 2013). The issues of power tied to language ideologies appear as asymmetrical power relations which can be justified through beliefs about language by the dominant culture in society wishing to preserve dominant norms (Lee, 2013). Gee (2012) characterizes language ideologies as theories, with linguists formulating overt or explicit theories describing what speakers actually do with language, and speakers formulating tacit or implicit theories that prescribe what is okay to do with language and which may be used to justify power imbalances.

For a linguist, then, bad language would consist of language that does not fit speakers' language rules or patterns, while to a casual speaker bad language might be deemed as falling short of well-educated speech (Gee, 2012). For example, although Spanglish is characterized by translanguaging between Spanish and English and using calques and borrowings from English in Spanish, linguists consider it to be linguistically viable as it follows typical grammatical rules and patterns between the two languages (Lipski, 2008). Despite the fact that it is spoken by more than 50 million speakers in the United States, monolingual speakers of Spanish often judge Spanglish as "bad Spanish" when normed with what is considered "good" monolingual Spanish. This dichotomy is illustrative of the power imbalance between monolingual, standard Spanish, and Spanglish, which is typical of a language contact environment and of dynamic bilingualism which draws upon speakers' full linguistic repertoires (García, 2009; Lipski, 2008). It is also illustrative of the power imbalance in the United States between monolingual English ideologies and other languages, including monolingual Spanish and Spanglish. Although language ideologies appear in a variety of forms, monolingual and standard language ideologies will be addressed here due to their prevalence in educational language-learning environments.

Monolingual Language Ideology

Monolingual language ideology can appear at societal, institutional, and individual levels (Cook, 2010). Part of the move toward nation states in the nineteenth century included a move toward single national languages as a manifestation of nationalism (Cook, 2010; Gurney & Demuro, 2022). Current examples of monolingual repression of other societal languages abound. Speaking to what he considers the dictatorship of monolingualism in regard to African languages, wa Thiong'o (2023) observed, "One of the things which often stands in the way of adequate policies for African languages is the false logic of monolingualism and particularly the notion of one national language which has to swallow up all the others. A variation of this is the assumption that only the languages of the big ethnic groups can become regional and national" (p. 29). Importantly, he highlighted the ideological perspective that one national language must subsume the others, and that only languages of large groups are considered important.

Economics also provides impetus toward societal monolingualism. According to García (2014), "To be a global language, a language not only has to be spoken by many, but it must have economic, political, and cultural power" (p. 71). Castilian Spanish, for example, serves as a form of economic and social capital for Spain, with its export positioning Spain as the global authority and producing economic benefits (García, 2014). Similarly, for many, British English is still at the epicenter of Kachru's (1992) inner circle of Englishes and is marketed as such internationally, with speakers of British English positioned as native-speaking experts best positioned to purvey the product and publishers positioned to benefit from sale of monolingual English as a Foreign Language (EFL) teaching materials (Carreres, 2014; Widdowson, 2003). Monolingual language ideologies at the societal level, then, represent cultural, social, and economic capital which in turn represent underlying dominant power structures.

Institutional monolingual ideologies tend to be linked to social monolingual ideologies. These ideologies may appear in multiple institutional environments, such as medical and legal, but the focus here will be on education. Language education policy (LEP) refers to the creation of educational policy which links societal language ideologies visible in national language policies to practice in schools (Shohamy, 2006). Societal monolingual ideologies thus appear in the structure of language teaching as LEPs. According to Shohamy (2006), an LEP is

> a powerful tool as it can create and impose language behavior in a system which it is compulsory for all children to participate in. It can further determine criteria for language correctness, oblige people to adopt certain ways of speaking and writing, create definitions about language and especially determine the priority of certain languages in society and how these languages should be learned, taught and used. (p. 77)

These policies may reflect monolingual language ideology as representing a single language of the nation state and, in the current globalizing world, may be at odds with the needs of multilingual, multicultural learners (García, 2014; Shohamy, 2006).

Returning to the concept of power in language ideologies, repression of non-dominant languages and language speakers is part of the role of language in nationalism and appears in language education policies in schools (García, 2014). Spanish in the United States will be used as an example. Some states, such as Arizona, California, and Massachusetts, have banned bilingual education, although some of these laws have been overturned in recent years (Pacheco et al., 2015). In primary schools, when programs for bilingual or EB students exist, these focus primarily on using the students' home language to support English acquisition. This limited use of home language support is generally removed in third grade in time to focus on English acquisition for high-stakes testing linked to federal funding (Babino & Stewart, 2018; García et al., 2017; Sikes & Villanueva, 2021). This process values the dominant societal language rather than giving learners space to master both languages and does not acknowledge years of research showing the long-term benefits to learners who are able to use their home language in school (Beaudrie et al., 2014; García, 2009).

In the US state of Texas, a state with over 1 million emergent bilingual students in public schools (Sikes & Villanueva, 2021), schools are required to provide bilingual education when the population of speakers of a different home language at any given grade level is above twenty. However, due to endemic bilingual teacher shortages, bilingual program waivers are common. As Spanish-speaking students exit the primary grades with their home language no longer the primary language and not having had the opportunity to acquire biliteracy, they enter most secondary language programs to have Spanish be taught as a foreign language, despite their bilingualism, reflecting the monolingual ideologies that contribute to language loss (García, 2014). Students thus tend to leave their K-12 schooling with English as their dominant oral and written language rarely having attained biliteracy. The non-dominant societal language has been repressed, fulfilling the role of language in nationalism and in line with monolingual language ideologies.

In multilingual Singapore, Lee (2013) documented the dominant institutional role of English despite the presence of four national languages. In universities, for example, English retains higher social and cultural capital (Bourdieu, 1991) over Mandarin Chinese. In a study of translation of literary Singaporean anthologies, Lee found that initial volumes reflected the hegemony of English, with English being the only language Mandarin, Malay, or Tamil texts were translated into. However, over time Lee reported a shift to translations moving between all languages. The directionality of translation in these texts therefore challenged the social and institutional hegemony of English. As discussed previously, these practices may be linked to the Direct Method pillars of bilingualism as two solitudes, or that they reside as two separate languages within one person, that the home language interferes with additional language acquisition, and therefore that languages should be taught in isolation of each other (Cook, 2010). Despite empirical evidence that bilingualism functions as a single repertoire within the mind of the speaker (Grosjean, 1989; García, 2009), these perceptions persist. According to Widdowson (2003),

The widely accepted idea that the first language should be avoided at all costs in the second language classroom, and translation resolutely discouraged, is based on the belief that contact between the two languages is the last thing you want. So, it would appear ... that if bilingualism is to be defined as two languages in contact in the individual, conventional language teaching procedures are designed to stifle rather than promote it. (p. 150)

Indigenous languages have also been subjugated beneath the language of the nation state in countries around the world, from New Zealand to Peru and Norway to the United States (Albury, 2015; Hornberger & Skilton-Sylvester, 2000). As with minority languages, the goal of indigenous language eradication has been cultural eradication and creation of linguistically and culturally homogeneous states. This socially and politically determined process largely fell within the purview of schools, with children in indigenous boarding schools in the United States and New Zealand beaten for speaking their home language and teachers in Norway receiving bonus wages for actively pursuing the "Norweigenization" of their students (Albury, 2015). Schools have also played a role in Maori and Samoan language revitalization efforts in New Zealand (Albury, 2015). However, responsibility for indigenous language revitalization efforts has largely tended to fall within the communities themselves. In many cases in the United States, in language revitalization movements it is largely adults rather than children who learn their community languages, leaving the future of the languages, and some would argue cultures, in doubt (McCarty & Nicholas, 2014). Similarly, in Brunei, Noorashid and McLellan (2018) describe the risk of loss of the indigenous language Dusun due to the dominance of Malay and English in schools and other institutions. While indigenous language revitalization reflects a post-colonial, post-nationalist approach, prior and current monolingual language ideologies still act in counterpoint to many efforts, including within schools.

Standard Language Ideology

As illustrated in Manyak (2008), monolingual ideologies are tied to standard language ideology. Standard language ideology is "a bias toward an abstracted, homogeneous spoken language which is imposed and maintained by dominant bloc institutions and which names as its model the written language, but which is drawn primarily from the spoken language of the upper middle class" (Lippi-Green, 2011, p. 67). This socially constructed idea that a single variety of a given language exists serves as "a measuring stick for normativity against which 'non-standard' speakers fall short. That such varieties do not actually exist empirically does not diminish their symbolic power" (Linares, 2022, p. 52). Symbolic power enables a dominant actor to gain power through symbolic means such as language which would otherwise be obtained through physical or economic force (Bourdieu, 1991). Standard language is considered mainstream and used by the well-educated; it typically is used in writing and in the mainstream media. Non-standard language, in contrast, tends to be oral and aligned with certain social groups, including immigrants (Gee, 2012; Shohamy, 2006). Non-standard language can arouse "moral indignation [which] derives from ideological associations of the standard with the qualities valued within the culture" (Woolard & Shiefelin, 1994, p. 64).

While standard languages serve ostensibly as the measuring stick for language norms, because they are imposed by dominant institutions such as governments or schools, their underlying purpose is to maintain dominant institutions and existing power structures. Through symbolic power, the dominant actor is able to suggest to a non-dominant actor what he or she is, thereby establishing a hierarchical relationship (Bourdieu, 1991). When used in formal schooling, standard language ideology can marginalize students who speak or write other languages or language varieties. Students positioned as non-standard speakers are therefore positioned as non-standard in general, or as outsiders to ways of being and knowing within a given society (Linares, 2022). Since it represents dominant norms, standard language ideology can be difficult to disrupt, yet strategies such as pedagogical translation can recognize bi- or multilingual learners' language practices as assets and position the learners themselves as knowledgeable, whether in a second, world, or heritage language-learning environment.

Additionally, recognition of and resistance toward standard language ideology may affect the selection and incorporation of texts for translation, permitting the inclusion of a wider variety of texts, such as hybrid texts which translanguage or those which draw upon a variety of dialects. Exposure to this broader selection of texts might foment critical, complex discussion regarding language use as well as decision making in the translation process itself, thereby challenging the underlying symbolic power of standard language. Similarly, recognition of and resistance toward standard language ideology may affect the types of writing activities designed for pedagogical translation activities. For example, students may be permitted to translanguage when writing, or to choose a dialect or dialects to write in, and then translate their own work, thereby becoming language architects through the agency to make deliberate language choices (Flores, 2020; see also e.g., Celic & Seltzer, 2013).

Ideological Clarity and Pedagogical Translation

Societal language ideologies impact the development of individual language ideologies. All language users formulate ideologies. In educational environments, individual language users such as administrators and teachers need to be ideologically clear regarding what these ideas are (Álfaro, 2019). Language ideologies manifested as LEPs are implemented by practitioners, described by Shohamy (2006) as "bureaucrats" (p. 79) who do the work but have no input in their formulation. In contrast, Babino and Stewart (2018), documenting the persistence of monolingual language ideologies, found dual language teachers taking action against strict separation of languages and incorporating translanguaging in their pedagogy. Similarly, French and Armitage (2020) found that in the "monolithic" (p. 92) monolingual English learning environment in Australia, instructors used multilingual teaching strategies, including translanguaging, to challenge the status quo. However, bottom-up efforts by practitioners may nevertheless be stifled by top-down LEPs. Similarly, while school administrators in a linguistically and culturally diverse school in the state of California ascribed to state-mandated monolingual language ideologies, a single teacher approached language use in her classroom from a multilingual, multicultural perspective (Manyak, 2004). In her classroom, EB students were able to make full use of their linguistic repertoires in composing bilingual books, and students from varying linguistic and cultural backgrounds were also able to better connect with each other through collaboration. However, because of the school's monolingual ideology, the teacher ultimately left, demonstrating the difficulty encountered by single stakeholders in challenging monolingual ideologies and the need for broader-based change supported by educational institutions and policy makers.

Within this site of tension, Álfaro (2019) maintained that language teachers must continually juxtapose their personal beliefs and values with established systems of belief as evident in LEPs in order to avoid perpetuating dominant power structures and passing those beliefs to their students. When established belief systems are passed along, students and their families can internalize them and develop their own ideologies about what is good or bad language, what is socially valued, and often whether they consider it of use to maintain or abandon a home language or acquire an additional language (Cook, 2010).

Additional Barriers

Barriers to the implementation of translation in language teaching exist beyond language ideologies and are also completely disassociated from pedagogic principles (Widdowson, 2003). These include disciplinary silos, narrow definitions of translation, educator discomfort and student affect. As previously mentioned, the typical disciplinary silos between language teaching and translation may be attributed to the lingering poor reputation of Grammar Translation and the resultant lingering ban on home language use in language teaching (Colina & Lafford, 2017). Translation may also not be understood in language teaching environments, underscoring the need for some theoretical understanding of translation across disciplines (House, 2016). This separation may result in a reluctance in language teaching, where the goal is language acquisition, to incorporate effective strategies used in TS for the training of translators (Colina, 2002).

Narrow definitions of translation may also result in barriers to the implementation of pedagogical translation. These definitions may align translation with word- or sentence-level searches for equivalence associated with Grammar Translation (Colina & Lafford, 2017) or be conflated with other types of translation, such as natural translation or concurrent translation. Breaking the barriers to incorporating translation will then rely in part upon clear definition of pedagogical translation, distinction from other forms of translation, and delineation of its benefits.

Instructor reluctance stemming from varying factors may also contribute to incorporation of translation. One is the absolutism of the Direct Method, as "a deep historical distrust of translation militates against it. Belief in the Direct Method is so deeply ingrained, and antagonism to translation so intense, that for many this route seems a step too far" (Cook, 2010, p. 52). Another factor is reliance on outdated research in bilingual education which alleged the advantages of language separation (Lin, 2015). Similarly, McLaughlin (2022) proposes that teacher reluctance may include "their linguistic background, institutional or departmental expectations that class be conducted monolingually, or a lack of experience in the practice of translation" (p. 109). McLaughlin's point that instructors' unease with incorporating translation may be linked to institutional or departmental expectations circles back to the previous discussion regarding institutional or individual language monolingual ideologies which may create layers of barriers, including monolingual policies, monitoring, and fear of job loss if the policies are challenged (Manyak, 2004).

Student affect may also impact the successful implementation of pedagogical translation. Negative affect may stem from students not valuing comprehension of texts due to a lack of relatability, including among minoritized or heritage language students or not valuing learning the language under study, often due to internalization of language ideologies (Linares, 2022). For example, in my own study, some secondary Spanish heritage language students expressed a lack of identification with the topic of the text being translated and therefore did not find the translation activity to be useful (Albrecht, 2024). However, "the onus of unseating standard language ideologies lies not with marginalized speakers but with '[listening subjects who] continually perceive deficiency'" (Linares, 2022, p. 53). Selection of authentic texts and considerations for teacher preparation will be addressed in Chapters 7 and 11, respectively.

Pedagogical Translation Reborn

In spite of the barriers, current literature paints "a relatively rosy" picture (McLaughlin, 2022) of the trajectory and growing momentum of pedagogical translation despite other relatively recent work concluding that the literature did not yet empirically support translation as a pedagogy (Carreres, 2014).

This forward momentum was given impetus by the multilingual and social turns, which provided needed recognition of the value of the home language in the language classroom and of bilingual practices (Kramsch, 2012; May, 2019). Thus, through a move in language instruction beyond monolingual ideologies, a "wide variety of opportunities arise for teaching bilingual students by means of bilingual instructional strategies ... Some of these instructional strategies involve encouraging students to use translation" (Cummins, 2007, p. 222). Given that pedagogical translation requires both a home and an additional language, recognition of home language use and bilingualism have therefore reopened the path for translation in language teaching.

Additionally, for some teachers and students individually, and again despite the barriers, translation as a language-learning strategy has also "stubbornly remained" (González-Davies, 2020, p. 436). For example, secondary students in one study asserted that they considered translation in language learning to be natural and beneficial, while university lecturers in another, in spite of official opposition to translation due to its connection to Grammar Translation, found translation to be a useful pedagogical tool and used it, albeit covertly (Canga-Alonso & Rubio-Goitia, 2016; Kelly & Bruen, 2015).

Scholarly work from varying language-learning levels and fields demonstrates the many benefits of pedagogical translation. These include support for multilingualism and multiculturalism (González-Davies, 2017; Phipps & González, 2004), fitting neatly within the multilingual and social turns in SLA and within the umbrella of translanguaging. Additionally, pedagogical translation supports acquisition of critical thinking skills, as students must acquire "new ways to think and act" (Phipps & González, 2004) as they analyze the language and culture of texts in one language and engage in the complicated decision-making process of determining the best approach for presenting these in another language. In Rowe (2019), for example, primary school students in a multilingual classroom in the United States worked together to translate each other's work, developing in the process a sophisticated understanding of identifying author intent. Similarly, in Sneddon (2012), two English–Albanian bilingual children in London engaged in composing dual-language books together, again engaging in a complex process of negotiating for meaning.

This negotiation process also includes decision making regarding audience and cultural similarity and difference as well as considerations of register and genre and various types of equivalence, including at the word, sentence, semantic, pragmatic, and discoursal levels (Butzkamm & Caldwell, 2009; Colina & Lafford, 2017). These considerations of equivalence may also include complex decision making regarding translation of metaphor, rhythm, rhyme, and untranslatable linguistic features such as wordplay (Escamilla et al., 2014; Kultti & Pramling, 2018). In Kultti and Pramling, for example, Finnish children in a bilingual preschool engaged in translation of the English phrase "piece of cake," meaning metaphorically that something is easy, into Finnish. With instructor prompting, they came up with the equivalent, "Simple sausage" and recognized the difference between figurative and literal translation. Similarly, in Axelrod and Cole (2018), primary students in the United States translating a school newsletter from English to Spanish engaged in lengthy discussion over semantic equivalence in the translation of an article title about a fall pumpkin sale. They eventually humorously determined that the literal translation of "The Pumpkins are Coming" simply did not work. They focused instead on the sale itself, titling the article, "La venta de calabazas," or "The Pumpkin Sale." These two early-grade examples illustrate that incorporation of translation can engage learners from a young age in Phipps and González's (2004) "new ways to think and act."

This enumeration of factors contributing to development of critical thinking skills overlaps with another benefit of key importance, namely, acquisition of literacy skills (Colina, 2002; Kern, 2000). In Jiménez et al. (2015), for example, emergent bilingual middle school students engaged in complex negotiation and collaboration to determine what they considered to be the best translation of a text excerpt from their English Language Arts course into their home language of Spanish. This included understanding nuance in new vocabulary in English and considering similar nuance to choose a translation in Spanish, thus developing reading comprehension skills through a bilingual strategy.

Changes in approach to translation in language teaching have also led to what some have termed the "translation turn" (Carreres & Noriega-Sánchez, 2021). From this perspective, pedagogical translation has shifted from being used solely as a means to learning language to the acquisition of translation skills as an end in itself (Cook, 2010; Council of Europe, 2020). Cook (2010) argues that if language learning is considered a bilingual process, the division between translation as a means and an end is a false dichotomy. As an end, translation is considered to have "intrinsic value in helping learners become well-rounded linguists" (Carreres, 2014, p. 125) and should therefore be added as the fifth skill to be acquired in language learning in addition to listening, speaking, reading, and writing (Carreres, 2014; Colina & Lafford, 2017). Part of the argument in favor of translation as a fifth skill rests upon the likelihood that multilinguals will be in a position in ordinary life situations beyond those of professional translators where they will need to translate or interpret (Carreres, 2014).

This argument for teaching translation as an end was made with post-secondary world language teaching in mind, but it may be applied to other environments. Amanti (2019), for example, studied primary bilingual teachers who regularly need to translate pedagogical materials from English into the language of instruction, demonstrating not only a need for more equitable environments for these teachers, but also that prior development of translation as a fifth skill would have been useful. Similarly, given the number of primary-aged children of immigrants who are placed in a position of translating and/or interpreting for their families, this perspective may be extended to additional age groups and to approaches using translation as a tool in literacy acquisition (Orellana et al., 2003; Welch, 2015). In a school following English-only policies, Welch (2015), for example, studied a teacher who built translation activities around her ESL students' skills as natural translators to support their biliteracy development as well as the translation skills they needed within their families, thus implementing translation as both a means and an end.

Beyond the linguistic and cultural learning benefits of pedagogical translation discussed in later chapters, in a broader sense, systematic implementation of pedagogical translation circles back and contributes to the ongoing classroom shift from monolingual ideologies focused on the idealized native speaker to focus on bi- or multilingual speakers (Linares, 2022) or, as in the CEFR, on Mastery in terms of ease of use (Council of Europe, 2020; González-Davies & Soler Ortínez, 2021). The shift in focus to multi- rather than monolingualism in turn holds the potential to disrupt dominant power structures evident in language policy and to contribute to the development of biliteracy (Hornberger & Skilton-Sylvester, 2000; Hornberger & Link, 2012).

However, despite the "rosy picture" (McLaughlin, 2022) regarding the future of pedagogical translation, the previously mentioned barriers remain, and there is work to be done in dismantling them and in replacing them with viable pedagogies and assessments (Carreres & Noriega-Sánchez, 2021). As McLaughlin also points out, it is the job of scholar-instructors to bridge theory and practice, and hence the need for books such as this volume.

2
Language Learning and Literacy

This chapter establishes the theoretical foundation for the book's approach of socially situated literacy and its connection to language learning. Definitions of language, learning, and literacy may be superficially simple but the underlying conceptions are much more complex. Following Block (2003), the terms language, language learning, and literacy will be problematized to establish a frame of reference for these key concepts and their interactions. Each will be addressed in sequence, followed by a synthesis of the concepts as language learning and literacy.

What is Language?

Language can be described cognitively, or as a linguistic system; and socially, or by its role in society. In exploring definitions of language, Block (2003) noted the SLA focus on language as linguistic systems, with language exchanges focusing on tasks or information exchange and speaker identity being limited to native or non-native. However, through the lens of both TS and of the social turn in SLA, language can be seen as social as well as linguistic (Kramsch, 2012; Pym, 2004). Thus, it is language that holds the vast array of varying components of social life together, it is language that places us within situational and cultural contexts, and it is language that we use to make sense of the world (Kramsch, 2012; Pym, 2015). Languages "are the medium through which communities of people engage with, make sense of and shape the world. Through language they become active agents in creating their human environment. This process is what we call *languaging*. Languaging is a life skill. It is inextricably interwoven with social experience ... and it develops and changes constantly" (Phipps & González, 2004, p. 2, emphasis in original). In this sense, a shift occurs from language as a static noun to languaging, or "to language," as a dynamic verb which describes what we do with language socially. The term "languagers" then describes who we are and who we become as users of language who are changed within this dynamic, social sense (Phipps & González, 2004). Similarly, as argued by García and Flores (2013), *translanguaging* is a verb which describes the social practices of bilinguals.

Beyond the description of language by sociocultural role, language can also be described in terms of boundaries. Distinction between languages is frequently defined by intelligibility, with dialects of a given language being mutually intelligible and separate languages being unintelligible. However, the drawing of boundaries may be much more complex. Boundaries, for example, may be geopolitical, with language identification being politically fraught and largely defined by the frontiers between nation states, as in the case of Croatian and Serbian (Greenberg, 2004). Socially speaking, dialects are often considered not only to be mutually intelligible variants but less-prestigious variants on a prestigious standard (Cai & Ebsworth, 2018), thus cycling back to standard language ideology. The connection of standard language to prestige implies a connection to dominant power norms. According to Lippi-Green (2011), "The myth of standard language persists because it is carefully tended and propagated, with huge, almost universal success, so that language, the most fundamental of human socialization tools, becomes a commodity. This is the core of an ideology of standardization which empowers certain individuals and institutions to make these decisions and impose them on others" (p. 61).

Linguistically speaking, however, all language variants have the same value (Labov, 1969). For example, languages in contact, such as Spanglish in the United States or portuñol/portunhol in Uruguay or Portugal, are linguistically rule bound and typical of language-contact situations but socially may be stigmatized (García, 2014; Lipski, 2008). Situations of multiple languages in contact can also be described as hybrid, with fluid translanguaging practices among speakers that transcend traditional descriptions of language (Makalela, 2013).

Ultimately, Makoni and Pennycook (2005) argued that languages are in fact invented, pointing "to specific contexts – as well as the specific agendas and conceptual beliefs – in which institutions, structures, language and languages are produced, regulated and constituted" (p. 140). The invention of languages cycles back to the invention of the nation state, they point out, with nations themselves "imagined and narrated into being" and "language, literacy and institutions" (p. 140) contributing to the process. Language invention is also linked to colonialism, with colonizers "identifying" indigenous languages incorrectly and thus inventing them (Niranjana, 1992).

While conceptions of language have become tied to the invention and identity of nation states with the common one-nation-one-language perspective, twenty-first-century globalization requires a shift away from language boundaries (Blommaert, 2015; Cook, 2010; Gurney & Demuro,

2022). When borders are considered permeable, "Such reimagination accepts languages and dialects as important resources for learning whether individuals live in the borderlands between nations, landlocked between states, or on an island" (Fránquiz et al., 2019, p. 136). For example, Makalela (2013) describes the (trans)languaging practices of university students in South African townships, noting the use of *Kasi taal,* a hybrid language consisting of Nguni and Sotho language groups together with Afrikaans and English. Language among these multilingual speakers is not limited to a spatial or temporal context, nor to a single language, but instead to speakers' desire to show unity in their multilingual, multicultural context. As part of making sense of and shaping the world, language is used not only for information exchange but also for developing relationships through showing solidarity or support (Block, 2003), which may involve fluid use of language that crosses and challenges historical, invented language borders.

To bring language back into the realm of language learning, it is important to recognize its macro and micro roles. On the macro level, colonial "invention" of language and the building of nation states has affected language institutionalization and instruction. Language ideologies which protect dominant norms appear in institutions such as schools and in language teaching practices. In contrast, micro language roles describe the way in which people "engage with, make sense of and shape the world" (Phipps & González, 2004, p. 2) and the way they use language to connect with each other, to think about language learning or to language. The term "language" will be used throughout the book to describe language in use, or discourse, and keeping these fluid conceptions of language and languaging in mind.

What Is Language Learning?

Generally speaking, language learning is "an act of critical appropriation of the world and ourselves" (Phipps & González, 2004, p. 143). This definition moves far beyond the often-applied view of language learning as acquisition of skills through explicit teaching. Krashen's (1981) influential division between language learning and language acquisition has played a long-standing role in describing language learning. According to Krashen, second language learning is explicit and occurs in the classroom, while SLA is implicit, following a process similar to first language acquisition, and occurs in natural environments or through exposure to comprehensible input. Although this claim has since been discredited (Cook, 2010), it is still commonly applied in classroom practice and is used to justify teaching only within the target language. However, as Cook asserts, "Any learner will inevitably both learn and acquire, translate and not translate, and it is not feasible to attempt a separation of the effects" (p. 94). Gee (2012) addresses the learning—acquisition dichotomy, noting that both the learning and acquisition processes have their benefits, as learning results in explicit knowledge and acquisition results in performance. In this sense, it might be argued that learning and acquisition are not so much a dichotomy but a continuum (see e.g., *Revisiting the continua of biliteracy: International and critical perspectives,* Hornberger & Skilton-Sylvester, 2000).

Language learning in terms of languaging focuses more on the effects of language learning on learners and returns to the conceptualization of learning as critical appropriation. The goals of languaging include meaning making, human connection, and "living in the language" (Phipps & González, 2004, p. 3) as opposed to "accuracy and measurable knowledge" (p. 3). Languaging therefore moves beyond the skills of reading, writing, and intercultural competence to the process of becoming an intercultural being. In describing this move, Phipps and González describe intercultural being as comprising the following:

1. Epistemology: Engaged with the whole social world; Reflective engagement with self and other
2. Situations: Discovered in action, reflection, and recursion; transdisciplinary
3. Focus: Skilful; Skilling as process
4. Education: Languagers-in-action, critical intercultural being, reflective sojourning
5. Learning context: Whole social world (including but beyond classroom)
6. Communication: Languaging; intercultural speaking, and listening
7. Value orientation: Border crossings
8. Boundary conditions: Being border crossers, translators, languaging links (p. 29, emphasis in original)

This is not to say that languaging leaves the skills of reading and writing aside, nor that accuracy is never a consideration. Instead, through languaging, reading, writing, and accuracy become part of the complex negotiation of meaning and development as an intercultural being.

In presenting the move toward intercultural being, Phipps and González are coming from a university-level, world language learning perspective. The question therefore arises of whether this goal applies in other environments such as second language learning in which learners need the second language to be able to function. However, Phipps and González's descriptors are relevant across environments. For example, EB students may be considered languagers in action who are learning language and culture within and beyond the school; they are translating for each other and their families and crossing physical and figurative borders; they are quintessential intercultural beings (Martínez et al., 2008). For the purposes of this book, language learning will be considered to be a process occurring within a classroom environment and therefore involving some level of explicit teaching. Nevertheless, the assumption is that language learning is affected by socialization and the social environment in and outside of the classroom, with the potential for acquisition to also be occurring.

What Is Literacy?

As with language, literacy has been and continues to be conceptualized across a broad range of perspectives and is often highly politicized. Frequently, literacy is simply viewed in terms of skill acquisition, that is, learning to read and write. This process requires the acquisition of linguistic and cognitive skills, with their application to reading and writing traditionally being considered as separate (Warner & Dupuy, 2018). Linguistic skills consist of being able to "recognize and produce graphic representations of words and morphemes, and knowledge of the conventions that determine how these elements can be combined and ordered to make sentences" (Kern, 2000, p. 25); they also consist of lexical, morphological, syntactic, semantic, and pragmatic knowledge (p. 28). In these terms, pedagogical translation can be used to make cross-linguistic connections between language systems (Escamilla et al., 2014). Cognitive skills include the ability to predict, infer, and synthesize meaning and draw upon activation of prior knowledge (Kern, 2000); pedagogical translation may also be used for these ends. Over time, however, reading and writing have come to be seen as linguistically and cognitively interconnected (Warner & Dupuy, 2018). Scholars within TS link home language literacy and translation competence. For example, Gile (2009) identifies home language literacy skills such as identifying register; nuance of meaning through word choice; and thematic knowledge as essential skills for students in translator training programs.

The acquisition of literacy skills fits within a variety of approaches in which literacy functions as a social practice influenced by power norms. These include traditional literacy, which views literacy as acontextual and skill based; ideological, which first presented socially situated literacy practices; New Literacies, which expanded approaches to socially situated literacy, including multiliteracies; and biliteracy. Each approach will be addressed in the following subsections.

Traditional Views of Literacy

Traditional, or autonomous literacy, is based upon learning to read and write and is considered to be situated in the individual rather than in society (Gee, 2012; Kern, 2000; Street, 1984). It is often implicit in literacy programs, with assessment scores driving decisions about instruction (Gee, 2012). In traditional literacy, reading is defined as decoding writing and writing is defined as coding (or encoding) language for reading, and literacy pedagogy is "formalized, monolingual, monocultural and rule-governed" (New London Group, 1996, p. 61). Readers then assign meaning to the text, because "If readers know the language, can decode writing, and have the requisite background 'facts' to draw the inevitable inferences any writing requires, they can construct the 'right' interpretation in their heads" (Gee, 2012, p. 38), with the "right" interpretation being more or less the same for all readers. In other words, traditional literacy is text based and allows for an academic monopoly over the meaning of written texts (Kramsch, 2012). This focus on the "letter of the texts" (Kramsch, 2008, p. 55) places their interpretation outside of social contexts and assumes that meaning is fixed, often in the minds of experts (Gee, 2012).

It is commonly believed that literacy itself, or autonomous literacy, leads to a change in economic or occupational social standing (Kern, 2000; Street, 1984, 2006). However, the social impact of traditional literacy is mythical, with the myth hiding underlying "cultural and ideological assumptions…so that it can then be presented as though they are neutral and universal and that literacy as such will then have these benign effects" (Street, 2006, p. 1). Instead, ethnicity and social class play a greater role in social mobility, with autonomous views of literacy, and accompanying approaches to teaching literacy, serving to maintain the hegemonic status quo (Street, 1984).

Problems therefore arise in schools when traditional literacy practices as defined by dominant groups do not fit the literacy practices of non-dominant groups. In her classic study on the literacy practices of three different groups in the southeastern United States, Heath (1982) noted the significant difference in literacy practices among groups within a small geographical area. Importantly, she found that only the "mainstream" group's literacy practices aligned with literacy practices as defined by the schools. As Gee (2012) elaborates, in schools students can build upon foundations of mainstream literacy acquired at home, but it is difficult to establish mainstream foundations when other foundations are already in place. This type of dramatic change requires a change in identity for non-mainstream groups, thus affecting their literate trajectories (Gee, 2012). If literacy practices were so diverse in the small geographical region studied by Heath, with only one group's practices aligning with sanctioned school practices, the implications of application of traditional views of literacy in a globalizing, multicultural, multilingual world are sobering. However, in response to the effects of traditional views of literacy, new approaches have been developed.

Ideological Views of Literacy

In contrast to traditional views of literacy, the ideological view of literacy is based upon Vygotsky's (1978) social constructivism. That is, knowledge is socially constructed, and this construction is mediated through the tools of language and culture, among others. Through the ideological view of literacy, the skills of reading and writing are socially situated and therefore culturally embedded (Street, 1984), thus describing the variation in literacy practices by social groups identified by Heath. In contrast to traditional literacy, within the ideological view of literacy, the socialization process is important for participant meaning making, and meaning making is therefore not considered to be a matter of determining an existing, static textual interpretation (Street, 1984). Instead, literacy moves beyond the skills of reading and writing to "The cognitive and sociocultural ability to use the written or print medium according to the norms of interaction and interpretation of a given discourse community" (Kramsch, 2008, p. 37). Literacy as a social practice also opens the way for critique of the social practices within which literacy is embedded, or for critical literacy. According to Freire (1970), this means that critically reading the systemic injustices in the world becomes an integral part of reading the word. An examination of how varying literacy practices as modeled by Heath are supported or not in the schools, followed by a plan of action, would be required through the lens of critical literacy.

Social contextualization of literacy occurs on both macro and micro levels, with contextualization at each level impacting the other (see e.g., Hornberger & Skilton-Sylvester, 2000). At the macro level, social contextualization includes examination of the role literacy plays in the social control and hegemony of dominant classes. It "distinguishes claims for the consequences of literacy from its real significance for specific social groups" (Street, 1984, p. 2), with reading and writing practices depending upon social stratification as described by Heath. At the micro level, social contextualization is based upon interactions among individuals, such as within families, communities, or schools. Parmegiani (2014), for example, documented how writing instructors' expectations for critical thinking and organization in writing at her community college differed from her Dominican students' autonomous literacy experiences in high school, creating a disconnect in the type of product students produced. In this case, "writing was related not only to second language acquisition issues, but also to divergent literacy practices" (p. 41), creating the need for instructors to socially contextualize their students' literacy practices and to "invite the mother tongue into the composition process" (p. 42), or to incorporate translanguaging, and to create a "pedagogical alliance" (p. 23) with a Spanish instructor. These steps helped to socially contextualize students' literacy practices and to provide a space for their biliterate growth.

New Literacy Studies

The move toward social views of literacy contributed to the formation of the new field of New Literacy Studies. Scholarly work in this field began in the 1980s, including the previously mentioned work by Heath and Street, with the field coalescing under this name in 1990 (Gee, 2012). In New Literacy Studies, literacy is defined only through observing it within social contexts and their ideologies (Bartlett, 2007; Gee, 2012). That is, the ability to read is placed within being able to read certain text types a certain way because one is a member of a certain social group or domain, including educational institutions (Bartlett 2007; Gee 2012). In this sense, the term "literacy practices" (Bartlett 2007) can be used to describe the socially determined patterns connected to literacy and their cultural significance. When literacy is considered a social practice, the focus shifts from mastery of text as the written medium to discourse, or language in use (Gee, 2012; Kramsch, 2012). Instead of asking what a text says or means, one might ask, "What does this text *do*?" (Phipps & González, 2004, p. 46) in conjunction with what the person does "with other humans ... and the material, social, and symbolic notion of 'being' literate" (Bartlett, 2007, p. 53).

In terms of "doing literacy" and its connection to discourse, Gee (2012) distinguishes between discourse with a "d" and a "D" (p. 2). Big D Discourse describes "saying (writing) –doing–being–valuing–believing combinations" (p. 151), which means there is always more than language involved. Discourses are key to personal identity, in that each person develops a "primary Discourse" (p. 153) based upon the environment, or Discourse community, in which they grew up. Discourse communities "implicitly share a stock of prior texts and ideological points of view that have developed over time" (Kramsch, 2008, p. 62). Recognition of the differing practices of Discourse communities is reminiscent of the literacy practices of the three groups in Heath's study, emphasizing that literacy is changeable and contextualized rather than static and autonomous. Bartlett (2007) also maintains that individuals make deliberate moves to position themselves as literate based upon social and cultural norms. These individuals may be outside a given Discourse community, but, given the symbolic capital of literacy within that community, seek to enter that community through developing "legitimate" (Bartlett 2007, p. 54) literacy practices. In sum, literacy is dynamic, drawing upon knowledge of written and spoken language and of cultural norms and ideologies (Gee, 2012; Kern, 2000).

Part of knowledge of cultural norms is genre, which describes social processes within cultures that are visible within language choice and register within oral or written texts. Recognition of genre is therefore a part of literacy, as "it is the capacity to understand and manipulate the social and cultural meanings of print language in thoughts, feelings and actions" (Kramsch, 2008, p. 56). For second language learners, understanding the social and cultural meanings within a genre may be particularly valuable (Tardy, 2011). Understanding of social and cultural meanings in text may result in greater attention being paid to register and style in the language in use, rather than to assignment of prescriptive norms which assume one interpretation of a text or one correct use of language. In contrast to the oral–literate divide, it also assumes a connection between oral and written discourse: "Because we read and write connected discourse and not just sentences, literacy also requires understanding of relationships between larger segments of text as well as knowledge of genres and styles ... [it] requires us to understand relationships between oral and written discourse" (Kern, 2000, p. 28). That is, a connection to orality is always required in literate societies (Yeganeh, 2022).

Multiliteracies

Multiliteracies will be explored within sociocultural views of literacy, initially framed through the discussion on ideological views in which literacy is socially and culturally contextualized (New London Group, 1996). Through the sociocultural perspective of literacy, "Reading and writing are communicative acts in which readers and writers position one another in particular ways, drawing on conventions and resources provided by the culture" (Kern, 2000, p. 34). The close connection of literacy to sociocultural practices in language provides the impetus for teaching language, literacy, and culture as one unit. In the initial manifesto, the New London Group explained the what, why, and how of the pedagogy of multiliteracies, and members have since periodically revisited and revised the initial pedagogy.

The Why of Multiliteracies

The pedagogy of multiliteracies was designed to "overcome the limitations of traditional approaches by emphasizing how negotiating the multiple linguistic and cultural differences in our society is central to the pragmatics of the working, civic, and private lives of students" (Cope & Kalantzis, 2009, p. 60), thus linguistically and culturally contextualizing literacy in contrast to traditional skills-based, decontextualized literacy approaches. The goals of multiliteracies were for students to: (1) use literacy to access the language needed for work, community, and power and (2) develop the criticality needed to "design their social futures and achieve success through fulfilling employment" (p. 60), with a focus on the multilingual and the multimodal. The multilingual component addresses multilingualism in terms of globalization and minority languages as well as in terms of social variation of discourse within a single language, including standard language and global Englishes. The multilingual component will be discussed in the "What" of multiliteracies.

The What of Multiliteracies

The pedagogy of multiliteracies entails a shift in how textual meaning is conceptualized. Instead of meaning being seen as an unchanging entity housed within texts, from a multiliteracies perspective, meaning "is considered an active and dynamic process in which learners combine and creatively apply both linguistic and other semiotic resources (e.g., visual, gesture, sound, etc.)" (Warner & Dupuy, 2018). A pedagogy of multiliteracies therefore focuses on designing meaning. Design of Meaning recognizes learners' agency in meaning making in contrast to traditional literacy practices in which learners are taught skills and are recipients and reproducers of knowledge (Cope & Kalantzis, 2013; Freire, 1970). This framework includes three design elements: *Available Designs, Designing,* and *the Redesigned.* Available Designs are dynamic, contrastive representations in meaning and replace static representations in traditional literacy such as "grammar" or "the literary canon." Instead, these representations must acknowledge the variability and dynamism or conventions and might include mode (as in multimodal), genre, and discourse (Cope & Kalantzis, 2013). Zapata (2018) linked the dynamic, contrastive representations of meaning in Available Designs to culturally relevant pedagogy, in that culturally relevant materials "connect closely with who the learners are and what they need both personally and academically" (p. 13).

Designing involves doing something new with, or transforming, Available Designs, in contrast to the transmission of static meaning in traditional literacy; pedagogical moves involved in Designing are discussed in what follows in the "How" of multiliteracies. The final element, the Redesigned, refers to texts that, through their Design, are now available to others in their Redesigned form and it also refers to the designer as having been Redesigned (Cope & Kalantzis, 2013). Translation may be seen as a Design process in which meaning is negotiated, with the translated product and the translator being considered Redesigned. Interestingly, the concept of the Redesigned through translation connects to Phipps and González's process of becoming intercultural beings through languaging.

The How of Multiliteracies

The initial pedagogy of multiliteracies presented four pedagogical orientations, namely, overt instruction, situated practice, critical framing, and transformed practice. These orientations were later presented in the Design of Meaning framework as the knowledge processes of experiencing, conceptualizing, analyzing, and applying (Cope & Kalantzis, 2013). These four orientations are described as "pedagogical moves" which may encourage instructors to expand their pedagogical repertoires but are not a pedagogy in themselves. Additionally, they are not to be considered linear but as a process of "weaving" (p. 18) among them all. *Experiencing* starts with experiencing the known and moves to explicit instruction which allows students to experience the new. This move may be related to the process of activating students' prior knowledge. *Conceptualizing* focuses on knowledge processes which are housed within disciplinary knowledge; on the process of making implicit knowledge explicit; and on conceptualizing by naming, such as by comparison and contrast, categorizing, making conceptual connections, and generating theory. Zapata (2018) weaves the elements of experiencing and conceptualizing together in recommending the pedagogy of multiliteracies for heritage language learners (HLLs), in that it enables them to build upon their implicit linguistic and cultural knowledge as they move toward new learning.

Multiliteracies and pedagogical translation have multiple areas of intersection. Both assume a bi- or multilingual foundation, with the home language scaffolding additional language acquisition and literacy (González-Davies, 2014; New London Group, 1996). The pedagogy of multiliteracies and pedagogical translation both promote metalinguistic awareness through language contrast with the potential for doing so through multiple modes (Hornberger & Skilton-Sylvester, 2000; Pym, 2010). Finally, as previously mentioned, both foster meaning making through negotiation of meaning, or Design, through authentic contexts (Cope & Kalantzis, 2013; González-Davies, 2014; Tymoczko, 2007;). Students may, for example, translate a text and need to identify the genre, register, and lexicon appropriate for this text type, contrasting language and noting differences in style between cultures. This type of activity promotes literacy, critical thinking, and cultural awareness (Pintado-Gutiérrez, 2019). Translation also encourages students to make implicit linguistic and cultural knowledge explicit, including through consideration (Design) of appropriate modes. For example, in research studying students' capacity to use language to represent cultural elements in a text, in two university-level courses, one English translation course in Korea and one beginning Japanese course in London, students considered appropriate modes such as visual, written, and aural while engaging in a translation project (Lee & Gyogi, 2018), which resulted in improving their intercultural competence. Similarly, Cano and Ruiz (2020) found that during a collaborative translation of a narrative text, primary grade bilingual students showed skill in translation at the sentence and discourse level, constructing meaning through discussion of grammar, syntax, vocabulary, and figurative language and analyzing the conflict and resolution.

Analyzing requires functional and evaluative critical capacity (Cope & Kalantzis, 2013). Functional critical capacity involves inductive and deductive reasoning and identifying cause and effect. Analyzing the function of a translated text from a TS perspective (see Chapter 3) might be linked to functional critical capacity. Through evaluative critical capacity, students evaluate systems of power, including others' perspectives and motives; in translation, this may be done through analyzing both what types of texts are being translated into what languages and how they are translated; for example, if the culturally "foreign" elements of the source text are maintained or modified to suit the target culture (see Chapters 4 and 7).

Depending upon the texts selected, pedagogical translation may be used as a tool for analysis of either type.

Applying includes applying appropriately and applying creatively. Applying appropriately involves the application of new understandings to the "diversity of real world situations and testing their validity" (Cope & Kalantzis, 2013, p. 18). Applying creatively involves making a creative intervention which takes into account the learner's agency, interests, and experiences. Kern (2000) addressed the potential of pedagogical translation to transform meaning within the initial pedagogical move of transformation, which is now applying. In translation activities, students become aware of the following: "(1) the importance of word choice in meaning design, and (2) the lack of simple one-to-one correspondences between expressions in the two languages. As they translate, students must closely analyze the particular context ... and then carefully weigh the semantic overtones of each potential rendering" (p. 159). Through this type of transformation, students must apply their knowledge of both languages appropriately and creatively as they generate the translated text.

Biliteracy

Expanding beyond biliteracy as reading proficiency and vocabulary knowledge, Hornberger (1989) defines biliteracy as "any and all instances in which communication occurs in two or more languages in or around writing" (p. 213), with the element of communication inherently implying a social element. Indeed, because of the influence of social, political, economic, and cultural factors, biliteracy practices can be considered to fall within the ideological, or socially situated, view of literacy (García, 2009; Nuñez, 2023; Reyes, 2012). According to Louie and Davis-Welton (2016), "Understanding biliteracy and how to foster it in classrooms is important for educators because this understanding can help teachers nourish students' intellectual possibilities" (p. 598), including through cultural and linguistic validation.

García et al. (2007) extend conceptions of biliteracy to pluriliteracy. Pluriliteracy practices "move[] away from the dichotomy of the traditional L1/L2 pairing, emphasizing instead that language and literacy practices are interrelated and flexible, positing that all literacy practices have equal value" (p. 11). Indeed, as students are able to move fluidly across languages, they are also able to move fluidly across literacies (Fránquiz et al., 2019). García et al. (2007) argue that pluriliteracy practices offer the potential for transformation and change as they permit dynamic, flexible language practices and open space for the agency of the learner. Flores (2020) describes this agency as language architecture, in which bilingual students, through reading the world and the word, are able to choose the domains of language they will use in their literacy practices as opposed to deficit approaches which see their language as deficient and require remediation. The dynamic, flexible practices of pluriliteracy also tie to translanguaging, or the written or oral use of a speaker's entire linguistic repertoire for meaning making (García, 2009). Gasca Jiménez (2019) explains that plurilingualism focuses on language users in general, while translanguaging focuses on minoritized speakers. For EBs or HLLs, developing biliteracy through bilingual reading comprehension strategies such as translanguaging and translation contributes to literacy achievement (Ganuza & Hedman, 2019; Gasca Jiménez, 2022; Pacheco et al., 2017). Translanguaging is further discussed in Chapter 4.

During the nineteenth century, the global West undertook a nation-state project in which single nations are identified with a single language. Institutions vested in promoting and protecting what the nation state stands for therefore "work hard to validate their favored status in that state, in part on the basis of language" (Lippi-Green, 2011, p. 69). As part of the nation-state project, monolingualism became aligned with national identity, as did mass monolingual literacy (Phipps & González, 2004). However, a shift to socially situated literacy places literacy as "the relationship of learners to the world through an act of cultural politics" (p. 36). It is logical, then, to also socially situate biliteracy (Reyes, 2012), especially as "the value placed on bilingualism relates to the ability of the language learner to write the language as well as to speak it. But that in its turn is calculated ... by assessing the weight of what Bourdieu terms 'symbolic capital,' with 'community languages' usually only being seen as 'oral codes'" (Phipps & González, 2004, pp. 24–25). The connection to symbolic capital is key, as it identifies the typically lower symbolic capital of bilingualism, which can then be linked to biliteracy (see also Hornberger & Skilton-Sylvester's critical continua of biliteracy, 2000). The development of biliteracy from a dominant language into an additional language involves a much higher level of symbolic capital than the development of biliteracy from a non-dominant language into a dominant language (Hornberger & Skilton-Sylvester, 2000), resulting in decision-making processes which make biliteracy development in educational environments socially, politically, and economically fraught.

Various models describe educational programs for the development of biliteracy. According to García (2009), there are four models in the United States. The first is convergent monoliterate, in which there are two languages in communication to work with a text written in one language, which is usually dominant. This is a subtractive model, in which the first language is used only to support SLA, and the support for the first language is then removed (Sikes & Villanueva, 2021). Many bilingual programs in the United States follow this model. For example, in the state of Texas, the home language may be used to support English acquisition, then removed once adequate progress has been made or prior to the beginning of standardized state testing, with the monolingual belief that students will do better on the state tests if they are only working in English. The goal of this model is English acquisition rather than biliteracy.

The second model is convergent biliterate, in which two languages are used to work with a text in both languages. However, the minority literacy practices are based upon dominant language literacy norms. For example, some bilingual programs in the United States teach Spanish literacy based upon translated English language curricula, not addressing the differing structure of Spanish. The third model is separation biliterate, which follows monolingual views of bilingualism, or that languages are "two solitudes" (Cummins, 2017, p. 404) in the speaker's head. In this model, one of the two languages is used to work with a text in the same language. Although this is an additive framework, biliteracy is better approached holistically. This distinction highlights underlying views regarding language boundaries, as through a holistic approach, languages are seen as integrated rather than separate systems (Makoni & Pennycook, 2005).

The last of García's four models is flexible multiple. According to this model, multiple languages are used to work with texts in multiple languages and/or other media. These can be integrated or separated. The flexible multiple model permits translanguaging and is an additive framework. Because multiple languages are used to work with texts in multiple languages, pedagogical translation would also be permitted within this framework. In the United States, primary grade one- and two-way dual-language programs apply the flexible multiple model. In one-way programs, all students speak the same first language, which is used and developed while English is acquired. In two-way programs, half of the students speak a home language other than English, and half speak English. Students are paired with a speaker of the other language in order to support acquisition of both languages. Bilingualism and biliteracy are also the goals of both one- and two-way programs. For EB learners, dual-language programs have the highest positive student outcomes (Reyes et al., 2012; Sikes & Villanueva, 2021). However, there are challenges to consistent implementation. First, two-way programs are more expensive to develop and implement than traditional bilingual or English as a second language programs. It is also difficult to find qualified teachers, and families need to buy into the structure and goals of these programs. Finally, dual-language programs generally end after the primary grades, and support for biliteracy ends at this time.

Hornberger's (1989; Hornberger & Skilton-Sylvester, 2000) continua of biliteracy is another model for studying the development of biliteracy in various environments. This complex model presents nested continua of four facets of biliteracy, namely, contexts, development, content, and media, each with its own sub-continua, and each sub-continuum intersecting with the others.

According to Hornberger (1989), learners allowed to utilize all points of the continua have a greater chance "for their full biliterate development" (p. 289). Revisiting the continua of biliteracy, Hornberger and Skilton-Sylvester (2000) added a critical component which addresses the role of language ideologies and power asymmetries within sociopolitical contexts. Each continuum falls within social contexts, with each end weighted as more or less powerful. Despite the typically higher symbolic capital of developing biliteracy from a dominant language into a non-dominant language, the critical continua of biliteracy sets up a model for challenging the traditional social power weighting of the elements of biliteracy development. Hornberger and Skilton-Sylvester argue that traditional power weightings can and should be contested "by paying attention to and granting agency and voice to actors and practices at what have traditionally been the less powerful ends of the continua" (2000, p. 99).

For example, within contexts of biliteracy, on the sub-continuum of bilingual to monolingual language use, and linked to monolingual language ideologies, monolingual language use is weighted as socially more powerful. Similarly, in the development of biliteracy, on the sub-continuum of oral to written language use, written language use is weighted as socially more powerful, again highlighting dominant views of home languages as worthy only of use as oral codes (Phipps & González, 2004). At the intersection of the two sub-continua, then, lies the point of dominant monolingual literacy. However, this and each sub-continuum may be challenged such that the power weighting shifts. This can be done through deliberate pedagogical moves: "The continua model posits that what (content) biliterate learners and users read and write is as important as how (development), where and when (context), or by what means (media) they do so" (Hornberger & Link 2012, p. 268). These pedagogical moves will be addressed in the context of translation throughout the book. What, or the content, of biliteracy will be addressed in Chapter 7 on selection of authentic texts, while by what means (media) will be addressed in Chapter 8 on multimodality. Where and when are interspersed throughout the book.

Revisiting the critical continua of biliteracy, Hornberger and Link (2012) explored the connections between the continua, translanguaging, and transnational literacies. They defined translanguaging as a pedagogical stance which intentionally permits oral and written alternation of languages (and their varieties), and transnational literacies as "literacy practices that draw on funds of knowledge, identities, and social relations rooted and extending across national borders" (p. 262). Viewing translanguaging and transnational literacies through a biliteracy lens contributes to shifting away from dominant norms that favor monolingual, written, and decontextualized (autonomous) literacy practices toward multilingual, oral, and contextualized (ideological) practices. Hornberger and Skilton-Sylvester (2000) proposed that although "It is perhaps the New Literacy Studies which have done the most to draw our attention to ... contestations of macro-level, dominant, monolingual literacy practices" (p. 104), all stakeholders, from students and teachers to administrators and policy makers, should play a role in resisting dominant literacy norms.

The continua of biliteracy has been used as a model to study biliteracy in multiple environments. For example, Hornberger and Link (2012) found that standardized tests in an English–Spanish bilingual program privileged decontextualized, monolingual, written forms of literacy which did not recognize or draw upon students' contextualized, bilingual, oral forms of literacy, thereby not reflecting students' full knowledge or capabilities. Similarly, in the Liangshan region of southwestern China, Yao and Turner (2024) found that because standardized, written Nuosu Yi language was emphasized in bilingual schools rather than students' oral forms, the Nuosu Yi taught in schools was seen as irrelevant in everyday life and relevant only to high-stakes examinations, as reflected in decreased enrollment and school closures.

Some efforts have been made to recognize biliteracy from the macro, or policy, level. For example, the Seal of Biliteracy was conceived of in the state of California in the United States in an effort to recognize the biliterate development of students speaking home languages other than English (Davin & Heineke 2017). Since its initial implementation in 2011, all states have implemented the Seal. However, the Seal has largely been implemented in world language programs in higher socioeconomic environments, thus not effectively shifting dominant power norms as seen through the lens of Hornberger's critical continua of biliteracy (Davin & Heineke, 2017). The Global Seal of Biliteracy (GSoB) recognizes biliteracy development throughout the world (Global Seal Statistics, 2023). It applies the Common European Frame of Reference (CEFR) to measure language proficiency, approaching biliteracy through plurilingual and pluricultural practices, which will be addressed in Chapter 4.

Literacy in Language Learning

Using a socially situated literacy perspective (Kern, 2000), this book moves away from siloed emphasis in language instruction on structure or communication and toward discourse. That is not to say that there is no incorporation of structure or communication, but instead that it is about the combined development of communicative competence, structural elements, and the ability to "analyze, interpret, and transform discourse and ... ability to think critically about how discourse is constructed and used toward various ends in social contexts" (Kern, 2000, p. 303). These social contexts include political and educational institutions and the power relations embedded within them (Barton et al., 2000). Kern (2000) identifies seven principles of a socio-cognitive view of literacy, which involve the following:

1 Interpretation, both by the writer and the reader
2 Collaboration between writer and reader
3 Culturally based conventions for reading and writing

4   Knowledge of culturally based norms
5   Levels of problem solving, from relationships between words to social contexts
6   Reflection, including self-reflection
7   Knowledge of contextualized language use (discourse) (p. 17)

Kern summarizes the seven principles by stating simply, "Literacy involves communication" (p. 17). From this perspective, language teaching must involve authentic literacy events and incorporate literacy at every level, not just higher-level literature courses.

Literacy-based language teaching therefore reflects the shift in SLA from native-speakerism based on monolingual norms to the multilingual and social turns, in which students are "apprentice discourse analysts and intercultural explorers" (Kern, 2000, p. 306). Consequently, learning objectives will revolve not just on knowing (language forms) or doing (language functions), but on the relationships between knowing and doing or between form and function. Being *in* the language then involves "communicative appropriateness informed by metacommunicative awareness" (Kern, 2000, p. 304). In socially situated, literacy-based language learning, students make sense of texts produced by themselves or others to "expand their awareness of a new language and culture ... reading and writing are treated not just as linguistic skills, but also as cognitive and social processes" (p. 15). This type of literacy should be learner-centered, focused on cross-cultural connection, and, as with Principle 6, involve learner reflection (Kramsch & Nolden, 1994).

A socially situated literacy approach, including biliteracy, requires an in-depth consideration of context. Kramsch (2008) describes context for literacy events as including social and cultural dimensions. Literacy events involve interaction between reader and text and are defined by "their members' common social practices with written language...and common ways of interpreting those practices" (p. 60). The social dimension of context includes event, audience, textual purpose, and register, while the cultural dimension involves the Discourse communities' relationship to prior texts and narrator point of view, including ideological. The critical continua of biliteracy add consideration of power weighting in social and cultural practices between two written languages and the role of power in interpreting those practices.

What, then, is the role of pedagogical translation in socially situated, literacy-based language learning? First, translation may either support or challenge dominant power norms (Niranjana, 1992). Niranjana, for example, chronicled the translation of Indian literature into English to support the British colonial enterprise through "othering" (p. 11), which positions "the knowledge and ways of life in the colony as distorted or immature versions of what can be found in 'normal' Western society" (p. 11). While it is not anticipated that pedagogical translation activities will function on this scale, the ongoing role of language ideologies and autonomous literacy practices in the maintenance of dominant power norms must be taken into consideration. In post-colonial thought, this propensity may also be looked at in terms of essentializing (language, literature, culture) within a given society to the detriment of minoritized citizens (Niranjana, 1992). For example, insistence upon monolingual language teaching or the sole selection of "high culture" texts for translation would play a role in validating dominant norms, languages and literacy practices.

On the other hand, translation may also challenge dominant language and literacy practices. As noted in Chapter 1 discussion on the SLA multilingual turn, pedagogical translation requires moving between or within languages, which immediately challenges monolingual teaching norms. Translation activities might also include translation of students' own vernacular or other vernacular texts, such as poems from David Bowles's (2018, 2020) *They call me Güero/Me dicen Güero*. Translation of oral texts from student cultures with a strong oral tradition might also serve to validate these language and literacy practices.

Additionally, incorporation of translanguaging pedagogy and acceptance of students' translanguaging practices during translation activities validates bilingual students' linguistic and cultural practices. Translanguaging has been linked to literacy studies, focusing on the practices of multilingual readers and writers "which go beyond traditional understandings of language, literacy, and other concepts, such as bi/multilingualism and bi/multilingual literacy" (García & Kleifgren, 2019, p. 553). That is, institutionally aligning language practices with the dominant state language(s) and adding a new language without socially situating it ignores the fact of language in use. Translanguaging, on the other hand, releases political and institutional restraints on language use, allowing bi/multilingual learners to engage in a literacy process in which they create "more diverse texts, enjoy more confianza as literate beings, and experience a deeper critical multilingual experience" (p. 568). Ultimately, this is the goal: to create a space through socially situated literacy processes like pedagogical translation in which learners feel that they are confident, literate beings.

3

Translation and Second Language Acquisition

Recent research in TS has focused on its interdisciplinarity, or movement between and across fields. "An interdiscipline...challenges the current conventional way of thinking by promoting and responding to new links between different types of knowledge and technologies" (Munday et al., 2022, p. 21), including linguistics, modern languages and language studies (including SLA), cultural studies, and comparative literature. A growing body of scholars has explored and advocated for the link between translation studies and language education (see e.g., Carreres & Noriega-Sánchez, 2018; Colina & Angelelli, 2015; Gasca Jiménez, 2022; Mellinger, 2017). Although literacy is not on the list, the necessity of texts in the act of translation would certainly argue for its inclusion.

Building upon this interdisciplinarity, this chapter explores theoretical frameworks from the fields of TS and SLA that might serve as a foundation for establishing literacy-based strategies for pedagogical translation. It begins with an overview of the role of translation and the translator, followed by approaches to translation. These approaches are not intended to be exhaustive nor to provide a theoretical history, but instead to present approaches which may align well with pedagogical translation as a literacy-based strategy. The chapter ends by considering how translation theory and SLA theory might combine in practical classroom application of pedagogical translation.

Translation and the Role of the Translator

Translation is often described by its role. Benjamin (1968) describes the purpose of translation as making the relationship between languages visible. Similarly, wa Thiong'o (2023) defines translation as "the language of languages" (p. 63), or how languages and cultures talk to each other. Bassnett (2014) defines translation as "an endless series of rereading and rewriting" (p. 117) requiring the difficult negotiation of linguistic and cultural differences by the translator. She identifies this process as a journey across time and space, thereby highlighting the importance of context. González-Davies (2020), among many others, defines translation as mediation. According to sociocultural theory (SCT), signs and cultural tools like language *mediate* higher human cognitive functions and intercede in human interactions (Vygotsky, 1978). If we think about mediation in terms of a continuum, language mediates human activity and translation mediates languages and cultures (Block, 2003; González-Davies, 2020). The recurring theme of translation as movement across languages and cultures appears across these definitions of translation, giving us an idea of what is meant in describing translation as *mediating* languages and cultures.

While translation's role as a mediator between languages and cultures would seem to ascribe high importance to both translation and to translators, perceptions of the role of the translator vary, leading to differing perceptions of the importance of translation as well. When translation is seen as a simple process, the role of the translator is simple, unimportant, and available to anyone with some knowledge of two languages (Bassnett, 2014). However, when translation is seen as the complex negotiation between languages and cultures that it is, the role of both the translator and translation increases in importance: "In modern bilingual or multilingual cities, translation is an indispensable part of everyday life. The space of translation is normalized and becomes a space of exchange that can bring about cultural renewal" (Bassnett, 2014, p. 174). When modified to apply to education, this statement advocates powerfully for the use of translation not only for establishing multilingual space but also for language instruction in schools: "In modern bilingual or multilingual [*schools*], translation is an indispensable part of everyday life. The space of translation is normalized and becomes a space of exchange that can bring about cultural renewal" (Bassnett, 2014, p. 174). The normalization of translation would in turn normalize learners' bilingual practices and open the way for learners to draw upon their linguistic and cultural assets.

Approaches to Translation

The Role of Equivalence

Despite its contested nature, the concept of equivalence is always present to some degree in TS (Munday et al., 2022; Panau, 2013). According to Toury (2012), equivalence is assumed in translated texts, and the question becomes one of what is equivalent and what is not. Therefore, according to Cook (2010), "The quest for an understanding of the nature of equivalence, understood in the terms of linguistics, is in many ways the starting point of modern translation theory" (p. 57), with the degree to which a translator may deviate or not from the original a key consideration. Similarly, Bassnett (2014) describes translation in terms of the potential for equivalence, that is, as a process in which "something written in one language is moved into another, words and sentences are reshaped and remade, *although the assumption is that the original will somehow still be present in the reformulated version* [emphasis added]" (p. 3). In other words, some degree of equivalence is necessary in translation. Baker (2018a) chooses to use the term *equivalence* for its familiarity "rather than because it has any theoretical status" (p. 5) and with the understanding that equivalence in translation will always be relative given the various linguistic and cultural elements in play.

Frameworks in TS like functionalism can encompass and surpass equivalence while providing criteria for determining if or how much equivalence is appropriate. In functionalist approaches, translation strategy is based upon the function or purpose of the translation as stated in the translation brief (i.e., translation instructions), which should include the target audience and purpose (Nord, 2018). According to Nord (2018), the translation should balance the intent of the source text, as understood through careful analysis, with the indicated purpose and audience of the translation. In literacy-based language instruction, these elements would align with text comprehension, audience, and purpose. A functionalist approach in pedagogical translation may therefore contribute to learners' sense of authenticity in their work and guide the linguistic and cultural decisions they make for the target audience.

Reiss et al. (2014) built upon the concept of functionalism by applying informative, expressive, and appellative text types to translation strategy. From this approach, equivalence must be sought at the text level and meet the function of the source text type. Informative texts are factual and translations must be straightforward, with explications (explanations) given as needed. Expressive texts are creative and translations should reflect the author's perspective. Appellative tests are designed to appeal to the reader for a desired response, so translations should seek to have an "equivalent effect" on the reader of the translated text as the source text would have had on the source text reader.

From a functionalist approach, considerations of equivalence may still be useful in pedagogical translation depending upon the objectives of a translation activity. For example, in a translation activity in an intermediate-level secondary Spanish class, most students collaboratively translated the word *llantas* in Spanish to *wheels* in English (from the poem *Wheels*, Bowles, 2018, English edition; *Wheels*, Bowles, 2020, Spanish edition) (Albrecht, 2024). Upon examining Bowles's initial English version, they learned that *llantas* had been translated from *whitewalls*, a specialized type of tire placed on lowrider cars as part of their overall aesthetic and cultural significance (Ortega, 2020). Students discussed whether their own translation to *wheels* or *whitewall* mattered, and most, being unfamiliar with lowriders, thought it didn't. However, one student commented that it did matter for people who were interested in this particular type of car, which is representative of Chicano culture within the United States. Therefore, if the reader is interested in Chicano culture or if the goal is to depict Chicano culture, then the selected term should be whitewalls. On the other hand, if the goal is to domesticate, or make the translated text more familiar to non-Chicanos, the term wheels would be selected. The goal of this study was to determine whether a translation activity contributed to heritage and world language learner reading comprehension, and a functionalist approach was used to determine if translations demonstrated comprehension of the source text.

Let's look at another type of intersection between levels of equivalence. In one of the author's mixed secondary intermediate Spanish classes, the students engaged in a discussion of a saying used in Spanish to make children who have hurt themselves feel better: *Sana, sana, colita de rana. Si no sanas hoy, sanarás mañana*. World language learners quickly determined that the literal translation, "Heal, heal, frog's little tail. If you don't heal today, you'll heal tomorrow," did not work functionally in terms of offering a meaningful consolatory ditty in the target language. Bilingual speakers of Spanish offered possible translations such as, "Do you want me to kiss it better?" which is completely different linguistically but more appropriate pragmatically, and works functionally. These types of discussions may leave students with a deeper understanding of degrees of correspondence in translation between languages depending upon the purpose of the translation and how cultural understanding may play a role (see also *Así se dice* in Escamilla et al., 2014).

Like discourse, pragmatics also concerns language in use. Intercultural pragmatics in play during additional language acquisition address cultural norms in the home and additional language that underlie how meaning is inferred (McConachy, 2019). This may include understanding that an utterance involves a given emotion, irony, or sarcasm; or a cultural norm such as routine, politeness, or friendliness. However, unrecognized pragmatic assumptions based upon one's home culture may result in "othering" members of the new culture (McConachy), pointing to the value of pragmatics when considering translation activities. For example, when discussing pragmatics in one of my classes for pre-service teachers, bilingual speakers of Spanish offered different inferences regarding when one stops saying "good afternoon" and starts saying "good evening/night." Many agreed that one would start saying "buenas noches" when the sun sets, or around 6.00 pm. One student indicated that she would say "buenas noches" after dinner, which culturally for her would be around 9–10 pm. In this case, the translation between languages would be the same, but pragmatically, for a cultural insider, the assumption upon hearing "buenas noches" would be that dinner had been eaten. For cultural outsiders, the broader assumption would simply be that it was evening. The translator would therefore need to determine whether or not to add an explication to the translation, or domesticate the text, so that the target audience would pick up on the nuance.

Equivalence in translation is therefore closely aligned to cultural transfer, including in text types. Within systemic functional linguistics, the term *genre* describes the way that cultural norms are manifested in texts, such as articles, speeches, or essays. Because cultural norms are involved in the structuring of text types, genre may not translate directly between cultures or may in fact be impossible (Cook, 2010; Halliday, 1964; Reiss & Vermeer, 2014). Tardy et al. (2020) maintained that pedagogical translation functions as a strategy for teaching genre to multilingual university students because of the recontextualization required across languages. A sample task might be for students to select a magazine article on a given topic in the home or additional language and to then provide a translation for an audience of their choice. In completing the translation, students must take into account "translation difficulties related to culturally specific information, historical or geographical references, presumed shared knowledge, and humor" (p. 310).

In Even-Zohar's (1990) polysystems theory, the sociocultural, sociolinguistic environment is assumed to play a role in translation. This includes the types of texts selected for translation and in the typical direction of translation from the dominant language into the non-dominant language (Munday et al., 2022). In turn, these decisions are representative of sociocultural power imbalance, with symbolic power resting in the dominant language. According to Lee (2013), there is a dominant (hegemonic) language in a multilingual society and one or more dominated (non-hegemonic) languages; tensions between them are "in high relief in a translational relationship" (p. 107). While polysystems theory refers specifically to literary translation, it might be applied in educational environments in terms of the following: (1) what translated texts are available for students to read; and (2) what texts are available for students to translate. In the United States, for example, few children's books published in other countries are imported, translated, or republished (Goldsmith & Huang, 2017). Teachers searching for texts which reflect their students' diverse backgrounds are therefore largely limited to books published in English in the United States. Nevertheless, applying pedagogical translation as a bilingual, biliterate teaching strategy is a way to resist dominant power norms in biliterate contexts (Hornberger & Skilton-Sylvester, 2000) as texts selected for translation may be representative of the non-dominant culture and directionality of translations may change.

Translation across multiple levels of equivalence can create meaning in unforeseen ways, in particular as students collaborate and negotiate (Cano & Ruiz, 2020; Cook, 2010). Given the impossibility of achieving equivalence on every potential level, there is always the assumption that there will be loss in translation, including loss of sound patterns, word order, connotation, and lexical and cultural meaning, including through differences in genre as previously mentioned. As a result, only certain types of equivalence may be achieved (Cook, 2010). The degree of correspondence desired in a translation may be determined by the function of the translation (Colina, 2015; Cook, 2010). Bowles (2014), in discussing the decision-making process in translation from Nahuatl to English, observed, "I have tried to strike a balance between the features of the original Nahuatl performance and the expectations of modern readers of poetry" (p. 39), also noting the text's translation journey of rereading and rewriting across time and space from the original Otomí composer, the Nahua adapter of the text, the indigenous transcription, his own translation to English—and the considerations toward equivalence at each step. Ultimately, Bowles reflected upon his objective in finding a balance between the source text and his modern audience. Skopos theory might be applied here: if the final translation meets the purpose of or instructions for the translation, then ultimately the level of equivalence is of secondary consideration (Reiss & Vermeer, 2014).

The multiple levels of equivalence that may be considered between texts, and the certainty of loss, illustrate the potential of pedagogical translation as a literacy-teaching strategy: "Attention is on neither the 'first place' of the student's own language nor the 'second place' of the new language but on a 'third place' of the interaction between the two" (Cook, 2010, pp. 72–73). It is the interaction between the two that provides learners with the opportunity to recognize similarity and difference on varying levels of equivalence and thus to more fully comprehend a text. Jiménez et al. (2015), for example, found that translation of an excerpt from an English Language Arts middle school text into students' home language of Spanish resulted in increased metacognitive and metalinguistic awareness, both of which are indicators of reading comprehension. In this study, students did struggle with concepts of equivalence. In translation of idiomatic expressions, they first attempted word-for-word translations which made no sense, as idiomatic expressions have no lexical and often no syntactic equivalence. However, the authors pointed out that student recognition that they had "correctly" translated and yet the result still made no sense can be a strategy for helping students recognize when they are dealing with an idiomatic expression. They must therefore look at the function of the translation. The cognitive processes required for this type of translation are complex and demonstrate the range of linguistic skills students must draw upon:

> Although idiomatic expressions were uniquely problematic for students to translate, they were particularly fruitful for providing insight into student thinking. Working on idiomatic expressions, students recognized semantic problems with a literal translation, thought about alternate meanings of words and word synonyms in English, made inferences about what the passage might be saying, related the English phrase to idioms in

Spanish, and assessed the resulting translations for syntactic correctness and semantic fit. As such, these episodes made visible the cultural and linguistic understandings that students either brought with them or developed during the activity of translating. (Jiménez et al., 2015, p. 266)

Students were therefore evaluating equivalence at semantic, syntactic, and pragmatic levels while addressing the functionality of their translation.

This degree of correspondence as determined by the function of the translation—or "reprocessing an existing text" (Council of Europe, 2001, p. 95)—can be connected to mediation. What has been termed the "mediation turn" in translation "encourages learners to explore beyond culturally bound connotations, acquire a wider scope by looking at the nuances inherent to non-binary errors, develop multileveled skills – from the lexicon to pragmatics – and negotiation principles" (Pintado-Gutiérrez, 2022, p. 44). From a functional perspective, learners will base their decisions regarding lexical and pragmatic nuance on the purpose of the text. For example, in the author's advanced-beginner secondary Spanish course, learners had to determine the purpose of a translation in terms of the target audience before translating a medical intake form. That is, they noticed both informal and formal medical terms could be used, ultimately deciding on the less-formal terms given that the text was for lay people, not medical professionals.

Augustyn (2013) argued that the bilingual practice of translation allows language learners access to high-frequency vocabulary as well as to compare levels of equivalence between words or phrases. For example, similar to Jakobson's discussion of the non-equivalent translation from the Russian *syr* to *cheese* in English due to different types of cheese available in each environment (Panau, 2013, citing Jakobson, 1959), in one of my intermediate university courses for heritage speakers of Spanish, students engaged in a discussion of the translation of *cheese* in a bilingual children's book and how the type of cheese involved represented cultural difference, noting that it needed an explication in English but not in Spanish. In this sense, translation of even simple lexical items points to the need not only for textual comprehension but also for the development of intercultural being as a part of socially situated literacy.

According to Cook (2010), early language learners might focus primarily on linguistic levels of equivalence in translation, while intermediate and advanced students would move toward pragmatic or discourse equivalence as their skills improve. However, from a bilingual education perspective, Escamilla et al. (2014) proposed the incorporation of pedagogical translation as a bilingual teaching strategy as early as in the third grade, and texts selected for translation should be short and conceptually dense. Butzkamm and Caldwell (2009) recommended that in this search for equivalence, "translation unit[s]" (p. 200) be at the sentence or paragraph level, while keeping in mind the overall context of the text being translated. The goal for equivalence may be literal, with a focus on lexicon and syntax, but it may also be conceptual, as would occur with texts such as poems or riddles that are rich in culture and idiomatic language use. Escamilla et al. (2014) have found that "children argue vehemently and eloquently" (p. 75) over word selection, thus augmenting their comprehension.

Domestication and foreignization of texts are additional considerations toward equivalence. Through domestication, translated texts reflect target linguistic and cultural norms, making the translated text fluid and easy to read in the target language (Venuti, 2018). Through foreignization, translated texts reflect linguistic and cultural difference. According to Venuti (2018, p. 15), domestication is an ethnocentric process and dominates the Anglo-American translation culture—thus rendering the translator invisible—as well as the source language and culture. In translating his own works from Gikuyu to English, wa Thiong'o (2023) noted that in his first translation he tried to preserve the rhythms of the source language, using a foreignizing approach, but that his later translations were more concerned with capturing "the spirit of the novel" (p. 51), which he deemed more important than capturing the sense of the source language. Venuti (2018) maintained that all translated texts must be domesticated by the nature of translation from one culture into another and that foreignizing is in fact adding foreign*isms*, or the insertion by the translator of cues which signal the source language and culture. Nevertheless, according to Tymoczko (2002), foreignizing or defamiliarizing a literary text is a post-colonial act as it draws attention to linguistic and cultural differences and calls standard language into question. Additionally, the choice to domesticate is influenced by dominant societal hierarchies, particularly in the United States and Great Britain, thus resulting in translated texts which mirror dominant linguistic and cultural norms. Cook (2010) proposed that beyond choosing between the voices of domestication and foreignization, translators may choose a third voice: their own, thus aligning with wa Thinog'o's (2023) view of translation as the language of languages. The choice to domesticate, foreignize, or "rewrite" a text in one's own voice requires an understanding of the options, a profound linguistic and cultural comprehension of the source text, and the linguistic and cultural skill to effect the type of textual equivalence desired. For a student of language, acquisition of these complex skills would require explicit instruction and modeling and the ability to read the world as well as the word (Freire, 1970).

Finally, Lefevere described literary translation as an act of rewriting by those with ideological and institutional power to do so (Lefevere, 2017). This approach was directed toward a target audience of professional and student translators (Munday et al., 2022). However, translation as rewriting implies a critical approach which may be applied in pedagogical translation as well, in particular as students translate source texts and then compare their own translations to an already-existing translation. While advanced language students may work with existing literary texts, primary or secondary students may work with excerpts, depending upon their level, or with bilingual or dual-edition children's literature (Colina & Lafford, 2017). A translation activity may be designed as a guided writing activity in which one of the objectives is acquisition of a certain element of writerly craft. In Lefevere's sense of rewriting, critical conversations regarding ideological or institutional elements which may have been in play in the target audience may also aid students in their growth as languaging, intercultural beings working with socially situated texts.

In analyzing a multilingual literary anthology in Singapore, Lee (2013) noted that the editors' perspective on translation moves beyond ideological and institutional power, in that translation is "always vulnerable to misreading, misinterpretation, misshaping" (p. 130), in which case no one language (namely, English) can be "the single transcendental language that travels across linguistic barriers" (p. 130). In the critical continua of biliteracy (Hornberger and Skilton-Sylvester, 2000), biliterate practices are assigned a typical power weighting in society, with monolingualism being the dominant power norm. Lee's analyses of translations between the four official languages of Singapore rather than only between English and Chinese, English and Malay, or English and Tamil is an example of how acts of rewriting may in fact challenge and reverse dominant power norms. A return to wa Thiong'o's (2023) conceptualization of translation as the language of languages may be useful here in terms of its mediating role between all languages, not only as a replicator of dominant power norms.

Second Language Acquisition

This section links translation and SLA theory, pointing toward the interdisciplinary foundation of pedagogical translation. SLA theory is currently dichotomized between cognitive and social processes. Some SLA theorists continue to focus primarily on cognitive processes as seen in the IIO model (Block, 2003; Gass et al., 2020). Through the cognitive approach, external influences on SLA may include the home language speaker's linguistic and psychological background and learner motivation and affect, but the multilingual and sociocultural influences incorporated in the multilingual and social turns are not included.

However, as described in Chapter 1, SLA theory has broadened over the past fifty years from a primary focus on cognitive processes to include social and multilingual turns. SCT is a primary lens used "to explain the relationship between language acquisition and language socialization ... SCT reverses the notion that language acquisition takes place in the head and that language use merely applies the acquired knowledge to the social world" (Kramsch & Stevenson, 2008, p. 21); instead, socialization is equated with language acquisition. Pedagogical SCT approaches are inclined toward authentic task-based, collaborative learning, such as that found in pedagogical translation.

Similarly, May (2013) described the effect of the multilingual turn in SLA as "multilingualism, rather than monolingualism, as the new norm of applied linguistic and sociolinguistic analysis" (p. 1). As discussed in Chapter 1, the multilingual turn allows home language use in the classroom. This typical bilingual practice not only validates student identity but also provides scaffolding for additional language acquisition and mediates student thinking (Stachl-Peier, 2020). This new focus on multilingualism centers multilingual learner identities in selection of language-teaching pedagogies which develop "translingual and transcultural competence" (Laviosa, 2019, pp. 181–182) and require the ability to move between languages and cultures, a skill also developed through pedagogical translation.

These competencies align with CEFR (Council of Europe, 2018) goals of plurilingual and pluricultural competence as well as with American Council on the Teaching of Foreign Languages (ACTFL) goals of understanding cultural perspectives and for effective communication based upon cultural understanding (The National Standards Collaborative Board, 2015). They also align with the literacy goals of the pedagogy of multiliteracies, namely, for students to have "access to the evolving language of work, power, and community, and fostering the critical engagement necessary for them to design their social futures and achieve success through fulfilling employment" (New London Group, 1996, p. 60). However, given the monolingual focus of content-area standards such as the Common Core State Standards (CCSS) in the United States, second language theory is not applied, which is problematic for bi/multilingual teaching and learning. This requires extension of the standards, which may be through the addition of bilingual strategies like translanguaging and pedagogical translation within the context of second language standards such as the English Language Proficiency Standards (ELPS) in the United States (Fenner & Segota, 2023; García & Flores, 2013).

Translation and Second Language Acquisition

Due to its dominant role in language teaching, the field of SLA generally determines what is considered best practice (Cook, 2010; Laviosa, 2014). Therefore, whether to use translation in language teaching is influenced by conceptions of best processes for language teaching within SLA. Process is in turn influenced by conceptions of the purpose, or desired outcomes, of language instruction (Laviosa, 2014). When monolingual language ideologies are in play, desired outcomes are generally seen as parallel monolingualism in one person, leaving no room for the use of pedagogical translation. For example, traditional SLA objections to translation in language teaching include that it impedes development of fluency and that it promotes home language interference and transfer of home language vocabulary and structures into the additional language. These claims align with monolingual approaches to language teaching. However, Cook (2010) pointed out that the existence of simultaneous interpretation argues against claims of the detrimental effects of translation on language acquisition, and that "Any learner will inevitably both learn and acquire, translate and not translate, and it is not feasible to attempt the separation of the effects" (p. 94).

Beyond the persistent presence of translation in SLA, key theories of SLA align with both translation theory and the use of pedagogical translation. For example, according to Krashen (1981), learners acquire language through language input that is slightly above their current level and when their affective filter has been lowered. Carefully designed translation tasks can provide comprehensible input through the home language while lowering the affective filter for students who are permitted to use their home language. Cummins's (1979, 1981) common underlying proficiency (CUP), basic interpersonal communication skills (BICS), and cognitive academic language proficiency (CALP) also align with pedagogical translation use. The theory of CUP maintains that underlying cognitive and academic skills, including literacy, are transferable across languages, thus supporting the use of home languages for content or language acquisition. Similarly, Hartmann and Hélot (2020) maintain that "implementation of translation as a pedagogical practice may be considered as a logical outcome of [Cummins'] *Linguistic Interdependence Hypothesis*" (p. 98). According to the linguistic interdependence hypothesis, "the development of competence in a second language (L2) is partially a function of the type of competence already developed in the home language at the time when intensive exposure to L2 begins" (Cummins, 1979, p. 3). Implementation of bilingual strategies such as pedagogical translation may therefore be expected to scaffold both home and additional language competence (González-Davies, 2017; Hartmann & Hélot, 2020).

Cummins's frameworks for SLA are commonly and globally applied to bilingual education. BICS and CALP differentiate between social and academic language use. Cognitive academic language proficiency takes 5–7 years to develop, while BICS takes only about two (Cummins, 2007). The acquisition of CALP tends to be the focus in schools, as academic language is considered essential for academic success, including for standardized testing, the results of which are often tied to governmental funding. In contrast, as BICS deals with social language, it is linked to communicative competence in informal environments and tends to receive less educational focus. However, BICS can be linked to teaching pragmatics, or saying the right thing at the right time given that speakers judge each other "on the basis of pragmatic triggers" (McConachy, 2019, p. 170).

Once cognitive, literacy, and academic proficiency in one language have reached an adequate threshold, it is possible for "concepts, skills, and learning strategies" (Cummins, 2016, p. 940) available through CUP to transfer across languages. Translation can facilitate this transfer through its inherent contrastive analysis (Pym, 2012). The CUP approach supports the development and use of students' home languages and literacies in the classroom, with the intent that these skills will transfer. This approach refutes the still-common, monolingual-approach concerns of policy makers, educators, and parents that "less instructional time through the majority language would have adverse consequences for students' literacy development in that language" (p. 942).

Translation also aligns with Swain's (1995, 2005) pushed output theory. In response to Krashen's theory of comprehensible input and its focus on listening and reading, Swain argued that output—namely, speaking and writing—is also required for language acquisition. This output should be *pushed,* that is students should be pushed to generate correct, understandable language; to notice gaps in their learning; to reflect on language form; and to refine their language production (Swain & Lapkin, 1995). These processes require the negotiation for meaning which may be accomplished through translation (Panau, 2013; Pintado-Gutiérrez, 2022). Building on Schmidt's (1990) noticing hypothesis, Ellis (2003) proposed that learners must notice language features in order to internalize them, and task-based language teaching (TBLT) can be designed to encourage noticing through focus on form, comparison, or negotiation of meaning. While Ellis was careful to distance TBLT and Grammar Translation, he affirmed that translation could be used as a task for meaning making. Finally, translation also aligns with SLA work on bilingual identity development (see e.g., Norton, 2013; Pavlenko, 2006), which will be further addressed in Chapter 6.

Translation Theory, Second Language Acquisition, and Pedagogical Translation

How, then, are translation theory and SLA linked with pedagogical translation? The key elements will be the functionality of a translation, including considerations of equivalence, in combination with the multilingual turn in SLA. This leads to the assumption of social-situatedness of both source and target texts or of cultural considerations in translation. A focus on the functionality of a translation, including pragmatic factors, may contribute to learner perception of communicative utility of the activity and hence positive affect. Cultural learning will be directly addressed in Chapter 6 and is also closely linked to linguistic learning as addressed in Chapter 5, in particular, as it overlaps with pragmatics. First, however, we turn to approaches to pedagogical translation in Chapter 4.

4

Approaches to Pedagogical Translation

As pedagogical translation has gradually found its way into more language-learning environments, differing approaches related to its end goals have emerged. García et al. (2020) differentiated pedagogical translation into three strands, all of which rely upon the multilingual turn in SLA. The first strand is traditional pedagogical translation. This initial approach does not focus on social contexts but instead on language-learning benefits through translation. Second, the CEFR (Council of Europe, 2020) incorporates translation to develop and assess plurilingual and pluricultural competence. The plurilingual approach advocates for the use of translanguaging in the sense of allowing movement between languages as a unitary system, but it does not include power weightings between languages. It was designed for both second and world language environments. The final translation approach is that of translanguaging, which also allows movement between languages as a unitary system but which comes from a critical, decolonial stance. Initially conceptualized by Cen Williams in Wales for equitable teaching of Welsh in English-dominant British society (García et al., 2020), this approach is more common in bilingual or second language than world language-learning environments and takes into account students' home, often minoritized, languages (Axelrod & Cole, 2018; Cano & Ruiz, 2020; David et al., 2019). This approach has also appeared in heritage language–learning environments (Belpoliti & Plascencia-Vela, 2013; Pacheco et al., 2015).

Although the three approaches vary in their alignment with social contexts, the role of translation as a mediating activity is in play across them all. Because translation serves to transfer meaning in its role as a language mediator, regardless of the pedagogical approach, translation will be considered to function as a mediator (Colina & Lafford, 2017).

After elaborating upon each approach, the chapter will discuss how the three strands might appear in examples of translation activities throughout the book.

The Traditional Approach to Pedagogical Translation

Along with the multilingual and social turns in the field of SLA, studies from a traditional pedagogical translation approach began to appear around the turn of the twenty-first century. These largely focused on language-learning benefits. From this perspective, "The real usefulness of translation in foreign language classes lies in comparison of grammar, vocabulary, word order and other language points in the target language and the student's mother tongue" (Dagilienė, 2012, p. 125). Laufer and Girsai (2008), for example, studied different approaches to teaching additional language vocabulary to Hebrew-speaking secondary EFL students, including contrastive analysis in tandem with translation. In the study, participants who had participated in a contrastive analysis/translation approach retained more vocabulary. The authors therefore recommended that contrastive analysis and pedagogical translation be included in additional language teaching to raise student awareness of linguistic equivalence issues and to improve vocabulary retention, noting that, in terms of communicative language teaching, "the best method for achieving this goal may not be identical to the goal itself" (p. 712). Augustyn (2013) also argued for the reinstatement of bilingual strategies such as translation for high-frequency vocabulary learning in post-secondary world language courses, noting the link between vocabulary teaching and acquisition of literacy skills. Similarly, Goundareva (2011) found that post-secondary students of Spanish in British Columbia who participated in translating an excerpt from a short story in Spanish to English were better able to produce new vocabulary than their peers who did not participate in the translation activity.

Park et al. (2015) presented Poetry Inside-Out, a literacy program based upon poetry and translation designed for EB secondary students and implemented in ESL classes in the United States. In this program, students translated poetry from their home language into English, then used the translated poems as models to write and present their own poems in English. Through the process, students "played with word meaning and used their expertise in their respective countries as evidence" (p. 55). While some elements of intercultural competence and/or intercultural being were present in the study, its focus was largely on how the translation activity helped students to acquire academic literacy in English.

Barnes's (2018) study on reinstating pedagogical translation in the language classroom provides a bridge between traditional and plurilingual approaches. The author studied British secondary students' perceptions regarding the usefulness of translation in world language learning, looking for a methodology that would contribute to world language students' exposure to authentic application of the new language. With 100 percent of participants finding translation to be useful in the classroom, and some finding more interest in learning about the target culture, Barnes recommended teaching with a range of explicative and communicative translation. Explicative translation is used for contrastive analysis to make language functions clear in the additional language and largely aligns with traditional translation and communicative translation, which is "a more 'realistic' dimension to language teaching" (p. 253) that aligns somewhat with plurilingual translation, as will be seen in the next section. Although Barnes linked traditional and plurilingual translation, overall, studies such as these largely demonstrate the linguistic benefits of pedagogical translation but are not focused on cultural components of translation. This is in contrast to both plurilingual and translanguaging approaches, which will be discussed next.

The Plurilingual Approach to Pedagogical Translation

Because translation entails cultural as well as linguistic choices, approaches to pedagogical translation have evolved to include cultural learning. Plurilingual approaches to pedagogical translation under the CEFR, for example, focus on using translation for plurilingual and intercultural competence. Plurilingualism is the ability "to use languages for the purposes of communication and to take part in intercultural action, where a person, viewed as a social agent, has proficiency, of varying degrees, in several languages and experience of several cultures" (Coste et al., 2009, p.11). In contrast, multilingualism centers on "the coexistence of several languages at the social or individual level" (Council of Europe, 2020, p. 30), thereby focusing principally on linguistic components of language without cultural considerations. The goal of the plurilingual approach is to allow learners to use all their linguistic repertoires to make meaning and to encourage them to identify how languages and cultures are similar and different (Council of Europe, 2020). From a plurilingual perspective, the act of translation implies "crossing borders between languages and building bridges between cultures" (Hartmann & Hélot, 2020, p. 96). Translation from a plurilingual approach has been broadly applied across the globe.

The plurilingual approach has multiple characteristics, moving beyond communicative language teaching and instruction of discrete linguistic skills (Corcoll, 2013). Instead, the integrated plurilingual approach (IPA) is characterized by purposeful, collaborative tasks with a focus other than language and which follow a didactic sequence (González-Davies, 2017).

As collaboration is a typical element, this approach also relies on co-construction of meaning (Council of Europe, 2020). Learners are encouraged to transfer skills between languages, to explore the potential of different forms of expression; and to use their entire linguistic repertoires, or to translanguage, and hence instructors must incorporate structured use of the home language through activities like translation (Corcoll, 2013; Muñoz-Basols, 2019). From a plurilingual perspective, translanguaging promotes "interlingualism," or the ability to compare and contrast across languages (Laviosa, 2018). Translation and translanguaging are also beneficial because they promote creativity and a multilingual identity. García et al.'s (2020) distinction between translanguaging within the IPA and translanguaging as a decolonial approach will be addressed later in the chapter.

While drawing upon their linguistic repertoire, "Plurilingual individuals are seen as drawing flexibly on their interrelated, uneven, and developing plurilinguistic repertoire to accomplish a variety of communicative tasks involving more than one language" (Laviosa, 2022, p. 12) or dialect or variety (Council of Europe, 2020). While drawing upon this repertoire, learners are expected to be participating in "intercultural action" (García et al., 2020, p. 84) and developing intercultural competence and mediation skills, or the "ability to work within more than one culture efficiently and to bridge cultures" (González-Davies, 2017, p. 5). In the process, students may also begin to question or develop their own cultural assumptions. Oprica (2016), for example, details a translation activity of brief, culturally rich texts from Romanian into Spanish for young heritage speakers of Romanian in Spain which was designed to foster both plurilingualism and pluriculturalism, as the heritage speakers were not familiar with many of the Romanian texts and their cultural ties.

The IPA involves two key shifts in language teaching and learning. First, a communicative focus on mediation and interaction must be added to a focus on reception and production, with mediation as a combination of the latter three (Council of Europe, 2020; Gónzalez-Davies & Soler Ortínez, 2021). Additionally, the focus on teacher and learner skill shifts from native-like proficiency aligned with monolingual ideologies to mastery, or the C2 level in the CEFR. The teacher's role, then, "is not to imitate an ideal native speaker, but rather to become a competent plurilingual speaker who takes on the dimension of a 'pedagogic mediator' to help students make sense of what they should do (norm), could do (affordance), and would do (intentionality)" (González-Davies & Soler Ortínez, 2021, p. 19). For these shifts to be effectively implemented, González-Davies and Soler Ortínez recommend that the rationale for the IPA be explicitly taught to both students and teachers to facilitate the pivot away from monolingualism and native-speakerism.

Translation is a key component within the plurilingual approach because it is "a natural communicative action carried out by plurilingual speakers" (González-Davies & Soler Ortínez, 2021, p. 19) that is used for mediation.

Within this approach, translation is considered both a means for language or other learning and an end in itself, or as a "fifth skill" added to the traditional four skills of listening, speaking, reading, and writing in language learning (Colina & Lafford, 2017; Council of Europe, 2020). Translation tasks may therefore be designed for linguistic, cultural, or content objectives or to demonstrate skill in translation itself.

Scholars from TS and Spanish linguistics have applied the plurilingual approach to heritage language learning. For example, in their study on pedagogical translation for heritage language lexical development, Belpoliti and Plascencia-Vela (2013) drew upon heritage learners' cultural backgrounds, including 70 percent as language mediators in family or community settings, and full linguistic repertoires, encouraging participants to consider the connection between cultural and lexical variation in Spanish. Mellinger and Gasca Jimenez (2017) explored the potential for HLLs to draw upon their cultural backgrounds, including language brokering experience, and full linguistic repertoires in interpreting courses. They highlighted the need for differentiating instruction between HLLs and additional language learners based upon these groups' different linguistic and cultural backgrounds. Gasca Jiménez (2017, 2019, 2022) has focused on translation as a plurilingual approach for HLLs through the incorporation of HLLs' language and experience into heritage language instruction, including through translanguaging and recognition of students' ideolects as a resource (Gasca Jiménez, 2022a & b).

Some of this scholarly work demonstrates an overlap between the plurilingual and decolonial translanguaging approach. For example, in a study on post-secondary HLL critical language awareness in the United States, described HLLs as plurilingual and engaging in plurilingual practices and also referred to power imbalances resulting from standard and monolingual language ideologies. Similarly, Carreira (2016) does not explicitly align with either approach but focuses on recognizing and building upon the diverse and often marginalized linguistic competencies and cultural backgrounds of HLLs in mixed heritage—additional language classrooms in order to support bilingual identity and language development. This critical plurilingual perspective points toward alignment or overlap with the translanguaging approach, which will be discussed next.

The Translanguaging Approach to Pedagogical Translation

As previously mentioned, the concept of translanguaging was first developed by Cen Williams as a pedagogical means to strategically utilize both Welsh and English in bilingual Welsh classrooms (Laviosa, 2018). Translanguaging has since been expanded upon conceptually within bilingual, second, heritage, and world language—learning environments and to include translanguaging theory, space, practice, stance, and pedagogy. A translanguaging approach to pedagogical translation takes all of these elements into consideration.

According to translanguaging theory, bilinguals have one linguistic repertoire which they use for meaning making, as opposed to named first and second languages (García & Leiva, 2014). Kumagai and Kono (2018) and Laviosa (2020) note the similarity between plurilingual and bilingual approaches to translanguaging in terms of meaning making. However, it is a decolonial perspective which marks the key differentiation between the two approaches, as bilingual and world language education programs, which are typically aligned with a plurilingual approach, have different "stakes and goals" (Kumagai & Kono, 2018, p. 251). From the bilingual approach described by García et al. (2020), the stakes and goals of translanguaging include a social justice component which is "a way to undo the process through which the knowledge base and linguistic/ cultural practices of colonized people was obliterated" (Li & García, 2022, p. 314). This is a political act. It attempts to eliminate hierarchical language practices, disrupt traditional views of bi- or monolingualism and the power weighting associated with them (García & Kleifgren, 2019; Hornberger & Skilton-Sylvester, 2000) and replace monolingual language ideologies with translanguaging as "a *language ideology* that takes bilingualism as the norm" (Mazak & Carroll, 2017, p. 5, emphasis in original). This perspective in turn empowers minoritized bilingual learners who tend to have inequitable education experiences in monolingually oriented countries (García & Leiva, 2014; Skutnabb-Kangas, 1988).

García et al. (2020) describe this translanguaging approach as typical to bilingual environments in the United States. However, research in other areas around the globe has shown a similar decolonial, social justice approach. For example, Omidire and Ayob (2020) describe positive student affect due to a safe environment which valued home languages as an affordance of translanguaging in culturally and linguistically diverse English-medium South African schools. The translanguaging pedagogy implemented in the classrooms under study demonstrated a disruption of language hierarchy as students' home languages were recognized, valued, and utilized. Similarly, Mazak and Carroll (2017) found that in Puerto Rican higher education, translanguaging disrupted the hegemony of English in academia and supported learner identity.

The second component of translanguaging is recognition that bi/ multilingual students engage in translanguaging practices such as bi- or multilingual discourse in their daily lives. These translanguaging practices involve the fluid use of all resources within a speaker's repertoire without regard to constructed language boundaries (García, 2009; Li & García, 2022). These language practices may be complex and may not fit within school or instructor conceptions of what exactly these practices are, making it critically important to understand where misperceptions may arise and to work to truly understand students' language practices and to leverage them for the students' benefit. Li and García (2022) describe students whose language practices are not understood and therefore incorrectly addressed in their schools. For example, Song, a student of Chinese heritage in London, considers himself an English speaker. However, his school, making incorrect assumptions about his language practices, puts him in an ESL class, where he is bored, and a Mandarin Chinese as a foreign language class, but Mandarin is not his home language. Li and García note that, "In isolating these categories as one named language or another ... the complexity of how they lead their lives is simply ignored. This means that they always fall outside of the school's understandings for inclusion" (p. 316). However, in classrooms which recognize and understand students' complex translanguaging practices, these practices may be drawn upon and used. For example, language users may speak or write in one language or another or in both, and everyone in the social environment is engaged in conversation whether they know all of the languages in play or not (Marrero-Colón, 2021).

In conjunction with translanguaging practices, Li (2010) has referred to translanguaging space, which is a space for translanguaging that is created as a result of translanguaging. In a translanguaging space, language users draw upon their linguistic repertoires for meaning making. The translanguaging space also promotes collaboration, cultural inclusivity and identity formation. Li stresses that "the consequentiality of translanguaging cannot be underestimated. It creates a social world in which the actor plays a number of roles and occupies a number of positions. It is also a social world where the individual feels a connectedness with others" (2010, p. 13). In his study, Li documented the multilingual identities of three university-aged Chinese men in Britain, including satisfaction with their multilingual, multicultural identities and the fact that as Chinese who had either immigrated to or been born in Britain, they were "not Chinese ... We belong to the world" (p. 12). For the three multilingual participants, this sense of place in the social world went beyond language boundaries which are tied to the one-nation-one-language concept of nationalism and monolingual language ideology.

In addition to the social benefits, translanguaging promotes language development, including enhancing critical thinking about language. Critical thinking about language leads to metalinguistic awareness, which has been linked to reading comprehension and positive literacy outcomes (Escamilla et al., 2014; Jiménez et al., 2015). Li documented the youths' breadth and depth of linguistic creativity as they moved between languages, noting that a higher level of literacy in Chinese contributed to a stronger connection to the language, popular literature and culture of China in one of the participants. While this study did not take place within a classroom, it demonstrated the high degree of linguistic dexterity that can be developed and drawn upon in the classroom as bilingual students have the opportunity to function within a translanguaging space.

In order for translanguaging practices to be capitalized on for language and literacy learning, instructors and other stakeholders must develop a translanguaging stance. Through a translanguaging stance, educators believe that (1) bilingual students' language practices work as one continuum, and (2) bilingual students' linguistic resources are an asset. This stance is ongoing and, particularly in second language—learning environments in which students are learning the dominant societal language, it is not withdrawn once language learners are deemed to have sufficient proficiency in the dominant language (García & Leiva, 2014). Given the ongoing existence of monolingual teaching practices, the development of a translanguaging stance at the institutional level will be more likely to produce sustainable, systemic change needed for the consistent opening of this type of space (Prilutskaya, 2021). Hartmann and Hélot (2020), for example, described the well-established institutional practice of language separation in bilingual programs in the Alsace region of France, as did Sikes and Villanueva (2021) for the state of Texas in the United States. A translanguaging stance may be difficult to establish and sustain without institutional buy-in.

Once a translanguaging stance is established, institutions and educators can develop and implement translanguaging pedagogy. Translanguaging pedagogy is characterized by releasing students from monolingual constraints and repositioning them as competent learners (Cano & Ruiz, 2020; García & Leiva, 2014). Students are able to use their voices to express questions and understandings; to use their agency to choose what language(s) to use for sense making and to use their understandings of language, culture, and audience to influence their language decisions (Axelrod & Cole, 2018; David et al., 2019). As part of the social justice component, students can have their academic and social needs addressed and their home languages and cultures, or "ways of knowing" validated (Omidire & Ayob, 2020).

Prilutskaya (2021) found that translanguaging is more likely to be utilized in content-based instruction than in world language instruction, due to concerns with proficiency in the latter. In world language environments, the distinction would need to be made between activities which involve sense making or negotiation for meaning, in which translanguaging could most certainly be implemented, and activities in which proficiency will be assessed. Nevertheless, implementation of translanguaging pedagogy also requires buy-in. In a systematic review of 233 empirical studies on translanguaging pedagogy in English-learning environments, Prilutskaya (2021) found that sustainable translanguaging classroom pedagogy requires ongoing professional development for teachers, administrators, and policy makers and ongoing collaboration between researchers and stakeholders.

Specific steps can contribute to effective implementation of translanguaging pedagogy, within which translation may be embedded. Areas in which translation might be incorporated will be elaborated upon; the reader may notice an overlap in translation approaches in the studies cited, demonstrating that translation activities might be adapted for different approaches. However, from a translanguaging approach, translation activities must maintain a decolonial approach which uses translation to make students' "bilingual lives visible to all" (García et al., 2020, p. 89).

First, new vocabulary can be introduced with multiple languages, cognates, and/or inquiry. For content-area lessons, Dougherty (2021) recommended adding translanguaging strategies to vocabulary and content instruction and group and independent practice. Pedagogical translation can then be used as a contextualized strategy to teach vocabulary in general or content-area vocabulary in particular, especially with parallel texts (Lo, 2023; Laufer & Girsai, 2008). Parallel texts are source-language texts with a target-language translation. They are commonly used in translator training to stimulate noticing vocabulary nuance or idiomatic expressions, among other things, but their use has been extended to pedagogical translation (Lo, 2023; see Chapter 7 on selecting authentic texts). Next, content can be taught using multilingual texts and dictionaries, to which translation activities such as guided writing (Translation Spotlight, Chapter 5), translation of proverbs (Translation Spotlight, Chapter 6) or bilingual editions of children's books (Translation Spotlight, Chapter 7) might be added. Syntax transfer can also be used as needed (see e.g., Jiménez et al., 2015).

For group practice of the content, collaborative, multilingual groups can be formed for discussion and projects, and projects might include collaborative translation projects (see, among others, Cummins, 2019; Jiménez et al., 2015; Manyak, 2004; and Translation Spotlight, Chapter 9). Again, multilingual texts and syntax transfer can be incorporated, to which translation activities which draw upon students' home languages might be added (see e.g., Jidai et al., 2017; Sneddon, 2009). Finally, multilingual reading and writing can be incorporated into independent practice of content. Peer-to-peer or home-to-school collaborative translation activities may again be considered a way to draw upon students' home languages and cultures while developing an additional language (Translation Spotlight, Chapter 9). However, Cummins (2019) cautions that, as represented by the Canadian experience, dual-language initiatives represent only a small portion of mainstream institutional practice and may in fact be seen as not counting.

Informal learning experiences may provide opportunities to explore the potential of both translanguaging and translation outside of institutional confines. For example, I participated in an informal science learning activity for under-represented intermediate school girls in which the varying components of a translanguaging approach were present. First, multiple participants were EBs who engaged in bilingual language practices in their everyday lives, including during the activity at a Texas state park in the United States. Both monolingual and bilingual staff who were facilitating the activity demonstrated a translanguaging stance, opening space for participants to engage in translanguaging in order to make meaning of the learning experience orally and in writing (Albrecht & Navarrete-Burks, 2025;

Jeffery et al., 2025). Upon arriving at the state park, participants were given laminated cards with photos of local flora and fauna with names in Latin, English, and Spanish. Participants were able to use the translations to discuss or write about their experiences in any language and were encouraged to share other names they might use for the items on the cards, drawing upon and validating their background knowledge. Participants therefore moved fluidly between languages, including in conversations with each other and with staff, in the nature journals in which they recorded their experiences, and on dual-language scavenger hunt worksheets in which they responded in multiple languages and with drawings to make meaning of their experiences. Participants were able to demonstrate their knowledge when, during the scavenger hunt for local flora and fauna, they found the activity prompt lacked the category of "amphibian" after they had seen a frog and wanted to record the observation. Across languages, they discussed the problem and came up with differing ways to represent their knowledge and meaning making. Some students opted to take their scavenger hunt worksheets home to show parents, who would be able to read them in their own language.

The fundamental role of translation from a decolonial translanguaging approach will therefore be quite different from the role of translation from a plurilingual approach. According to García et al. (2020), "Translation acts as a bridge between languages and cultures, but it is a crossing, enabling the monolingual reader to access material that has been written by a monolingual author, and expressing through another language the worldviews of another culture" (p.85). This bridge, however, leaves power hierarchies undisturbed. The language-learning environment will thus determine the language teaching approach, whether a plurilingual bridge or translanguaging "fluid corriente of practices that work within the entanglement of words and worlds in which many minoritized bilingual children live" (García et al., 2020, p. 85).

Although García et al. focus on translanguaging in primary bilingual environments, the need may also arise in other language-learning environments such as secondary monolingual, world languages in which both world and HLLs are present, or dedicated heritage language courses. In the first, for example, Jiménez et al. (2015) found that translation activities supported metalinguistic awareness and reading comprehension for intermediate EB students.

In mixed heritage–world language courses, simultaneous plurilingual and translanguaging approaches to translation may be appropriate. For example, for many reasons, including lack of emphasis, training, and resources (Carreira, 2016), it is common in the United States for secondary and post-secondary language classes to include both heritage speakers of a given language and learners of the same as a foreign language. Pedagogy in these classes generally supports foreign rather than heritage language learning, yet differentiation between approaches is required to meet all students' needs (Burgo, 2018; Carreira & Kagan, 2018). Albrecht (2024) found that translation in mixed secondary groups has potential for doing so. Similarly, Pintado-Gutiérrez (2022) found translation to be an inclusive tool through a plurilingual approach in "highly complex schools" (p. 7), with "'translanguaging as an approach to educating emergent bilinguals in mixed classrooms in schools. Translation is presented as a rich space where the use of translanguaging with emergent bilinguals fits particularly well'" (citing Floros, 2021, p. 287). In this sense, García et al. (2020) may argue that translanguaging from a decolonial rather than plurilingual approach would be more appropriate given the presence of EBs in complex schools and the assumed need for addressing power differentials visible through language.

The distinction between plurilingual and translanguaging approaches underscores the importance of identifying the underlying purpose of translation activities, such as functioning as a culturally sustaining pedagogy (Albrecht et al., 2024). While García et al. (2020) refer to translation as a monolingual endeavor, Cummins (2019) describes a range of pedagogical translation activities incorporated in various learning environments within a translanguaging stance and designed to support students' socially situated literacies. For example, at International High School in New York City, EB students may choose to write in their first language or in English, with other students or community members translating their work if the teacher does not speak the language. At the primary level, the instructor may read a book in the additional language and ask for student home language translations of some of the vocabulary, thus validating students' language practices. Using books modeled in class, children can also be encouraged to write bilingual books or newspaper articles individually, collaboratively, or with their parents. As one student noted, "It makes it faster to be able to use both languages instead of just breaking your head to think of the word in English when you already know the word in the other language" (Cummins, 2019, p. 30, citing Leoni et al., 2011). This range of activities suggests many possible configurations that might be modified by age or language level, depending upon the need.

A decolonial approach to translanguaging has also been placed within the umbrella of translingual pedagogies which "build on and develop the practices associated with mobilizing and meshing diverse linguistic resources" (David et al., 2019, p. 252), including language brokering, code meshing, and translanguaging. The socially defined goal of translingual pedagogy is to "leverage students' full linguistic repertoires towards pedagogical aims" (p. 258). David et al. (2019) place pedagogical translation within translingual pedagogy and as such have developed the TRANSLATE protocol as a type of translingual pedagogy. For this instructional routine, instructors follow seven steps. First, they connect students to a text by activating background knowledge related to the theme. Students then read a set amount of text independently and subsequently share what they thought was the main idea. At this point, either the instructor or the students select one or two sentences to translate, with the instructor commenting on why the selection would be good to translate or not. Students then work collaboratively to translate in pairs or small groups, with the instructor scaffolding the translation with vocabulary and comprehension strategies, and then share and discuss the translations with the other groups. This involves negotiation about areas of disagreement with special attention to nuance in vocabulary or misunderstandings of the text. Finally, the instructor leads a discussion regarding how new comprehension through the translation relates to the characters or themes in the text. Throughout this process, students may engage in translingual problem solving, including through translanguaging. David et al. (2019) cautioned that application of the protocol should be flexible and determined by local contexts, with teachers discussing their "evolving understandings" (p. 272) during professional development sessions and students having input through reflection on their translingual practices, including translanguaging. Student reflections can help instructors better understand how to capitalize on their understanding of student translanguaging to better capitalize on it for desired learning outcomes.

Translation Approaches in Translation Spotlights

Translation from traditional, plurilingual, or translanguaging approaches aligns to varying degrees with the frameworks used for standards, objectives, and evaluation in the Translation Spotlights in Chapters 5–11. However, because the focus of traditional pedagogical translation tends to be limited to linguistic learning, this approach will not be directly addressed in the Translation Spotlights. Instead, linguistic learning will be incorporated within the other approaches. As already indicated, the CEFR aligns directly to a plurilingual approach, so CEFR standards and objectives will be assumed to be plurilingual.

Neither the ACTFL World-Readiness Standards nor the CCSS directly align to any of the translation approaches. However, translation activities may still be used to meet ACTFL proficiency benchmarks, as will be illustrated in the Translation Spotlights. As the CCSS are used to model application of content-area standards for second language learning in this book, a translanguaging approach to translation should be assumed for these learners as well. García and Flores (2013) contended that the CCSS should be read through a bilingual lens, or as Bilingual Common Core State Standards. Through a bilingual lens and translanguaging approach, bilingual students would be provided with different progressions of content mastery in English and their home language to meet these standards. This process in turn leads to validation of translanguaging pedagogies, including translation.

Part II: Translation for Linguistic and Cultural Learning

5

Literacy, Translation, and Linguistic Learning

While professional translation requires highly developed language expertise, educational practices may also be informed by the field of translation (Colina, 2002; Munday et al., 2022). According to Cook (2010),

> Linguistics, language teaching, and translation theory have, over the last hundred years or so, all taken similar paths ... the focus of attention in linguistics has moved from an exclusive interest in the "lower" levels of linguistic forms, to one which is more interested in the use of those forms in action as discourse. This shift echoes and has informed a similar movement in language-teaching theories from a preoccupation with normal accuracy to one with communication ... Translation theory has followed a similar trajectory, with a developing interest in pragmatic and discoursal equivalence. (pp. 56–57)

This connection between linguistics, language teaching, and discoursal equivalence in translation theory demonstrates not only the links between these fields but also to literacy.

Chapter 5 begins a more practical examination of classroom translation for literacy acquisition through linguistic learning. It begins by examining the role of translation in literacy acquisition. It then moves to translation and metalinguistic awareness, a key element of reading comprehension (Jiménez et al., 2015; Laufer & Girsai, 2008). This is followed by the mediation of translation for linguistic learning, such as phonology, morphology, lexicosemantics, syntax, and pragmatics (Colina & Lafford, 2017; González-Davies, 2017; Mellinger & Gasca Jiménez, 2019), the connection of growth in these skills to acquisition of literacy (Jiménez et al., 2015; Park et al., 2015; Kultti & Pramling, 2017) followed by translation for acquisition of writing skills, including register awareness (Colina & Lafford, 2017; Escamilla et al., 2009). The chapter will end with a Translation Spotlight on guided writing.

Translation as a Literacy Practice

Translation is a literacy practice that is "complex and authentic" (Keyes et al., 2014, p. 17), requiring analysis, comprehension, and ability to rewrite in the target language (Hernández, 1998). According to Washbourne (2010), "One inescapable fact is essential to internalize: 'Translators are writers' ... Everything that a writer has to do well, a translator has to do well" (p. 26), supporting arguments in favor of using translation to support literacy acquisition. As part of this process, translators must pay careful attention to context in order to make appropriate decisions regarding word choice.

Translation also links to the common bilingual practice of translation within the community. Martínez et al. (2008), for example, found that bilingual intermediate-grade students' natural translation practices in the community could be drawn upon for audience awareness in academic writing. However, students initially viewed their translation practices as social and required multiple attempts to help them see the connection between their natural translation abilities and academic literacy. Through engaging in translation simulations at school, students were able to make the connection between how they modified their speech in different natural translation contexts to how they could change written language depending upon the audience.

Through pedagogical translation, students have the opportunity to make cross-linguistic connections needed for literacy acquisition in an additional language. According to Pacheco et al. (2015), "By making cross-linguistic comparisons, students can begin to question how languages vary in both form and content, and can examine the relationship between language and culture" (p. 58). Escamilla et al. (2009) maintained that cross-language strategies contribute to linguistic growth, writing improvement in both monolingual and bilingual classrooms, and biliteracy development. They recommended the *Así se dice* translation activity as a thoughtfully planned cross-language strategy, noting in particular highly engaged student discussions, particularly over lexical choices. A more detailed explanation of the strategy is offered in Chapter 6.

The Role of Background Knowledge in Literacy Acquisition

The activation of background knowledge is a well-established strategy for reading comprehension. "In a top-down model of reading comprehension, the reader 'relies on world knowledge (i.e., background knowledge, contextual information and other higher-order processing strategies) to understand a text'" (Colina, 2015, p. 158). Butzkamm and Caldwell (2009) highlight the importance of background knowledge in clarifying key details, while Rydland et al. (2010) found that prior topic knowledge was correlated with additional language vocabulary and reading comprehension. They recommended that students' prior topic knowledge be developed in both first and additional languages for content-area text comprehension. Finally, Velásquez (2020) found that activating background knowledge and explicitly teaching vocabulary contribute to HLL reading comprehension. Kern (2000) advocated for application of schema for additional language reading comprehension. Linguistic knowledge falls within formal schemata, as do rhetorical organizational patterns such as register, genre, and style. Topical, cultural, and experiential knowledge fall within content schemata.

Thinking in terms of multiliteracies pedagogy, drawing upon Available Designs like linguistic and content-area background knowledge can set the stage for a translation activity, or for Designing. Underlying background knowledge can also serve as Available Designs and affect translation approaches. For example, in Heugh et al. (2017), students at an Australian university with varying cultural and linguistic knowledge used differing approaches to the translation of a document in Japanese to English. One student with a deeper cultural connection to Japan made more deliberate changes to the translated document out of cultural sensitivity, while another paid greater attention to the linguistic equivalence of the translation. Awareness of students' linguistic and cultural backgrounds, and attention to background knowledge activation, can align with creation of specific linguistic learning objectives, such as metalinguistic awareness or lexical acquisition.

The Mediation of Translation for Linguistic Learning

Pedagogical translation mediates for linguistic learning, which in turn is linked to literacy. However, it is important to underscore the ongoing reluctance in some quarters to use translation in language teaching because of its prior focus on grammar and linguistic assessment (House, 2016). In response, House (2016) emphasizes the importance of incorporating pragmatics to fully take advantage of translation as a language-teaching tool. House's point is illustrated by Jiménez et al. (2015), who used a modified guided reading approach, incorporating translation to investigate how EBs use linguistic knowledge in two languages while translating and constructing meaning. Using "conceptually and linguistically rich excerpts from the English literature curriculum" (p. 253), they found that intermediate-grade EBs "employed their conceptual understandings about lexicon, syntax, and semantics to comprehend source texts and to create their target texts, and in the process, they signaled broader conceptual understandings about language and literacy" (p. 258). The authors concluded that translation was a key element in meaning making due to the close attention required for moving within and between languages and cultures.

Metalinguistic Awareness

Development of metalinguistic awareness has been identified as key in additional or second language learning and reading comprehension (Gasca Jiménez, 2017; Jidai et al., 2017; Nagy, 2007). Metalinguistic awareness involves paying attention to the structure and meaning of language (Bialystok, 2001) through "the ability to identify, analyze, and manipulate language forms" (Koda, 2007, p. 2). It may involve attention to phonology, morphology, lexicon, semantics, syntax, and/or pragmatics (Jiménez et al., 2015), all of which are tied to reading comprehension (Nagy, 2007).

Translation has been described as a metalinguistic task. "Translation requires attention to how meanings change across languages and cultures, which in turn develops learners' metalinguistic awareness and intercultural sensitivity. It also trains the learner to make decisions and solve problems under conditions of uncertainty – skills that are transferable beyond the language classroom" (Pym, 2010, p. 151). As such, it requires understanding the meaning of the source text and conveying that meaning to some degree of equivalence in the translated text (Jidai et al., 2017). This description speaks to the complexity of the skill involved in translation. During translation activities, students may be asked to explain their translation choices to the group and may also do so spontaneously during collaborative work. This requires the ability to think metalinguistically and to express metalinguistic reasoning (Jiménez et al., 2015; Linares, 2022). Cross-linguistic connections between phonological, morphological, lexicosemantic, syntactic, and pragmatic linguistic components can be useful additions to translation activities, as these stimulate metalinguistic awareness given the explicit nature of the comparisons which are being made (see Beeman & Urow, 2013, or Escamilla et al., 2014 for detailed pedagogical explanations of cross-linguistic connections in bilingual classrooms. These may be adapted for other language-learning environments).

Phonology

Phonological awareness can contribute to word recognition, oral fluency, and reading development across languages. For example, Kultti and Pramling (2017) utilized phonological awareness during a preschool translation activity to raise children's metalinguistic awareness of words that sound similar in Finnish as well as in English, introducing the concept of homophony. Additionally, during the activity, the instructors created a translanguaging space. Children were encouraged to translanguage, moving fluidly throughout their linguistic repertoires, to be able to negotiate meaning. Importantly, the authors concluded that "despite children being immersed in a bilingual program, the development of linguistic and metalinguistic insights is challenging and something that teachers may need to target specifically" (p. 723). That is, instruction for varying linguistic aspects such as phonology should be incorporated into teaching objectives so that phonological awareness can be explicitly taught.

Phonological awareness may also contribute to language learning between languages that are dissimilar. In a systematic literature review, Yang et al. (2017) found significant overlap in phonological skills between Chinese and English, noting that despite the different sound systems, phonological tasks require attention to sounds in each language and awareness of similarity and difference. While this study was not oriented toward translation tasks, it nevertheless illustrates a phonological function that a translation task such as that developed in Kultti and Pramling (2018) could play between languages that are dissimilar.

Morphology

Morphology, or the study of how words are put together, can be useful in cross-linguistic comparison between languages which are similarly structured. These comparisons may not be productive or possible between ideographic and morphological languages. Nevertheless, morphological awareness in the home language has been shown to contribute to reading development in an additional language (Yang et al., 2017). Morphology includes morphemes, or the smallest units of meaning in a word: these are affixes, which are attached to the beginning or end of a word or embedded within the word, and roots, which may stand alone (free morphemes) or have affixes (bound morphemes) attached to them. Morphemes are derivational if a word changes meaning through the addition of a morpheme; often, the lexical category of the word changes as well. For example, addition of the suffix *-ero/-era* to a noun in Spanish changes the meaning of the original noun to *someone or something that does something to the original noun*. Therefore, the addition of the suffix *-ero* to the noun *sombra*, or shadow, creates the new noun *sombrero:* something that makes a shadow—or, a hat. A cross-linguistic connection between the morphology of the two would make apparent that the Spanish word requires an affix, while the English is a stand-alone morpheme and does not.

Morphemes can also be inflectional. Inflectional morphemes are added to change tense, aspect, mood, person, and number in verbs and gender, number and case in nouns and adjectives but do not change the underlying meaning of a word (Ortega, 1996). Returning to the example of *sombrero* and *hat*, the inflectional morpheme *-s* can be added to the end to make each word plural: thus, *sombreros* and *hats* demonstrate that pluralization in these languages may involve similar inflectional morphemes. Inflectional morphemes may differ between languages, such that *hats* becomes *hattar* in Swedish, or *children* in English becomes *niños* in Spanish, illustrating that the inflectional morphemes for number are not always the same. Fois (2020) noted the efficiency of translation activities for teaching grammar and morphology at beginner levels, although they could of course be applied at other levels.

Pedagogical translation can be used to draw attention to linguistic similarities and differences, and cross-linguistic connections can be paired with translation activities to highlight these similarities and differences. Cross-linguistic connections help to make linguistic comparisons explicit, or to increase students' metalinguistic awareness (Escamilla et al., 2014). They may be informal during instruction or practice or may be presented in cross-linguistic comparison charts which are then displayed in the classroom. For example, students might notice linguistic components such as phonological, morphological, or syntactic similarity and difference during a guided writing translation activity. These observations can be discussed and recorded on a cross-linguistic connections chart after the translation activity, with the instructor asking targeted questions to teach the objectives. For example, phonologically, students may notice that [f] in English and Spanish makes the same /f/ sound, while [b] and [v] sound the same in Spanish but have different sounds in English. A text for translation containing elements to be addressed in the objectives might be selected.

Lexicosemantics

Semantics involves the embedding of meaning within written or oral texts. This might involve creating or identifying textual coherence and nuance (Koda, 2007; Kramsch, 2008). Coherence can be established through markers such as pronouns, including demonstratives like *this* or *these* in English; conjunctions; or repetition of sounds (Kramsch, 2008). In the dual-edition children's book *La Matadragones/The Dragon Slayer* (Hernández, 2018), for example, the story of Ratoncito Pérez is told with repetition in both languages, but only the version in Spanish demonstrates textual cohesion through rhyme, which indicates an equivalence issue the translator needed to address. One difficulty with comprehension of written compared to spoken dialogue is that signs such as tone of voice or gesture are not naturally present in writing (Kern, 2000). Hence, these elements must be added in through lexicosemantic strategies such as punctuation or word choice, and, in a translation activity, functionally carried from one language to another.

Jiménez et al. (2015) anticipated that EB students would encounter semantic difficulty in capturing shades of meaning, or "larger ideas" (p. 257) represented by idiomatic expressions in their translation activity. In the study, students translated an idiomatic expression literally and determined that the translation was syntactically correct but made no sense, thus, as the authors noted, flagging an idiomatic expression that required further discussion and negotiation. During a guided writing translation activity in one of my post-secondary heritage language classes, students negotiated over the translation of *white cheese* into Spanish, noting that the descriptor *white* had been added so that cultural outsiders would understand the type of cheese being referenced. They determined, however, that based upon the context of the text, *white* would not be needed as cultural insiders would understand without the descriptor. This discussion demonstrated depth of understanding based upon both the context of the text as well as of two potential audiences. Kern (2000) also highlighted the importance of teaching punctuation conventions between languages, as differing conventions can cause confusion and misunderstanding.

Second and heritage language reading comprehension have been closely linked to vocabulary knowledge, with a threshold of about 98% of vocabulary understood for comprehension to occur (Koda, 2007; Velázquez, 2020). Vocabulary knowledge is often characterized in terms of depth and breadth. Breadth of vocabulary knowledge refers to the number of words known, including collocations in which more than one word is typically placed with another (Ganuza & Hedman, 2019). Depth refers to how well a word is known and includes "denotative meaning; pronunciation; spelling; morphology; syntax and collocations; meaning, including connotations, antonyms and synonyms; register; and high or low frequency" (Qian, 1999; Qian & Sched, 2004). Many of these concepts do not always translate directly between languages. For example, care must be taken to recognize the inexact nature of synonyms, including when "carrying over" meaning from one language to another. Hypernyms or more general terms such as the verb "watched" may be selected instead of a closer match like "scrutinized." Care must also be taken when the denotative meaning of a word in one language has a different connotative meaning in the other (Washbourne, 2010). Prepositions may also differ. For example, English often adds a preposition after a verb to change its meaning, such as *look* and *look for* or *ask* and *ask for*, while other languages would use different verbs. Similarly, the verbs *fazer* in Portuguese or *hacer* in Spanish have two separate verbs, *to make* and *to do*, in English. For polysemy, or a single word with multiple meanings in one language, this word will generally have a separate word for each meaning in another language, often causing translation challenges (Washbourne, 2010). In Albrecht (2024), multiple intermediate secondary learners commented on their heightened awareness of polysemy through a translation activity, noticing that simply looking up items in a dictionary could be confusing due to the disconnect in meaning or the array of choices, and that negotiation through collaboration and using context clues were also needed.

Qian (1999) found that university ESL students should be taught polysemy, synonymy, and collocations to improve depth of academic vocabulary understanding. Similarly, Zhang et al. (2019) found that HLL oral vocabulary knowledge only transfers to reading comprehension through direct vocabulary instruction, including morphology. Therefore, attention to vocabulary acquisition is key in literacy instruction. Semantic differences may become apparent in various language-learning activities but are particularly apparent in translation, given the negotiation required and working within a context.

In heritage language and EB instruction, vocabulary knowledge has been shown to be the key factor in reading comprehension. Belpoliti and Plascencia-Vela (2013) studied the impact of translation on depth of HLL vocabulary development, focusing on false cognates and the nuance of lexical phrases such as idiomatic expressions. Participants experienced gains in accuracy of translation in both areas, although idiomatic expressions proved to be more difficult. Similarly, Albrecht (2024) found that secondary HLLs showed gains in breadth of lexical knowledge after a translation activity, although, as in Belpoliti and Plascencia-Vela, some did not move beyond literal to functional translation, thus demonstrating depth of vocabulary knowledge. Albrecht suggested that this may have been due in part to student affect, as several participants indicated that they already knew everything in the text to be translated, yet translated word for word as opposed to by collocation. Similarly, after targeted lessons in meaning-centered translation, EB students in Keyes et al. (2014) still defaulted to literal translations. However, Jiménez et al. (2015) found that students negotiated for meaning as they translated, arguing for their lexical decisions based upon their understanding of the text. Similarly, analysis of figurative language through translation led EBs in Cano and Ruíz (2020) to deeper textual understanding. The findings in these varying studies demonstrate the utility of translation for breadth of vocabulary acquisition and the potential for depth. However, depth of vocabulary learning may be tied to other factors, such as metalinguistic awareness and collaboration, and the tendency to default to literal translation points to the need for careful modeling and guided writing prior to independent practice (see e.g., *Así se dice* in Escamilla et al., 2014). Washbourne (2010) recommends that vocabulary be addressed prior to attempting a full translation, where the focus will be at the sentence or higher level. If vocabulary is terminology, it should be translated the same every time; if not, context will determine if variation is appropriate.

Syntax

Metalinguistic awareness includes syntactic awareness or awareness of sentence structure. Pedagogical translation contributes to syntactic awareness across ages and learning environments. For example, Finnish children in a bilingual preschool noticed that sometimes they needed to change word order to arrive at an equivalent meaning as they translated a children's song from Finnish to English, thus becoming aware of functional versus literal translation and showing early capacity to think about varying language structures (Jidai et al., 2017). Additionally, while comparing the song *Twinkle, Twinkle Little Star* in English to an existing Finnish translation, they also noticed that at times different words were used to arrive at an equivalent meaning, highlighting the simultaneous interaction of varying components of metalinguistic awareness. In other environments, secondary EB students in the United States and university students in Spain also increased their syntactic awareness in English through translation activities (González-Davies, 2017; Jiménez et al., 2015).

Pragmatics

Pragmatics involves socially situated language use, but the line between where semantics ends and pragmatics begins is unclear. "The meanings of words as they are linked both to the world and to other words establish a speech community's pool of semantic resources" (Kramsch, 2008, p. 23). However, because meaning is also determined within a speech community, there is overlap between the two. As Kramsh (2008) noted, "Despite the general translatability from one language to another, there will always be an incommensurable residue of untranslatable culture associated with the linguistic structures of any given language" (p. 12). Because of the "incommensurable residue of untranslatable culture," pragmatics may be difficult to teach (Lertola & Mariotti, 2017). Nevertheless, it is essential for language learners to learn the pragmatic, socially situated component of language in order to be able to communicate effectively in the new language. This points to the complexity of skills being acquired in language learning beyond grammatical competence and to the fact that grammatical competence without pragmatic competence may still result in a failure to communicate. This complexity is reminiscent of the New London Group's (1996) multiliteracies framework, in which learners acquire literacy skills beyond "formalized, monolingual, monocultural, and rule-governed forms of language" (p. 61) which are needed to navigate a changing, diverse, multimodal world. In language learning, then, pragmatic skills are essential.

Due to the requirement for noticing cultural differences, pedagogical translation may be used to help language learners identify cultural differences visible in texts. Bilingual children's literature or children's literature written in the additional language may be a valuable resource across grade levels, including lower-level post-secondary language courses. For example, the bilingual children's book *Somos como las nubes/We Are Like the Clouds* by Jorge Argueta (2016) addresses migration from El Salvador to the United States through a series of poems. It was written in Spanish, then translated to English, centering Spanish language and culture in the text. Translation of a poem from Spanish to English could be used to identify how language is used to address cultural realities, and translation from English to Spanish could also demonstrate language variation when compared with the version of the text in the book, as the Spanish version uses regional vocabulary.

Audiovisual translation (AVT) has also been used to teach pragmatics and other language objectives. AVT activities might include speaking tasks such as dubbing or voice over, or written tasks such as subtitling. Subtitling may consist of a written translation from one language to another (interlingual) or a condensed written text within the same language (intralingual) (Lertola & Mariotti, 2017). When the language of dubbing or subtitling is different from the source language, the process is considered to be reverse dubbing or subtitling. Italian university students studying English found reverse dubbing and reverse subtitling enjoyable and motivating while improving pragmatic awareness (Lertola & Mariotti, 2017). The constraints of subtitling often require students to express the meaning of a video message in a shortened text and/or to decide which elements are key to the message and which can be left out. This process draws students toward using language pragmatically as they interpret the message, rather than simply effecting a literal translation.

The following dialogue between two characters from the movie *Shrek I* (Adamson & Jenson, 2001) has been widely extracted and subtitled or dubbed across languages:

Gingy: Do you know the muffin man?
Lord Farquaad: The muffin man?
Gingy: The muffin man.
Lord Farquaad: Yes, I know the muffin man ... Who lives on Drury Lane?

This type of brief excerpt can be used in multiple ways to teach pragmatics. First, pragmatically speaking, both speakers are fulfilling the expected role in the English dialogue because the entire exchange is based upon the common nursery rhyme *Do You Know the Muffin Man?* which follows the same sequence. Listeners for whom the nursery rhyme is part of their cultural memory will make the connection between the rhyme and the dialogue and recognize that it is a joke.

If the dialogue were used as a subtitling or dubbing activity for English learners unfamiliar with the rhyme, the instructor would need to explain the connection between the nursery rhyme and the movie, and learners would then need to decide whether to directly translate the dialogue, losing the humorous connotation present in English, or to determine if there was a similar short text within their own culture that might pragmatically function the same way. For example, for the Latin American Spanish version of Shrek, translators chose the children's song *Pin Pon* as an alternative to *Do You Know the Muffin Man*, and for the Portuguese version, translators chose *O soldado com a cabeça do papel* (Equipboard, 2019), thus fulfilling the humorous functional role of the text through cultural reference. An extension of a subtitling activity involving these types of pragmatic decisions would be to review the movie's translation after class members complete their own translations and to discuss the varying approaches and their effects.

Translation for Literacy Acquisition

Linguistic choices can be linked to literacy acquisition through analysis of "the appropriateness of linguistic forms to specific communicative purposes ... and the relation between text and context" (Figueiredo, 2010, p. 121), which can in turn be linked to register and genre in reading and writing (Figueiredo, 2010). That is, a reader might use linguistic cues to identify a more or less formal register or a certain genre, like an informal ad, a newspaper article, a speech, or a formal report. Translation is a pedagogical tool which can be implemented for teaching register and genre because it requires analysis of linguistic features in a source text and decisions about levels of equivalence in a translated text to meet the desired function of the translation.

Pedagogical translation, then, can simultaneously contribute to development of both reading comprehension and writing skills. Indeed, two axioms from translation studies maintain, "If you can't understand something, you can't translate it," and "If your translation can't be understood, you probably didn't understand the source" (Washbourne, 2010, p. 36), providing a powerful argument in favor of using translation as a reading comprehension strategy. Translation has been described as "the most rigorous test of understanding" (Butzkamm & Caldwell, 2009, p. 196) and can contribute to reading comprehension due to the attention to detail which students must pay to both languages simultaneously (Lee, 2013). While some consider translation a factor for reading comprehension with the introduction of literature for advanced language acquisition, others have advocated for the introduction of short, conceptually challenging texts in bilingual classes as early as third grade (Butzkamm & Caldwell, 2009; Escamilla et al, 2014). Collaborative translation activities can encourage students to discuss, negotiate, and sometimes argue for translations that best meet the desired function (Jiménez et al., 2015) and can in turn lead to thematic discussion which demonstrates deep comprehension of a text (Keyes et al., 2014).

Pedagogical translation can also contribute to the development of writing skills. Butzkamm and Caldwell (2009) noted somewhat humorously that "Unfortunately when I was young nobody told me that you can learn to write German by translating from another language, otherwise I would have started to do it sooner" (p. 202). The guided writing activity in this chapter builds upon learning to write through translation. Guided writing may be used for acquisition of writing skills in a first or additional language and typically involves a scaffold such that students have a model to follow when acquiring targeted skills. Scaffolds will vary across learning contexts and might include mentor texts (Kittle, 2022), sentence stems or frames (Sentence Frames and Sentence Starters, n.d.) or photos (Lee, 1994). Translation may be considered a bilingual guided writing activity, highly appropriate for bi- or multilingual students or in language-learning environments where bilingualization is the goal. When using translation as a guided writing activity, the structure of the text is already present and students should by definition follow this structure as they translate into the target language.

Introduction: Translation Spotlights

Prior to beginning the Translation Spotlights at the end of this and subsequent chapters, it is important to address several considerations. First, in the field of professional translation, directionality of translation typically moves from the translator's additional language into the translator's original language, a process known as direct translation (Washbourne, 2010). Moving from the home language to the additional language, or inverse translation, is not widely accepted, although exceptions exist. However, just as translator training programs often require some inverse translation, pedagogical translation activities may also use inverse translation depending upon the learning objectives.

Pedagogical translation assignments may range from activities to a series of activities (tasks), to projects, although projects typically combine pedagogical and professional objectives toward an authentic product and often are used in translator training courses (González-Davies, 2016). Instructors incorporating pedagogical translation tasks that encompass more than one class period may want to follow Washbourne's (2010) recommendation for translators in training to "translate in waves" (p. 25) yet to not leave off at a difficult spot, but rather to stop at a less-complex passage so that it will be easier to regain momentum.

The Translation Spotlights in this and subsequent chapters will include model objectives which will be more fully explained and developed in Chapter 10, which is dedicated to objectives and assessments. However, it is important to note here at the beginning of the Translation Spotlights that language-learning environments may be drawing upon a wide variety of standards. These include the Japan Foundation for Japanese Language Education (JL Standard) which is linked with the CEFR; the Chinese Proficiency Grading Standards for International Chinese Language Education; and China's Standards of English Language Ability. Additionally, the CEFR is not designed for specific ages of learners, although a supplemental *Collation of Descriptors for Young Learners* has been developed (Goodier & Szabo, 2018a; 2018b), with learners grouped by ages 7–10 and 11–15. The CEFR descriptors for these age groups are the same, providing the use of "age appropriate tasks and with support and guidance given" (Council of Europe, 2020, p. 138). Second, environments that incorporate content-based language instruction (CBLI) may require both language and content-area standards. For example, to meet the needs of the high number of students speaking other languages in their schools, some states in the United States have developed content-area standards in other languages. New Mexico has developed CCSS in Spanish, while Texas has Spanish Language Arts standards that align with state standards in English but reflect unique linguistic aspects of Spanish. Similarly, many states have varying English language development (ELD) standards. Many other nations with bi- or multilingual students in their schools have similar complexity in the layers of language and content-area standards which may be applicable in their contexts but which are beyond the scope of this book. It is also important to note that for simplicity, fewer standards and objectives are included in the lesson samples than might be incorporated into an actual lesson, including, for example, specific linguistic elements. The standards and objectives in the translation spotlights are therefore intended to model alignment between standards, objectives, translation activities, and assessments with the assumption that standards and objectives will be modified as needed according to learning contexts.

Translation Spotlight: Guided Writing Activity

Chapter 5 began a more practical examination of classroom translation for literacy acquisition through linguistic learning. It examined the mediation of translation and metalinguistic awareness, a key element of reading comprehension. It also examined the mediation of translation for linguistic learning and the connection of growth in these skills to literacy acquisition. Practically speaking, linguistic skills addressed through translation may link to writing skills, as addressed in the first Translation Spotlight. Chapter 6 moves to an examination of the complex interconnection of language and culture, and the mediation of translation for cultural learning.

Table 5.1 Translation Spotlight: Guided Writing Activity

Sample guided writing activity (Adapted from Colina & Albrecht, 2020). Assumed direction of translation will be from the target language into the home language.
Estimated time: 50-minute class period

Objective(s): Through a guided writing translation activity, I can:

CEFR (Council of Europe, 2020):
- *Produce clearly organized translations from (Language A) into (Language B) that reflect normal language usage but may be over-influenced by the order, paragraphing, punctuation, and particular formulations of the original (p. 103).*
- *Produce translations into (Language B), which closely follow the sentence and paragraph structure of the original text in (Language A), conveying the main points of the source text accurately, though the translation may read awkwardly (p. 103).*
- *Write clear, detailed descriptions of real or imaginary events and experiences marking the relationship between ideas in clear connected text, and following established conventions of the genre concerned in my home and an additional language (p. 188).*

ACTFL (2017, pp. 4, 15):
- *Understand the main idea and some pieces of information on familiar topics from sentences and series of connected sentences within written texts.*
- *[Through translation of a bilingual text,] in my own and other cultures, I can make comparisons between products and practices to help me understand perspectives.*

CCSS (National Governors Association, 2010):
- CSS.ELA-Literacy.W.7.3: *I can [translate] a narrative to develop imagined experiences, using well-structured event sequences.*

Prior Skills:
- Content: For this activity, students will be learning about narrative writing. Prior to the activity, they should know how to recognize the beginning (exposition), middle (action) and end (climax, denouement) of a narrative.
- Language: Intermediate mid-high (A2-B1) learners should be able to navigate past, present, and future tenses and conversations on familiar topics. They should have some knowledge of continuous and perfect tenses.
  ○ Students should have some skill using a bilingual dictionary. You may need to distinguish between using a dictionary and translation of an entire text through AI or a tool like Google Translate. What skills will learners acquire through doing the translation themselves? What will they miss out on in the process if they use AI?

Materials:
- Bilingual children's book for translation excerpts; model book: Garza, C. L. (1996). *In My Family/En Mi Familia*. Children's Book Press.
  ○ This book works particularly well for a narrative activity focusing on beginning, middle, and end, as it consists of short vignettes which include these elements.
- If you will project students' translations (this will be the assumed method, to be modified as needed by context):

- Projector
- Google or PPT slide presentation shared with the class. On the presentation, include instructions; a model text in the target language for translation, the excerpt for translation in the target language and blank slides on which each group will place their translation. You may also include the book's translation into the home language at the end, although students should not see this until their own translations are complete.
- If you will work by hand:
  - Copies of the translation excerpts in both languages for each cooperative group
  - Paper for groups to write their translations

Guided Writing Activity:

Before translating:
- Activate background knowledge: Ask students to think of a special family tradition or of a memorable time or activity from childhood that they would like to share. Have students share with a partner or in small groups where they are seated, then have some volunteer to share with the class. Talk about how to identify the beginning, middle, and end of the story.
- Tell students that they will be translating an excerpt from a children's book in the target language to the home language to model narrative writing, including how to include a beginning, middle, and end.
- Use the model text to
  - Translate from the target into the home language as a class. Model a "think aloud" to orally demonstrate your thought process (Escamilla et al., 2014), for example, choosing between a literal or functional translation or between vocabulary terms. Students may practice looking up terms for which they don't know the translation and determining which is the most appropriate.
  - Identify cultural elements in the source text that may differ in the translation. In bilingual books written as mirrors for one language/culture and windows for another (Bishop, 1990), this type of issue in translation may arise. For example, the model text, *In My Family/ En mi familia,* includes some explanations in English that are not needed in Spanish as the source culture should already understand the cultural context of the term.
  - Identify the beginning, middle, and end of the text.

Translate:
- Project the translation excerpt.
- Have students open the slide presentation on their own devices.
- In collaborative groups of 3–4, have students translate the excerpt from the home language into the target language on a blank slide. Ask them to pay attention to areas that are linguistically or culturally difficult to translate.
- Have students highlight the beginning, middle, and end of the text in their translation.

After translating:
- Project and discuss students' translations. How are they similar and different? Do the differences matter? Why or why not?

(continued)

Table 5.1 (*continued*)

- Project the book's translation. In their groups, have learners compare their own translations with the book's. How are the translations linguistically similar or different? Culturally similar or different? Do the differences matter? Why or why not?
- Have students share their linguistic and cultural conclusions with the class.
- As a class, discuss what the students identified as the beginning, middle, and end of the text. How did they recognize these elements? Discuss any differences of opinion.

Evaluation:
- **Formative:** Circulate among groups while students translate or discuss to make sure they understand and are on task. Pay attention to the translation strategies they are using and to whether dictionary use is effective.
- **Summative:** Summative assessments will differ depending upon the standards-based objectives but should demonstrate student mastery of the objective(s). A possible evaluation might include an additional collaborative translation after which students individually identify beginning, middle, and end of the narrative. If you are going to evaluate linguistic features, be sure to add these to the objectives.

Expansion/Modification:
- Many different types of texts could be used for this activity, particularly if the guided writing activity is to model a certain genre of text, such as narrative, expository, biography, or poetry.
- Additional linguistic and content-area standards and objectives could be included, including identifying similarities and differences in written conventions between languages, figurative language, description, and so forth.
- Depending upon the learners, more-advanced narrative elements could be included.
- After students have completed a guided writing activity, they can write their own narratives, including in a brief vignette style. Consider having them use one of the ideas they thought of during the activity in this lesson to activate background knowledge.

6

Literacy, Translation, and Cultural Learning

This chapter continues the practical classroom application of translation, this time connecting translation, culture, and literacy acquisition. Although culture is a common component across humanity, its definition is broad and problematic (Phipps & González, 2004). The chapter therefore begins with various approaches to defining and teaching culture and to connecting language and culture. Cultural learning will then be placed within the CEFR's intercultural competence and the ACTFL framework of cultural products, practices, and perspectives. The interconnectedness of translation, culture, and literacy; and translation, culture, and linguistic learning will then be presented as foundational considerations for the use of translation as a language-learning strategy. The chapter ends with two Translation Spotlights on proverb comparison and advertisement translation.

Culture Defined

The complexity of defining culture complicates the relationship between language and culture, and the relationship between SLA and culture. Block (2003) characterizes culture as providing the structure within which actors exert individual agency. In this sense, culture may be characterized as constantly changing through a series of social encounters (Phipps & González, 2004). Importantly, Byram (2020) defines culture for foreign language teachers (which might be expanded to language teaching in general) as "the beliefs and knowledge that members of a social group share by virtue of their membership. To describe these as 'shared meanings' is to open a link to language, in which they are embodied, and to a view of language learning as the meanings of a specific social group" (pp. 110–111).

In weighing the range of extralinguistic influences on linguistic choices, Pym (2015) notes that "the tongue becomes the foremost symbol of the resulting cultural identity. Hence its particular importance and power" (p. 127). The view of translation as a process of moving in (for bilingual speakers) or across (for world language learners) languages and cultures links directly to Byram's definition and will be further addressed in the translation activities at the end of this chapter. Additionally, Byram socially situates language learning, which aligns with this book's approach to literacy as socially situated.

Culture and the Identity of the Nation State

Culture has also been aligned with identity as part of a nation state and will be addressed in detail here due to the nation state's role in how language teaching is approached in educational institutions. Language, literacy, and translation have all been part of the alignment between the nation state and culture. Language, for example, has been used to show political allegiance and exclude outsiders, with the dominant language wielding symbolic power and the dominated language(s) being stigmatized (Kramsch, 2008), particularly when the dominant language is tied to an artificially created standard language. Along these lines, wa Thiong'o (2023) claims that knowing many languages but not knowing the language of one's culture is equivalent to enslavement, while knowing the language of one's culture with additional languages is empowerment. In other words, separating people from their language is equivalent to separating them from their culture and how they connect to the world, thus stripping them of identity and their power base.

Given the global dominance of English, separation from language and culture have often taken place in the contexts of English acquisition and colonization (Skutnabb-Kangas, 2017). Native American residential schools in the United States and Canada serve as an example of a deliberate move to separate children from their culture through removing their language. The colonial English-only policy was an assimilation tactic, with verbal and physical punishments for speaking the home language (Reyhner, 2018). Similarly, MacGregor-Mendoza (2000) has chronicled the experiences of Spanish-speaking students in primary schools in the state of New Mexico in the United States. Many of the individuals interviewed recounted verbal and physical punishments for speaking their home language at school. Although there has been a move away from such dire punishments, many language programs are still oriented toward assimilation into the dominant society, with English acquisition and first language loss being the vehicle for doing so (García, 2014).

Cummins (2019) identified multiple more recent studies in other environments in which home language use continues to be prohibited in schools. These included research by Agirdag (2010) in Belgium, in which students were not permitted to use their home language at school, thereby sending messages to multilingual, multicultural communities about the value of their language and identity in the dominant society, and by Pulinx et al. (2017) in which one-third of teachers in Flemish-speaking environments believed students should be punished for speaking the home language at school. These monolingual language orientations stem from the belief that the additional language is acquired more quickly through maximum exposure. While the maximum exposure belief is not supported by the literature, change in practice based upon ideologies about language, culture, and identity can be difficult (Cummins, 2016).

Translation and culture in terms of the nation state have been used as a colonial process of othering between dominant and subjugated nation states, with culture being "national, exclusive and defined by its univocal qualities" (Phipps & González, 2004, p. 64), on the one hand, and "exotic" and "what other people have" (p. 64), on the other. Similarly, colonial translation has been used by the dominant nation state to justify its portrayal of the inferior culture of the subaltern state (Niranjana, 1992).According to Venuti (2018), translation is cultural and political, as noted in current Anglo-American dominance in the field of translation. National cultures, therefore, "resonate with the voices of the powerful, and are filled with the silences of the powerless" (Kramsch, 2008, pp. 8–9), including in the availability of translated texts. As a result, in national moves toward literacy, "high" culture texts might be chosen for or in translation from what are considered to be other strong nation states (Phipps & González, 2004). In contrast, pedagogical translation can serve as a culturally sustaining practice that resists the common practice of separation from home languages in schools (Albrecht et al., 2023).

Intercultural Competence, Intercultural Communicative Competence, and Intercultural Being

The converse to separation from language as equivalent to separation from culture (wa Thiong'o, 2023) would be that connection to language is equivalent to connection to culture. In wa Thiong'o's context, this would be a connection to one's own language and culture. However, as language acquisition has typically been linked to cultural understanding, then connection to an additional language would also mean connection to another culture. According to Kramsch (2008), "The ability to acquire another person's language and understand someone else's culture while retaining one's own is one aspect of a more general ability to mediate between several languages and cultures, called cross-cultural, intercultural, or multicultural communication" (p. 81). This is often described as the meeting of two languages across political boundaries of nation states, although languages and cultures often meet within a single nation state, including within an educational system (Byram, 2020).

Intercultural competence, intercultural communicative competence (ICC), and intercultural being are all concepts that are considered in language teaching and learning. According to Byram (2020), intercultural competence occurs between interlocutors of different cultures but who have the same home language. ICC adds a layer of complexity as it includes interactions in a second language for at least one interlocutor, or both if the additional language is a lingua franca. Koshiba's (2017) definition of intercultural competence seems to align with Byram's ICC, as Koshiba also describes it as the negotiation of meaning between individuals with different linguistic and cultural backgrounds. From a foreign language teaching perspective, Byram (2020) proposed that the factors involved in intercultural competence include five ways of knowing. These are presented with knowing how to engage through education as the central point, with the assumption that all ways of knowing will be interconnected, and are drawn upon in the CEFR general competences for language proficiency (Council of Europe, 2020). The five ways of knowing are summarized as follows:

1. Knowing how to engage through education, including political education (*Bildung*) and critical awareness
2. Knowing about one's own and the other's cultures and identities; knowledge about how to interact individually and as a society
3. Knowing the skills of interpreting and relating
4. Knowing how to be, namely, one's attitudes in interactions with those whose "cultural meanings, beliefs, values and behaviors" (p. 100) are different than their own
5. Knowing how to learn or do, discover or interact (Byram, 2020)

Most of these ways of knowing assume interpersonal interaction, although Point 3, interpreting and relating, may involve translation of written texts and draw in the other factors in this way. A translation will therefore require knowledge of one's own and the other culture, bringing Point 2 into play as it will be necessary to make one's own implicit cultural knowledge explicit in order to be able to make cultural comparisons and contrasts. Understanding or knowing about the new culture will also be necessary. If this is not already the case, learning about the new culture will be required, as indicated in Point 5, knowing how to discover or interact. Discovery might include "the ability to recognize significant phenomena in a foreign environment and to elicit their meanings and connotations and their relationship to other phenomena" (Byram, 2020, p. 109). If discovery is taking place between interlocutors, which could take place in a translation activity such as a classroom simulation, it will be necessary to draw upon prior knowledge, to have an open attitude toward difference in ways of doing and being and to mediate these differences. Byram defines an individual able to navigate difference in this way as an "intercultural speaker" (p. 100), thereby identifying the language learning goal as interculturality as opposed to native speaker capacity.

Koshiba (2017) studied the development of bilingual and heritage language learner intercultural competence through a translation activity carried out by advanced bilingual speakers of Japanese and English at an Australian university. Through translation of texts from Japanese to English, students reflected on how linguistic and cultural norms and worldviews were demonstrated through the differing sign systems. Depending upon their own linguistic, cultural, and ethnic backgrounds, students also approached their translation tasks differently. One, who considered herself Japanese, reflected more on the historical context of the source text and how her translation would position her as a translator as well as the text in the target culture. Another ethnically Japanese student who considered himself Australian reflected more on linguistic issues in the translation.

Koshiba concluded that the task was most valuable for addressing Hornberger and Link's (2012) call for a pedagogical approach to bilingual and heritage language education "that can foster the whole range of languages and skills that bilinguals bring to a classroom ... This study has highlighted the effectiveness of translation in engaging bilingual learners in 'social literacy practices that reflect, explore, and question different worlds'" (Koshiba, 2017, p. 240, citing García, 2009, p. 352). In this study, students' knowledge of their own culture and consideration of the additional culture influenced translation decisions, demonstrating both the potential of designing translation activities to develop ICC as well as the need to recognize that learners' linguistic and cultural backgrounds may affect their approach to a translation.

Byram (2020) distinguished between intercultural competence and ICC, proposing a threshold for ICC which depends upon three factors. These are learners': geopolitical context; teaching and learning parameters; and when and how learners might use their ICC. Geopolitical context includes how learners might foreseeably need to use ICC, such as for business or political relationships with speakers of the language or as a lingua franca. However, ICC might also be considered for relationships with immigrant speakers of the language within one's own community, including in educational environments. Teaching and learning parameters include when students begin learning and how often; whether and how it is anticipated that they will be in contact with other speakers of the language; and instructional materials available.

Situations in which learners may need their ICC vary widely. Byram noted that secondary learners of French in the Northeastern United States, for example, have little instructional time and may never have the opportunity to interact with another speaker of French. However, ICC skills learned while studying French will be transferable to other encounters with other cultures and can be related to ACTFL's World-Readiness Standards (The National Standards Collaborative Board, 2015). In this case, "The rationale for language learning is founded on the underlying concept of world readiness/global competence" (Byram, 2020, p. 216). On the other hand, learners of English in Taiwan begin studying in the primary grades and will have many opportunities to use the language and to practice ICC in their environment. Similarly, in bilingual educational environments, learners by definition will be developing and using ICC.

In any of these cases, pedagogical translation can be used to develop ICC, but the previous considerations must be taken into account in planning. Looking back to Byram's "savoirs," learners will be drawing upon different backgrounds and contexts as they develop the skills of *Knowing about one's own and the other's cultures and identities*. For example, bilingual students participating in translation of the school's newsletter in Cano and Ruiz (2020) humorously noted an article advertising a fall pumpkin sale titled "The Pumpkins are Coming!" worked linguistically and culturally in English but sounded "scary" if translated directly into Spanish; they altered the title in translation accordingly. In the case of learners who will probably have little chance of interacting with speakers who are members of a cultural community who speak the additional language, Byram recommended that learners read texts in both languages which will foster reflection upon the home culture and lead to cultural comparison. Both Translation Spotlights at the end of this chapter require this type of comparison, and bilingual learners can also use prior cultural knowledge to engage in the activity. In other words, the same activity can be used but with learners drawing upon different levels of knowledge.

Yang et al. (2015) described the development of ICC through a university-level translation project. For the project, students spent a year translating a book in English on Australian aboriginal cultures into Chinese and engaged in related activities designed to familiarize students with aboriginal culture, resulting in enhanced ICC. Among other supporting activities, students attended a seminar with experts on aboriginal studies and learned the negative connotation of the word "institution" in aboriginal culture due to its connection to colonial oppression, while the word did not have a similar connotation in Chinese. Students were able to use this type of new understanding in considering semantically appropriate translations. Although the project was for a translation course, the methods and findings might be transferable and adaptable for pedagogical translation on a smaller scale for primary or secondary learners. For example, an extension for the translation of proverbs spotlight in this chapter could be to study the cultural context behind a given proverb (or proverbs) prior to completing the matching activity described in what follows in order to increase ICC during the actual activity. If parents, family or friends are involved in the selection of proverbs that are contextually appropriate for the group of learners (Clark et al., 2016), they could also be asked to record a brief reflection on the contexts in which they or others have used the proverbs; these could be combined into a single video used to activate prior knowledge prior to the translation activity. This type of activity could be aligned with Social Studies as well as Language Arts standards and objectives.

Phipps and González (2004) took the concept of intercultural competence in a somewhat different direction, moving instead to intercultural being, in which one enters into other cultures and re-enters one's own. Intercultural being does not require travel; it is about living in and with cultures instead of learning or knowing about them. While ICC requires communication in an additional language, intercultural being is done through languaging. Of key importance, Phipps and González describe translators as border crossers, and languagers as those who move beyond being competent learners of culture to living within it.

Using translation to teach for intercultural being should therefore prepare language students in general to function within their own and other cultures at home or abroad. This is a process. For example, in one of my intermediate secondary Spanish classes with both heritage and world language learners, students were assigned the ad campaign as described in Translation Spotlight 2. Collaborative groups selected a one-page advertisement to translate into the target language. The assignment required a functional approach to translation: What was the function of the translated ad? Through discussion, students in various groups determined that if the ad was to be understood by and appeal to the target audience, both language and graphics would need to be changed, as both were socially situated.

For one ad including a well-known basketball player in the United States, for example, students recognized the appeal of sports in general in advertising but decided that it would be more appropriate to include a well-known boxer in the target culture. For another ad, however, students selected a visual representation of Puerto Rican culture, while their target audience was Mexican, thus making assumptions and overgeneralizing. Through this exercise, students drew upon knowledge of the social context of their own language and culture and demonstrated awareness of the need for adaptation in translation because the context had changed. However, not all had fully acquired the cultural understanding needed to fulfill the functional requirements of the translation.

The Common European Frame of Reference for Languages

The development of pluricultural competence, or the ability to function within multiple cultures, is expected within the plurilingual approach in order to "broaden the types of tasks carried out in language classrooms and to value all the developing language resources that use/learners bring"

(Council of Europe, 2020, p. 44). To foster pluriculturalism, González-Davies and Soler Ortínez (2021) recommend that students be familiar with Haywood et al.'s (2009) scale of possibilities for translating cultural elements. The four possibilities are as follows: exoticism, or foreignizing; explication, or keeping a "foreign" term or concept but adding an explanation; neutralization, or generalizing; and cultural transplantation, or domesticating an item so that it fits within the target culture. The decision for the type of translation should be based upon the function designated within the translation assignment, and the assignment should be graded based upon whether the translation met the function.

González-Davies and Soler Ortínez (2021) give an example in which the very brief phrase "bacon and eggs" from an excerpt from the children's book *Harry Potter and the Philosopher's Stone* (Rowling, 1998) was selected for the purpose of producing a functional translation. Students were given potential translations for each of the four components on the scale of possibilities. As the hypothetical publisher asked for the story to be adapted to a Mediterranean culture, the cultural transplantation option, or the equivalent of "bread and tomato with ham and cheese" (p. 32), was selected. This type of assignment would be graded not by "Why is this translation right or wrong?" but by "Why has the translator translated it this way?" (p. 32), that is, the translation and its function must align.

Similarly, in the bilingual children's book *In My Family/En mi familia* (Garza, 1996), which was first published in English, the Spanish term *cascarones* was written with an explication in English as *cascarones*, eggshells. In the Spanish translation, *eggshells* was removed, presumably with the assumption that the audience would already be culturally and linguistically familiar with the term. Examination of this type of text could be used to model the application of the scale of possibilities, with students new to translation asking the question, "Why has the translator translated it this way?" As part of the didactic sequence, students could move to creating their own translations for each component on the scale of possibilities, then to just one, based upon the function of the translation. These considerations are highly contextualized and align with socially situated literacy in terms of cultural perspectives.

Cultural Products, Practices, and Perspectives

In the United States, the World-Readiness Standards for Learning Languages (The National Standards Collaborative Board, 2015) describe culture in terms of products, practices, and perspectives. Products can be tangible, like art, literature, or architecture, or intangible, like oral literature or institutional systems. Cultural products are present within a given society due to its cultural perspectives, and cultural practices involve use of products and also reflect cultural perspectives. Students are expected to show their understanding of the connections between cultural practices and perspectives and cultural products and perspectives, to make new connections to the world through the target language and associated cultural perspectives, and to make linguistic and cultural comparisons.

According to Phipps and González (2004), "Cultures are messy, heavy, people-ridden; Culture – or culture packaged – is light and universal" (p. 61). Culture that is most visible or packaged has been described as "Big C" culture, which is generally reflected in language textbooks focusing on products and practices without linking it to perspectives. A sole focus on either products or practices is generally missing the complexities of culture visible in "Little c" culture, as these are tied to the underlying perspectives which affect cultural products and practices. In terms of socially situated literacy, "Every act of language, be it written or spoken, is a statement about the position of its author within the social structure in a given culture … linguistic behavior [is] a series of *acts of identity* in which people reveal both their personal identity and their search for social roles" (Le Page & Tabouret-Keller, 1985, pp. 13–14, emphasis in original, as cited in Kramsch, 2008, p. 108). Differing frames of interpretation, then, would signal a different culture.

The existence of differing frames of interpretation, or cultural perspectives, represents one of the challenges of translation and points to the view of translation as moving across both languages and cultures. wa Thiong'o (2023) links cultivation in agriculture and culture as social practice, pointing out that both environments involve "translation from one environment to another" (p. 35). For pedagogical translation, the challenge of addressing these differing frames of interpretation must be expected and may be built into the objectives for a pedagogical translation activity. For beginning world language learners who may be primarily working with vocabulary, such as a translation activity asking learners to fill in the blanks with words from a word bank, the cultural connection may not yet be as visible. Second language learners living within the context of the language they are learning may be exposed to and appreciate at an earlier stage that sociocultural practices are affecting language use. For example, Escamilla et al. (2014) recommended that EB students begin as early as their fourth year in primary school to translate short, complex texts such as poems or idiomatic expressions in which cultural perspectives are certainly in play.

Cultural Perspectives of World Language Learners

Language learning depends upon contexts such as the language-learner's linguistic and cultural background and current language-learning environment, including geopolitical and learning (Byram, 2020; Hornberger & Skilton-Sylvester, 2000). The connection to context is reminiscent of links to context in the multilingual and social turns in SLA theory and to socially situated literacy. The language-learning environment of world language learners tends to be characterized by isolation from the language being studied, although, as previously noted, it can no longer be assumed that "foreign" languages and their communities are all beyond one's geopolitical border, and the internet can also serve to cross or erase borders. Whether or not a learner might anticipate cultural interaction with a speaker of the additional language, "the pedagogical need for a focus on specific cultural others remains. Learners need to at least imagine interaction with specific people and not a generalized 'other'" (Byram, 2020, p. 210).

Cultural Perspectives of Bilingual Language Learners

The cultural perspective of bilingual learners, however, will be characterized by exposure to at least the home and additional language cultures. In learning environments where both world and bilingual learners are present, these differing perspectives will need to be taken into account when planning translation activities. For example, Albrecht (2024) found that in a mixed heritage—world language group of secondary learners, a translation activity positively impacted reading comprehension in Spanish, but that the learners approached the activity from different cultural perspectives. For example, one HLL compared the process of writing the translation from the heritage language into the dominant language to the mental "chunking" of text when orally translating in the home environment. Another engaged in written translanguaging when reflecting upon the translation process. Two thought that the activity was irrelevant, one because although she had learned new vocabulary through the activity, it was not relevant to her language contexts; and the other because he thought he already knew all of the vocabulary, although there were errors in translation of collocations. World language learners, on the other hand, commented on looking for patterns in the text, looking for context clues as part of their process, noting the informality of the poem being translated compared to typical classroom texts and on the epiphany that Spanish was actually a language rather than a series of vocabulary words in translation. Ultimately, their process was affected by their context and learning parameters, but reflection upon the translation process itself was largely acultural. The HLLs, on the other hand, already had a bilingual cultural "anchor" to the language from which they were translating. This bilingual tie related directly to the learners' immediate community practices and not to the foreign, cultural "other" often conceived of in world language instruction.

Translation, Culture, and Literacy

Socially situated literacy is literacy tied to cultural and social contexts. Translation, culture, and socially situated literacy are then tightly intertwined given that translation is considered to be the use of language to "bring over" (Venuti, 2018) another culture. According to Schulte (n.d.), "The act of translation is always concerned with the reconstruction of a process rather than with the description of a particular content ... 'Reading is already translation, and translation is translation for the second time... The process of translating comprises in its essence the whole secret of human understanding of the world and of social communication'" (n.d., citing Gadamer). The human understanding of the world through reading and translation might be interpreted as moving beyond socially situated literacy to socially situated literacy within biliterate contexts.

Translation, Culture, and Linguistic Learning

Translation, culture, and linguistic learning have been closely connected in the literature. According to Cazden (1974), teaching is "a linguistic process in a cultural setting" (p. vii). The field of pragmatics illustrates this connection, as decisions about what the right thing is to say when and where is a cultural determination. Placing translation into this process, Cook (2010) affirmed that "translation mediates between monolithic linguistic and cultural blocks" (p. 79). Chesterman (1998) distinguished between bilingual and translation competence, with the bilingual speaker mediating linguistically *in* two cultures and the translator mediating linguistically *between* two cultures (as cited in Stachl-Peier, 2020), although it seems that translators who are bilingual could also be mediating linguistically in two cultures as well. Adding pedagogical translation into this equation, one might conclude that pedagogical translation mediates either in or between linguistic processes (cognitive mediation) and multiple cultures (relational mediation). Washbourne (2010) recommends that translators in training study "culturally bound terms" (p. 59) which may have some overlap in meaning but which do not fully align due to cultural connotation, sharing a list of these terms between Spanish and English for novice translators to investigate in terms of cultural connotation and similarity or difference in register. This type of vocabulary exploration could also be used prior to a pedagogical translation activity, in which the instructor extracts key vocabulary from the text for students to examine per Washbourne's investigation.

Translation for Inter- and Intracultural Competence

Viewing interculturality as living in diversity at home and abroad acknowledges and encourages the complex interactions between languages and cultures without the politically drawn boundaries of nation states aimed at establishing economic, political, and cultural power (Phipps & González, 2004). Along these lines, wa Thiong'o (2023) noted the role of translation as a mediator in African contexts, with translation of works within and between African countries fostering respect for other languages and cultures and also drawing attention to how languages share common culture and heritage. Similarly, Oprica (2016) detailed a translation of Romanian folklore activity designed to foster intercultural awareness in an extracurricular course for children of Romanian parents in Spain. The children, ages 9–12, selected 75 texts for translation which Oprica described as folklore, namely, "games, formula-songs, recital-stories, proverbs, household words, incantations and riddles" (p. 112). Folklore was selected for translation due to its inherent cultural representation, its brevity, and for the characteristics of rhyme and rhythm typically present in the text which create interesting dilemmas in translation. The students were generally not familiar with many of the texts, thus learning about typical names and mythological creatures in Romanian folklore. However, they tended to domesticate the texts in translation, making changes to reflect their cultural environment in Spain as opposed to maintaining Romanian cultural elements. While a critical conversation about these decisions was not mentioned in the article, this type of discussion could also be beneficial in developing intercultural competence in the presence of dominant linguistic and cultural norms. Oprica suggested that this activity could benefit other Romanian students in Spain, but I would argue that it could be adapted and utilized across many language-learning environments, particularly for HLLs.

In bilingual-learning environments, students are positioned to draw upon cultural competence within their own cultures in order to work through translation problems, thus applying their linguistic and cultural contexts. For example, David et al. (2019) found that intermediate-aged EB students built upon their own cultural knowledge as they collaboratively worked through translation activities. Similarly, Pacheco et al. (2015) found that EB intermediate students participating in translation activities were positioned as linguistic and cultural experts. These experiences contrast with monolingual approaches in which students are expected to forfeit linguistic and cultural identities to acquire the dominant language and culture and thus assimilate (Block, 2003). Pedagogical translation, then, may serve as a powerful vehicle through which students' intracultural knowledge or identity may be validated and drawn upon.

Explication is another strategy used by translators which can be implemented in language instruction as well. Through explication, "the translator interpolates an explanation of a lexeme bound to the source culture" (Washbourne, 2010, p. 128). For example, in the children's book *In My Family/En Mi Familia* (Garza, 2000), the author describes a musical group as a *conjunto band,* using the word "band" to explicate the foreign term "*conjunto*" to an audience who presumably is culturally unaware of its meaning. In the Spanish translation, only the term "*conjunto*" is used, as the audience will presumably be cultural insiders. Students could engage in this type of analysis by translating the text themselves (in either direction, depending upon the learning environment and the objectives), then compare to the text and discuss differences between their own translations and the text's. The use of culture-bound explication has always become evident to the author's students through these types of discussions.

Translation Spotlight: Translation of Proverbs

Because proverbs are short texts that are rich in cultural meaning, they have been used for training professional translators (Washbourne, 2010) and can also serve as fruitful texts for translation for language learners. However, the approach will vary based upon the type of learner. Proverbs may be used in bilingual science and literacy instruction to capitalize on what children already know (Arreguín-Anderson & Ruiz-Escalante, 2016). Arreguín-Anderson and Ruiz-Escalante's text selection process is instructive. They recommend that instructors first determine what proverbs are used by their students based on regional variation so that students can in fact make the desired connection to prior knowledge or their own contexts. In the author's bilingual teacher preparation courses, for example, students have identified proverbs used in their families and then tied them to their families' region(s) of origin. Some students have been familiar with their colleagues' proverbs, and others have not. Additionally, in terms of comprehension, some students found that although they had heard proverbs in their environments, they did not always understand them. This type of activity highlights the following: (1) instructors cannot assume that a text from a given society will be understood or related to by all students, (2) the need for understanding student backgrounds in the selection of texts, and (3) the need to address comprehension.

In bilingual learning environments, Escamilla et al. (2014) recommended the use of short, contextually rich texts such as proverbs as part of their *Así se dice* translation activity for primary grades, with objectives centering on both language learning and literacy acquisition. These types of texts must be carefully selected and translation activities carefully structured, given that even for professional translators "A short, challenging text that is four words in length … can take hours for a convincing final draft" (Washbourne, 2010, p. 28). Moving from the home language into the target language, the instructor models the process for students, demonstrating when literal translation is not effective and how to move to meaning-based translation, then moving students toward independent practice. In world language learning, Colina and Lafford (2017) recommended the use of proverbs or sayings in translation as a means for making cultural comparisons. In terms of function, the translation centers on bridging cultures with language as the vehicle for doing so. Equivalence will therefore be at the pragmatic level. Understanding the need for a meaning-based translation requires both understanding of the linguistic and cultural meaning of the original text and an attempt at a linguistic translation that is culturally accurate. The thinking skills required for these activities are complex and they could be expanded or modified for varying grades and/or with a reverse direction of translation.

Direction of translation may be determined by learning objectives as well as student proficiency. Once texts are selected, students can translate a proverb from their home language into the target language, keeping the functional purpose of the translation in mind in determining the level of equivalence. Because lexical or syntactic equivalence generally does not capture the pragmatic or cultural meaning of a proverb, it may be useful to translate the proverb directly first and discuss student interpretation of the meaning (Colina & Lafford, 2017), followed by an effort to match a proverb with similar meaning. A list of proverbs may be provided in both languages, which students then match by inferring meaning, a typical strategy in reading comprehension with an additional layer of complexity when moving between languages. Students may then compare cultural similarities and differences between proverbs.

Translation Spotlight: Translation of Proverbs Activity

This is a collaborative, intermediate translation activity which may be used and adapted across ages and language levels.

LITERACY, TRANSLATION, AND CULTURAL LEARNING

Table 6.1 Translation Spotlight: Translation of Proverbs Activity

Sample translation of proverbs lesson (adapted from Colina & Albrecht, 2020)
Estimated time: 50-minute class period

Objective(s): Through a translation activity, I can:

CEFR *(Council of Europe, 2020)*:
- *Produce clearly organized translations from (Language A) into (Language B) that reflect normal language usage but may be over-influenced by the order, paragraphing, punctuation and particular formulations of the original.*
- *Interpret and explain a document from another culture and relate it to documents or events from my own culture(s)*

ACTFL *(2017, pp. 5, 16)*:
- *Identify the underlying message in a proverb in another language.*
- *In my own and other cultures, explain how proverbs are related to cultural perspectives.*
- *Use proverbs in my home and an additional language to make cultural comparisons.*

CCSS *(National Governors Association, 2010)*:
- *Determine the meaning of words and phrases as they are used in a proverb in two languages, including figurative and connotative meanings; analyze the impact of rhymes and other repetitions of sounds*

Prior Skills:
- Content: Students should understand what a proverb is and how it is used prior to translating. This may be done at the beginning of this lesson or in a prior lesson.
- Language: Students should understand how to identify literary devices like rhyme and alliteration that may be used in proverbs. If language conventions are going to be discussed and/or graded, these should have already been taught and should be added into the standards and objectives.

Materials:
- Projector, computer and electronic devices for students
- Two lists of ten proverbs selected for similar meanings in Language A and Language B.
  - A four-column worksheet similar to the sample below. Language B proverbs should be added to column 1.
  - The proverbs in Language B should be cut apart.
  - Have enough of both lists for dyads or groups of 3-4.

(continued)

Table 6.1 (*continued*)

Sample Worksheet

Proverbs in Language B (target language)	Literal translation	Equivalent proverb in Language A (home language)	Cultural comparisons
Model: *A quien madruga, dios le ayuda*	Whoever gets up early, God helps	*Early to bed, early to rise makes a man healthy, wealthy and wise*	Both focus on routine and personal industry. Language B: Personal benefit includes relationship to deity. Language A: Personal benefits include wealth, health and wisdom.

Translation of Proverbs Activity:

Activate prior knowledge by having students do one or more of the following:
- Describe what a proverb is
- Look at sample proverbs in their home language(s) and explain why they are proverbs
- Think of proverbs they have heard in their families or other environments; alternatively, they may have asked family members for typical proverbs used in their home or community and bring back samples for the next class session. These could be illustrated, shared and explained.

Translation Activity:
- Hand out the lists of proverbs in Language A and Language B as indicated in Materials.
- Have students do three things with their lists of proverbs:
  - Translate the Language B proverbs (target language) into Language A (home language) in column 2.
    - Once this step is complete, ask students for their responses to the translations, which will probably include comments that they don't make sense. If students are not already familiar with literal vs. functional translation, explain that sometimes a text in one language must be translated for the overall meaning, not literally. Discuss the overall meaning of each proverb.

LITERACY, TRANSLATION, AND CULTURAL LEARNING

- Tell students that you will be giving them ten more proverbs in the home language which match the overall meaning of the proverbs in the target language.
  - Have the students match the proverbs, placing appropriate proverb in the home language into the appropriate space in column 3 and working in previously established groups.
  - Once all proverbs are matched, as a class, discuss student responses to the process. How did they decide which proverbs matched when they could not translate literally?
  - Have students note similarities and differences in cultural perspectives in the matched proverbs. Model the process with a set of proverbs first so that students can understand the thought process.
  - For example, students in the author's intermediate Spanish class noted that *A quien madruga, dios ayuda* and *Early to bed, early to rise, makes a man healthy, wealthy and wise* both had to do with the benefits of good habits and personal industry. However, the Spanish proverb included a religious component, while the proverb in English focused on wealth as a motivator.

Evaluation:
- **Formative:**
  - Literal translation of proverbs: Circulate and listen to student negotiation for meaning; answer questions as needed, but do not provide clues yet to the underlying meaning of the proverbs.
  - Translation matching: Circulate to make sure students understand the activity and to answer any questions. You may indicate if a match is incorrect.
- **Summative Options:**
  - Younger students could create a bilingual, illustrated poster of a set of proverbs to hang in the classroom or in the school hallways.
  - Have students reflect in writing on the cultural similarities and differences between the proverbs.

Expansion/Modification:
- Have students translate 2-3 proverbs from the target language into the home language, then rotate groups using a jigsaw strategy to share translations and discuss their prior groups' reasoning about the translation choices.
- For multilingual classes, have parents help provide proverbs in the home language and, if possible, a description of the meaning that can be used to help align with a proverb in the target language.
- For more advanced classes, have students find their own proverbs in their home language(s) which functionally match the target-language proverbs, then continue on to a cultural comparison of the matched proverbs.
- As a pre-translation activity, analyze the translations in a bilingual book of proverbs like *Mi primer libro de dichos/My First Book of Proverbs* (González & Ruiz, 2014). Ask students if they agree with the translation strategies and to defend their reasoning.

Translation Spotlight: Translation of an Advertisement

This translation activity offers the opportunity to incorporate various language, content, and cultural learning goals. First, translation of an advertisement of necessity incorporates multimodality and considerations of how different modes work together to create the desired message in the source language, then how these modes may need to be modified to create the desired message in the target language. Taking into account functionality in terms of selling a product, due to cultural nuance, the desired multimodal effect in the source language may not work in the target language. While the activity is modeled at the intermediate level, due to the brevity and high interest of the text involved, this activity might lend itself well to adaptation for earlier learners (Goundareva, 2011).

Socially situated literacy is linguistically and culturally contextualized. As illustrated in this chapter, culture is complex, which makes learning about culture complex. Nevertheless, pedagogical translation serves as a cultural mediator, offering students the opportunity to move in and between—rather than learning "about"—cultures while negotiating for meaning between the source and target texts.

LITERACY, TRANSLATION, AND CULTURAL LEARNING

Table 6.2 Translation Spotlight: Translation of an Advertisement

Sample translation of an advertisement activity (Adapted from Colina & Albrecht, 2020): For this activity, students will choose an advertisement from a printed or digital magazine in the home language to translate into the target language. Text in the advertisement should be minimal.
Estimated time: 50-minute class period

Objective(s): Through a translation activity, I can:

CEFR (Council of Europe, 2020):
- *Produce clearly organized translations from (Language A) into (Language B) that reflect normal language usage but may be over-influenced by the order, paragraphing, punctuation, and particular formulations of the original.*
- *Interpret and explain a document from another culture and relate it to documents or events from my own culture(s)*

ACTFL (2017, pp. 5, 16):
- *Identify the underlying message in an advertisement in another language.*
- *In my own and other cultures, explain how advertisements are related to cultural perspectives.*

CCSS (National Governors Association, 2010):
- *Determine the meaning of words and phrases as they are used in an advertisement, including figurative and connotative meanings; analyse the impact of rhymes and other repetitions of sounds*

Prior Skills:
- **Content:** Students should be familiar with the persuasive strategies of logos, pathos, and ethos.
- **Language:** Advertisements often use commands, so students should know how to formulate commands in the target language (the author has used this assignment to teach commands). They should also be familiar with written conventions in both languages.
- **Technology:** Students will need to know how to copy and paste images into a Google or Word document and to put text on top of the image.

Materials:
- Projector (if unavailable, the assignment can be modified to hard copies of materials)
- Model advertisement in the home language with simple text and graphics, ideally with elements representing cultural perspectives
- Hard or digital copies of advertisements in the home language
  - You may want to choose some sites in advance to recommend to students or think about places where they might look for ads, like their social media accounts.
- Hard copy or digital dictionaries
- Paper, scissors, and glue if students are not working digitally

(continued)

Table 6.2 (continued)

Activity:

Before translating:
- Activate prior knowledge: Ask students to think of a printed advertisement that has caught their attention. Discuss what graphic or textual elements have helped them remember this advertisement.
- Explain: Tell students that they will be choosing an ad in their home language, identifying the persuasive strategy used in the ad and translating it into the target language.
- Model: Show students the model advertisement you have chosen. In cooperative groups, have students identify the persuasive strategy used in the ad. As a class, discuss the strategy(ies) identified and why. Next, discuss who the target audience is for the advertisement. How are text and graphics used to reach this audience? Finally, discuss considerations in translating the text, such as audience and level of formality (register), specialized vocabulary and cultural considerations in the graphics.

Translate:
- In pairs or groups of 3–4, have students find a simple advertisement in their home language to translate into the target language.
- Have students translate the text into the target language.
- Have students choose new graphics, if needed. Tell them to be prepared to explain why they needed new graphics and why the one they chose is more appropriate.

After translating:

Evaluation:
- **Formative:** Circulate around the room to make sure students understand the activity and that they are able to find an appropriate advertisement.
- **Summative:** Summative assessments will differ depending upon the standards-based objectives but should show mastery of the objective(s). Possible products for evaluation might include the advertisement together with individual reflections on figurative or connotative meanings and/or on similarities and differences between cultural perspectives in the advertisement in the source and target languages. If you are going to evaluate linguistic features, be sure to add these to the objectives.

Expansion/Modification:
- Choose the advertisements that students will translate.
- To save class time, explain the assignment and have students choose their advertisements before coming to class.
- Depending upon the amount of text in the advertisement, leave blanks and offer a word bank to fill in the blank.
- Depending upon the level of your students and your objectives, direction of translation may be changed.

7
The Potential of Authentic Texts

Chapter 7 focuses on selecting linguistically and culturally authentic bilingual and dual-edition texts for translation activities and how these activities can contribute to socially situated literacy. Bilingual and dual-edition texts should be assumed to be written in a home and additional language, with all text presented in two languages. This would be in one book for bilingual books and in two books for dual editions. While this format may reinforce conceptions of language separation, translanguaging may also occur in these texts (Daly, 2018). Semi-bilingual texts, or texts which are written predominantly in one language but which code switch into another language (Chen, 2019), will be specifically identified and addressed at some points in the chapter, particularly in terms of bilingual practices and translation considerations. The role of power and language ideology in the production of these texts will be included, as well as research-based suggestions for selecting bilingual or dual-edition texts; creating and using text sets; and selecting paired texts for translation activities. How use of these texts for translation activities can contribute to biliteracy development will also be addressed. The chapter will end with a Translation Spotlight on using bilingual and dual-edition texts, text sets, and paired texts in the classroom.

The Role of Texts

A literacy-based approach to language learning draws upon linguistic, cognitive, and social relationships between readers, writers, texts, and cultures; between form and meaning; between reading and writing; and between spoken and written communication (Kern, 2000). Because literacy by definition involves texts, textual analysis becomes an immutable appendage to literacy acquisition. For this chapter, bilingual or dual-language texts which can be used for pedagogical translation are the proposed focus of textual analysis. The question then becomes, what texts should be selected? From a translator-training perspective, without authentic texts and contexts, translation pedagogy slides back toward Grammar Translation (Baer & Koby, 2003). Translation situations should also be varied, relevant, and imitate real life, pointing to the need for authentic texts (Kelly et al., 2000; Schaffner & Adab, 2000). Authentic texts also provide examples of genuine language use and language patterns which learners might transfer to new contexts (Washbourne, 2012b). Importantly, authentic materials contribute to novice translators' reading comprehension, text-to-self connections, and cultural similarities and differences across source and target texts. As students connect to the texts, schema within their minds are activated, again contributing to comprehension (Washbourne, 2012a; 2012b).

For language study, the dominant culture's literary canon has typically been privileged, which brings up the question of who determines what belongs in the literary canon and what purpose it serves (Phipps & González, 2004). According to Phipps and González (2004), "*Literature* lives within a narrow and defined role constrained by genre, enclosed by period, chained, unchained then rechained to movements or schools" (p. 137, emphasis in original); reading in this way leads to predetermined teaching outcomes as opposed to reading to develop critical thinking and interculturality.

Authentic texts should include oral and written texts that are representative of cultural practices and perspectives (Kern, 2000; Phipps & González, 2004). Fois (2020) recommended "small translating tasks related to the main topic" (p. 567) such as translation of famous quotes, book covers, or flyers that can be adapted across levels and prompt cultural as well as linguistic analysis. Similarly, beyond literature, these texts might include "advertisements, songs, magazine articles, recipes, medical advice, radio programs, [and] theatrical performances" which constitute "meaningful language acts" (Phipps & González, 2004, p. 95).

These types of texts will be addressed more fully in Chapter 8 on multimodality. For texts to facilitate the development of intercultural being through comparison and complexity, a variety of texts representing multiple perspectives should be available. This points to the benefits of utilizing text sets, which will be discussed later in this chapter, as well as to typical processes in pedagogical translation. According to Kramsch (2008), a signifying difference between oral and written texts is that "truth in oral mode is jointly constructed, while truth in literate mode is based on the logic and the coherence of the argument being made" (p. 40), thus affecting the functional role of a translation.

Dual-language texts are a valuable resource when approaching language learning as a process of bilingualization and biliteracy acquisition, as these texts "promote literacy transfers and solid development of literacy strategies, resulting in additive bilingualism" (Chen, 2019, p. 192). However, selecting high-quality, authentic texts is of key importance. Determining what constitutes an "authentic" text has been extensively problematized. Fox and Short (2003), for example, have devoted an edited volume to varying approaches to identifying textual authenticity, including considerations of language and culture. Simply speaking, Phipps and González (2004) describe authentic texts as those with "complexity embedded within them" (p. 104) as opposed to those constructed for classroom use. In this sense, "complex texts" which "enrich and fill out the semantic context of the original utterance" (p. 104) are often those which are recommended for translation activities (Park et al., 2015).

Translation and the Decolonization of Texts

As discussed in Chapter 3, language and translation have historically been sites for power struggle (Munday et al., 2022). The privileging of one language over another in the translation process is representative of dominant power structures (Lee, 2013) as well as ideological perspectives among "cultural gatekeepers" (Munday et al., 2022, p. 201) such as translators, translation commissioners, editors, or varying institutions. These perspectives may become embedded in the target text. Editors, for example, are often not fluent in the language of translation yet have considerable power in the shaping of the text, with their main objective being readability. An editor's interpretation of the function of a translation may therefore differ from that of the source text author and the translator. Similarly, publishers in the UK and the United States often choose works that are easily culturally assimilated, with the role of the translator becoming invisible (Venuti, 2017). Because these tensions between cultural or linguistic communities frequently appear through languages, language-contact environments help make post-colonial or other minority power differentials visible, with English or dominant languages of ex-colonizers tending to be favored (Lee, 2013, Niranjana, 1992). These manifestations, apparent in situations of language contact, are often based upon monolingual or standard language ideologies. Power differentials may become visible in texts considered for pedagogical translation in various ways.

Bilingual or dual-edition (texts available in two languages) children's books can be useful in translation activities in language-learning environments beyond primary grades. Bintz and Ciecierski-Madara (2022) argued that picture books should be incorporated in middle-grade curricula as they can be used and enjoyed by everyone and promote thoughtful analysis of the interconnection between text and illustration. Thinking in terms of translation, literacy, and language learning, the gap between pictures and words broadens to a linguistic and cultural gap between languages, with pictures playing a mediating role in meaning making. As long as older learners buy into the reason for using picture books, a strong argument may be made in favor of their use.

Bilingual children's books can serve multiple important roles in translation activities. First, when students complete a textual translation, bilingual books provide an existing translation with which to compare (Colina & Albrecht, 2020). Students can translate a section of text in one of the languages, compare translations with their classmates and then compare with the published translation. Additionally, as previously mentioned, illustrations can scaffold textual understanding. Translation of bilingual children's books activities can lead to rich discussion about variation in functional translations, nuance in lexical choice, and resultant nuance in meaning, and other linguistic or rhetorical considerations.

However, as dominant language ideologies are often in play in the translation and production of these texts, selection of bilingual or dual-edition texts for use in pedagogical translation should involve considerations of power differentials. Bourdieu's (1991) frameworks have been widely applied in studying language and power within translation. Examples of these frameworks may be useful in considering the selection of texts. For example, Lee (2013) maintains that the *symbolic power* differential between English and other national languages in Singapore threatens the maintenance of languages other than English, with symbolic power being "the measure of social capital accorded to a language in a specific socio-cultural context" (p. 19). Munday et al. (2022) draw upon Bourdieu's concepts of *field of social activity* and *field of power* in post-colonial analysis of translated texts. A field of social activity in translation would be the site of a power struggle between participants in the publication and translation of texts, with the field being translation and the participants including the source text author, the commissioner of a translation and the publisher(s), editor, translator, and reader. In the context of translation, the field of power controls operation of the literary field, or what gets translated and how.

The translation of children's books into Spanish in the United States is a case in point. In the United States, children's books are typically translated into Spanish only by specialized publishing houses and using standardized Spanish, and translation of children's books published in other countries is uncommon. Casanova (2004) highlights this phenomenon, noting that "Translation ... is a process of *littérisation,* whereby literary works written in dominated and less visible languages are accepted as 'literary' by being translated into dominant languages that hold stronger *linguistic capital*" [emphasis added]" (as cited in Lee, 2013, p. 138). On the other hand, as literatures of dominant languages are translated into a weaker language, the influence of the dominant language and culture expands through dissemination of the literature. This demonstrates that as a field of social activity in the United States, translation of children's books is not mainstream, standard language varieties are valued over vernacular or regional variants, and English is dominant. Therefore, in selecting texts for pedagogical translation activities, it is important to consider whether language ideologies are embedded within the texts.

An additional consideration in selecting bilingual texts for translation may be how code switching, or moving back and forth between languages (García, 2009), is used, as the facility with which one language may be used in code switching demonstrates its power positioning. Lee (2013) noted that a Chinese text with considerable code switches into English demonstrates the weak symbolic power of Chinese in Singapore and, in contrast, the high symbolic power of English. While these types of texts may be selected for translation activities, pragmatic objectives which make these power structures visible should be incorporated in activity planning. Other texts might be selected which challenge this power positioning. For example, in the middle-grade dual-edition volume of poetry *They Call Me Güero/ Me dicen Güero,* author and translator Bowles (2018, 2020) code switches into the other language in both volumes, validating bilingual practices and challenging the power weighting of English. Within the framework of the critical continua of biliteracy (Hornberger & Skilton-Sylvester, 2000), this code switching validates bilingual practices on the *bilingual–monolingual* subcontinuum of biliteracy within the continuum of *contexts* and challenges the dominant, monolingual power weighting of English.

Challenges to dominant power structures are also visible through translations. Hornberger and Skilton-Sylvester's (2000) critical continua of biliteracy provides a useful framework for analysis in determining how power is functioning or being challenged in biliterate environments. On the subcontinua of *vernacular-standard language use,* within the continuum of *content of biliteracy,* texts written in standard language, including the dominant societal language, typically represent dominant power structures. However, vernacular texts can challenge this dominant structure. Historically, Martin Luther's inclusion of vernacular language in his translation of the Bible served to challenge traditional ecclesiastical power (Munday et al., 2022). Modern texts may fulfill a similar role. Lee's (2013) analysis of translated anthologies in Singapore demonstrates a change in power weighting over time as translations shifted from non-dominant official languages translated to English to translations between languages. Similarly, most bilingual children's books in the United States are written in English first and then, often several years later, translated into an additional language.

However, the Spanish–English volume of children's poetry *Somos como las nubes/We Are Like the Clouds* (Argueta, 2016) challenges monolingual norms and decenters English as the dominant language as it was written in Spanish and then translated into English, with title and text appearing in Spanish first. Additionally, the book incorporates regional vocabulary from El Salvador rather than defaulting to standard Latin American Spanish, with some key terms not being translated into English at all but instead being translated in footnotes, thus challenging standard language norms in both languages and highlighting the fact that colonizing language practices can appear in any text in which the language is that of a colonizer. The role of translation in decolonization therefore needs to be considered in the selection of texts for translation in any language-learning environment.

Selecting Linguistically and Culturally Authentic Texts for Translation Activities

In a multilingual, multicultural world, text selection for any sort of analysis can be complex and should involve application of research-based criteria. Because of their contextual situatedness, texts should be linguistically and culturally relevant to students (Linares, 2022). When separated from these contexts, such as an excerpt in isolation from a larger written piece or from cultural, historical, or societal contexts, texts can lose their raison d'etre for the reader, or, in other words, their relevance (Phipps & González, 2004). Additionally, production of bilingual texts often points to colonial power imbalances, with the potential for these texts to embed dominant language ideologies, linguistic and cultural stereotypes, and erroneous representations (Alamillo, 2007; Niranjana, 1992); hence, the need for criticality in text selection.

A research-based list of criteria for selecting bilingual or dual-edition texts follows (Albrecht, 2022), although questions regarding translator and publisher may be modified or eliminated for monolingual texts to be translated into or out of the target language. Each element will be discussed sequentially.

1. What are the author's, illustrator's, and translator's relationships to the text? Who is the publisher? (Fox & Short, 2003)
2. How does the text portray status between languages? For example, in bilingual books, what language appears first in the title and in the text? How does this linguistic landscape affect portrayal of non-dominant cultures? (Chappell & Faltis, 2007; Daly, 2018)
3. Will the text be linguistically and culturally relevant to students? What types of changes are made in translation, and how do these affect the meaning of the text? (Alamillo, 2007; Linares, 2022; Nikolajeva, 2011)
4. What cultural values and representations appear in the book's text and illustrations? Who tells the story and who has power? (Chen, 2019; Fox & Short, 2003)
5. How do cultural representations change between the source text and illustrations and its readers, and the target text and illustrations and its readers? (Nikolajeva, 2011)
6. In a text set, what is the interplay between cultures? How do texts relate to one another? How does the combined perspective among texts contribute to critical understanding? (Brochin & Medina, 2017; Fox & Short, 2003)

Stakeholder Relationships to the Text

Ek et al. (2016) emphasized that using multicultural children's literature from a multiliteracies approach "decenters literacy definitions that focus on only one standardized national language and its accompanying 'authoritarian kind of pedagogy'" (p. 208, citing New London Group, 1996, p. 64). However, the relationship of author, illustrator, translator, and editor/publisher to the text impacts the final product. Typically, authors of bilingual or dual-edition texts who are cultural insiders will have a more "authentic" linguistic and cultural approach and connection to the content of the text than those who are not (Alamillo, 2007). However, this is a point of departure rather than a foregone conclusion. It is also possible for authors who are cultural outsiders to have a close connection to the content of the text; these may be teachers who saw a lack of availability of culturally and linguistically relevant texts for their students, so they started to write their own books (see e.g., Rivera-Ashford (2015), *My Tata's Remedies/Los remedios de mi tata*). The need for close consideration is illustrated by the case of Judith Byron Schachner's *Skippyjon Jones* series published in the United States. The English-based series about a Siamese cat's adventures has been popular and is widely available in school and public libraries. However, it has been criticized for incorporating mock Spanish and for culturally misrepresenting Latinos, raising the question of whether popularity is equivalent to high-quality literature (Martínez-Roldán, 2013). Martínez-Roldán argues that authentic linguistic representation should instead be evaluated when determining successful cultural representation.

Particularly in children's books, the illustrator plays a key role in contributing to the meaning of the text through use of artistic elements such as line, color, and style, but the illustrator's cultural relationship to a multicultural text can also be evident (Short et al., 2014). For example, the Nahuatl-Spanish children's book *Tonelhuayo uan Totlahtoltzin/La raíz y la voz* (Stromberg, 2018) is a compilation of Nahua folk tales illustrated by a group of artists from the state of Guerrero, Mexico, who also provided oral versions of the story which were then written and revised by another group of writers (*Los mejores libros*, 2018). The illustrations follow the Nahua artistic style and show the clear cultural connection between the illustrators and the text. Illustrated children's books that are translated and imported into target text language environments may result in cultural disconnects based on illustrations that make sense in the source but not the target culture, adding another layer of consideration in textual analysis (Spangenberg, 2022).

Attention to the translator's role in bilingual and/or dual-edition texts is important for several reasons. Venuti (2018) has maintained that the translator's invisibility in the Anglo-European world contributes to the domestication of translated texts, in other words, to the elimination of cultural difference by making the translated text appear as if it had always belonged within the source language and culture. Information on translators of bilingual or dual-edition texts can be difficult to find in books published in the United States, contributing to their invisibility and making it difficult to identify the translator's linguistic and cultural connection to the text (Short et al., 2014). Clearly, when authors translate their own texts, it can be much easier to identify the relationship of the translator to source and target language texts.

As previously discussed, publisher relationships to the text often reflect dominant monolingual and standard language ideologies. Through this stance, publishers are "'rewriting' literature and governing its consumption" (Munday et al., 2022, p. 169). Part of publishers governing what is consumed involves the ideological determination of whether or not to publish translations as well as who does the translating, as translator ideologies may also be in play (Munday, 2022). The ideological role of publishers in publishing translations, including in bilingual or dual-edition children's texts, merits investigation into the publishing houses in a given linguistic and cultural environment in order to determine what translations are being produced.

Linguistic Landscape

Text design or linguistic landscape within bilingual books implicitly portrays language status (Daly, 2018). This might be effected through language order, text size, translation accuracy, and accessibility in both languages, including whether dust cover flaps, acknowledgments, and reviews are translated (Huang & Chen, 2016). When readers see themselves in the linguistic landscape of a text, they can feel linguistically and culturally validated (Daly, 2018). However, the linguistic landscape can also send messages regarding language status in a given society at the same time. For example, Spanish–English bilingual children's books in the United States tend to put English text first, followed by Spanish, including in the book title. In a study on a Spanish–English bilingual children's book collection, Daly (2018) found that English was placed first in 74 percent of the books. The text of the dominant language is often also larger. The children's book *In My Family/ En mi familia* (Garza, 1996) was written to validate Latino culture in the United States, with short vignettes and illustrations by the author portraying significant memories and traditions representative of her culture. However, the linguistic landscape works somewhat in opposition to the illustrations and the text itself, as the title in English is first and much larger than the title in Spanish, with the body of the book maintaining the English–Spanish order throughout (Albrecht, 2022).

The linguistic landscape of the children's volume of poetry *Angels Ride Bikes/Los ángeles andan en bicicleta* (Alarcón, 2005) conveys an interesting message. The initial and ending poems are presented in English and then

Spanish, and present the city of Los Angeles, California, as a place where dreams can come true. The poems then portray family and community life in the city, and are presented in Spanish–English. The message in this linguistic landscape might be inferred that English is the dominant language and represents the dominant culture, while Spanish is the language representing home and family (Albrecht, 2022).

In an analysis of bilingual Chinese–English children's books in the United States, Huang and Chen (2016) found that most books were written in English first and then translated into Chinese, often with no cultural connection, with textual errors and with many lacking translation of the book's introduction, reviews, and author and illustrator information, thus making it impossible for monolingual Chinese parents to evaluate the books. Additionally, English text variation in font, size, and color to contribute to meaning and engagement was often absent in Chinese, sending an implicit message that English was more exciting and interesting to read than Chinese. In Chinese texts with both characters and pinyin, the pinyin word is generally placed above the corresponding character. Huang and Chen also found no textual correspondence in many of the books they analyzed, as well as errors in pinyin and Chinese characters that affected meaning.

Linguistic and Cultural Relevance

Linguistically and culturally relevant text selection might be approached from the framework of texts as mirrors, windows, and doors (Bishop, 1990; Botelho, 2021). As mirrors, texts reflect cultural experiences and identities. As windows, they offer a view to other cultures, and as sliding glass doors, they offer readers the chance to step into another world. Exposure to texts of all three types "can affirm and diversify readers' lived experiences" (Botelho, 2021, p, 119). Texts functioning as mirrors will be more linguistically and culturally relevant to a diverse student population, although those functioning as windows or doors may be thematically relevant to students' interests.

However, when instructors are cultural outsiders to their students, they may select texts which they think are culturally relevant but which in fact are not (David et al., 2019). Student involvement and, at the primary level, parent involvement in the selection of texts may therefore be recommended. As mentioned in Chapter 6, Arreguín-Anderson and Ruiz-Escalante (2016) recommended the use of proverbs for teaching primary science in order to increase the relevance of the content. However, students and their families should first be polled to determine which proverbs they use so that those selected will be relevant. The same process could be applied for a translation of proverbs activity (see Chapter 6) or a translation activity with lengthier texts such as poems, songs, or book excerpts.

Linguistic relevance is also key given the prevalence of standard language ideology and the many language varieties that exist within named languages. Linares (2022) pointed out that issues of linguistic identity may arise in any language-learning environment. For example, when the author was teaching intermediate secondary Spanish, students were required to read in Spanish for ten minutes at the beginning of every class period. Many of the books available had been written by English-speaking authors and then translated. HLLs in the course found many of these books unrelatable, despite having read them in English, because they were translated into Castilian Spanish and the students had been exposed to Latin American varieties of Spanish. This speaks to the linguistic connection students have to their home languages as they engage with texts and the need for linguistically relevant texts to support their identities. In the context of a translation activity, middle-grade students translating between Catalan and French in Spain also did not relate to the Catalan text they were translating as they considered themselves speakers of Gitan, which is linguistically similar to Catalan but which represents cultural differences (Linares, 2022).

Texts which employ code switching or translanguaging present interesting problems for analysis as well as translation. For a linguistically and culturally authentic effect, code switching should not have been added for "cultural flavor" (Barrera & Quiroa, 2003, p. 247) as in the case of the previously mentioned *Skippyjon Jones* series in the United States or to stereotype or disparage a language community. Instead, as Francisco Jiménez noted regarding his choice of using Spanish or English in his semi-autobiographical texts, sometimes the choice reflected the language in which an event took place, and sometimes it reflected what came naturally (Barrera & Quiroa, 2003). These types of texts present interesting translation problems, as the effect garnered through code switching may be lost, thus homogenizing what was initially hybrid (Lee, 2013). Bowles (2018, 2020) addresses this issue in some of the poems in his dual-edition volume, *They Call Me Güero/Me dicen Güero*. Many of the poems include code switching. In "*Textos de San Valentín*/Valentine Texts," for example, he has translated the poems but kept the code-switched lines the same in each poem. The cases for homogenization or maintenance of the code switch also present an interesting question in selecting text for pedagogical translation. Students would need to address why the code switch occurred in the source text, and, based upon functional considerations, including authorial purpose in the source text and linguistic and cultural authenticity, determine whether to employ a reverse code switch or not.

Selecting Paired Texts and Text Sets

Key among the rationales for incorporating paired, tri, or full text sets in literacy teaching is the potential for presenting multiple perspectives. Adiche (2009) argued about the danger of a single story, noting that through this incomplete perspective, stereotypes are born and proliferate. During her childhood in Nigeria, she read only British and American children's books, and when she started writing, her stories were about blond-haired, blue-eyed children who "... ate apples, drank ginger beer and played in the snow" (:51) despite never having experienced these things herself. She wrote instead about stereotypical versions of what she had been exposed to through reading. Strategies from translation studies align with the literacy strategy of pairing texts as well, focusing on authenticity of both the source text and the translation. According to Washbourne (2010), "Parallel texts – texts in the same subject field and ideally written by native speakers – are boons to the translator, and constitute one of the main resources for creating authentic target texts. If one is working into English, one looks for texts written in English on the same subject (and perhaps with the same audience)" (p. 91).

Grouping texts in pairs or in groups of up to 10–15 can help to fill out the story and avoid stereotypes. Including texts for translation, texts in multiple languages can also fill out the story linguistically and culturally in a way that is not possible monolingually. Nevertheless, when text sets only present "certain realities" (Alamillo, 2007, p. 28), whether cultural or linguistic, the possibility of stereotypes still exists. For example, if the theme for a text set is "heritage and tradition" (p. 28) among Latinos, care should be taken to avoid overemphasis on stereotypical foods such as tacos and enchiladas. Language stereotypes can also result if only one language variety, such as only standard, only one dialect or vernacular, appears in a text set. Because of these potential issues, critical textual analysis for groupings is key.

Varying options exist for incorporating text sets into the curriculum. One option is to create literature circles, which groups of students join based upon their interests after doing a "book walk" in which they are exposed to the texts and determine which ones they are interested in reading. Students then select 1 or 2 texts from the set and spend about a week reading them (Short & Cueto, 2023). At the end of the time allotted, students meet with their group to discuss connections that emerge between the texts that everyone has been reading. Reader response activities based upon transactional theory (Rosenblatt, 1978) can be implemented for these discussions.

Creating Text Sets

Text sets are valuable for multiple reasons. First, as previously mentioned, text sets can present multiple perspectives on a single theme, thus permitting as many students as possible to see themselves mirrored in the texts (Tshida et al., 2015). These might be linguistic and cultural perspectives intersecting with varying genres and modalities. Text sets can also be used to support inquiry-based projects, including for struggling readers (Hoch et al., 2019). Additionally, they can be used for building background knowledge to support comprehension of difficult texts (Lupo et al., 2018). Lupo et al. (2018) included at least one text aimed at increasing student motivation to explore the topic at hand and to read other, more-difficult texts in the set. Any of these rationales might be applied across the spectrum of language-learning environments.

Although the makeup of text sets may vary widely, several guidelines may be considered in their selection. A text set usually begins with an anchor text. Depending upon the objective(s) and the learning environment, this text might be a difficult academic text supported by other texts (Lupo et al., 2018) or thematically representative of the set. Beyond choosing texts which are related thematically, Phipps and González (2004) recommend selecting texts which foster "an intercultural process – of comparison, evocation, perplexity and illumination" (p. 136), leading toward intercultural being. However, while creating the set, it is important to examine the perspectives being represented. For example, a text set on cultural identity that includes only texts representing one community would still run the risk of perpetuating stereotypes, and, in environments where other communities are present, the possibility of mirroring some students but excluding others. Lupo et al. (2018) recommended a quad text set framework for text set selection. First, choose a challenging anchor text aligned with curricular objectives. Next, choose a visual text or texts like a photo or video to build background knowledge and motivate students; ultimately, these will help build comprehension of the anchor text. The final two components consist of informational texts and accessible texts, like fiction, non-fiction articles, or popular culture. While this type of set may work well for teaching a thematic unit, for example, text sets may vary widely depending upon the standards and objectives they are supporting.

Translation excerpts might be extracted from a larger thematic text set. Additionally, one or more texts that lend themselves to translation might be incorporated into a larger text set. As with Lupo et al.'s (2018) inclusion of texts designed to "hook" students on a topic, brief, linguistically and culturally relevant texts used to deepen comprehension and vocabulary knowledge through translation might be incorporated for any of the three prongs beyond the anchor text. Finally, depending upon learning objectives, text sets might be specifically designed only with texts that lend themselves well to excerption for translation, including poems, songs, brief biographies, or vignettes (Albrecht, 2022). Oral texts that are representative of a culture's oral tradition in literature such as proverbs, riddles, myths, and legends might also be included. Although some written compilations of these texts may be available, these types of texts may in fact be collected from students and their families with a strong oral tradition, written down, and translated.

A model of the text selection process using a modified version of Lupo et al.'s (2018) framework follows, selecting a small translation text set for the theme of cultural identity.

Book 1, the "hook": *Mi primer libro de dichos/My First Book of Proverbs,* by Ana Ruiz and Ralfka González. Ana Ruiz is a Spaniard living in the United States and Ralfka González is Mexican-American. They selected the proverbs for this book by traveling through Mexico and collecting them. The proverbs are written in standard language. The short, contextually dense texts lend themselves to translation. While the proverbs could be used in an additional translation-of-proverbs activity, one or two could be used to activate students' background knowledge and be connected to the theme.

Book 2, Anchor Text: *The House on Mango Street/La casa en Mango Street* (Cisneros, 1983, 1994). This middle-grade coming-of-age novel is used in both English language arts and Spanish as a foreign language courses. It lends itself well to translation activities as the story is presented in a series of stand-alone vignettes, some of which are short enough to easily excerpt, and is also used in some middle-grade language arts curricula in the United States. Jiménez et al. (2015) used a short excerpt from one of the vignettes during their study on translation for EB students selected for its language complexity. As the protagonist is the child of Mexican parents, this book represents a Mexican-American, urban experience. Spanish and English are presented in standard language.

Book 3: *Yes! We Are Latinos!/¡Sí! Somos latinos!* (Ada & Campoy, 2013, 2014). This dual-edition text explores the multitude of different Latino identities such as Afro-Latino, Indigenous American-Latino, and Chinese-Peruvian through brief expository texts and corresponding poems portraying a fictitious character living this experience. The brief poems and expository texts could be excerpted for a translation activity, although some might need to be divided by stanzas or paragraphs among groups. The book is often used in social studies curricula and has been selected as a supporting text due to its accessibility and broad representation of the different cultural identities. Spanish and English are presented in standard language.

Book 4: *They Call Me Güero/Me dicen Güero* (Bowles, 2018, 2020). This is a dual-edition coming-of-age volume of poetry with a Mexican-American protagonist living in the Mexico–Texas borderlands. The poems lend themselves well to translation due to their length, regional language variation and language complexity. Albrecht (2024) used a poem from this volume for a translation activity in a mixed heritage–additional language intermediate Spanish class.

Book 5: *Somos cómo la nubes/We Are Like the Clouds,* (Argueta, 2016). This bilingual children's book was written first in Spanish then translated to English and details a family's migration to the United States through poetry. The author, himself a Salvadoran refugee, uses regional vocabulary. This text lends itself well to translation as it is easy to excerpt and there is cultural and linguistic variation.

Evaluation of the truncated set: This set demonstrates linguistic diversity through standard and regional language variation. It demonstrates cultural diversity through the Mexican-American experience in two very different regions of the United States, the Texas borderlands and New York City, and through inclusion of the *¡Sí!¡Somos latinos!* And *Somos cómo las nubes* texts. To fill out the set, more variation in language, culture, and modality could be considered.

Another consideration for inclusion in a text set might be texts designed for readers' theater or choral reading. Participation in readers' theater or choral reading contributes to development of oral language skills and helps participants gain confidence in reading and pronunciation (Short & Cueto, 2023). Readers' theater is "the oral presentation of literature by two or more actors and a narrator reading from a script. Unlike plays, there is little or no costuming or movement, no stage sets, and no memorized lines. Literature becomes a living experience for readers through facial expressions, voice, and a few gestures" (p. 229). There is little research on translations for theater (Bassnett, 2014, p. 153), but readers' theater is recommended as a strategy to improve reading fluency (Short & Cueto, 2023). As texts designed for readers' theater tend to be scarce, instructors may need to modify other existing texts for use as a readers' theater. Texts that lend themselves well to modification tend to have "natural-sounding dialogue, strong characters, drama or humor, and a satisfactory ending" (p. 230).

In a primary EFL environment, Gu and Lornklang (2021) found that readers' theater utilizing traditional four-character Chinese Cheng-yu stories translated into English activated background knowledge, contributed to vocabulary learning and was enjoyable to students. The text selected, therefore, was linguistically and culturally relevant to students and worked well for additional language vocabulary acquisition. If the text is not available in translation, this type of activity might be extended into a guided writing translation activity in which students could participate in translating sections of the text relevant to their own assigned parts, thus contributing to vocabulary learning as well as modeling writing within the genre, character development and reading comprehension through considerations such as voice, tone, audience, and lexical nuance.

Choral reading consists of reading aloud in unison in small groups, with the entire class or even with a recording (Short & Cueto, 2023). Texts that lend themselves well to choral reading have predictable content, such as rhyme or repetition. While choral reading is designed to help struggling readers feel more confident due to the repetition and to their voices being joined with others, its use might be extended in language-learning environments to help learners feel more confident with reading in a new language as well as with pronunciation. Again, this type of activity might be extended with a translation activity in which students translate a section of the text to be read, including a repeated element. This might be modeled as a guided writing activity with the class, then divided into sections to be translated collaboratively in groups with final translations being shared and compared with the class. Participation in translation of the text might contribute to greater confidence in the readers' theater or choral reading as well as to comprehension of the text.

Biliteracy and Implementing Text Sets

How, then, does pedagogical translation fit into this process? We can think in terms of a multiliteracies pedagogy and designs of meaning, with Available Designs, Designing and the Redesigned (Cope & Kalantzis, 2013). Available Designs would be the texts in the set, including linguistic, cultural, and visual components. These might include texts in two or more languages such as bilingual or dual-edition texts; or poems, songs, or advertisements from the source language, the target language, or both. Designing would involve response to the texts, including activities aligned with reader response in which readers interact with the text and generate their own meaning instead of looking for a "correct" interpretation. Additionally, pedagogical translation activities such as *Bilingual Editions of Children's Books* might be incorporated at this point (this chapter). The Redesigned would be products produced during Designing, including translations. The implementation of dual-language children's books, particularly through paired texts or text sets, illustrates how power weighting might be shifted away from dominant language and culture. As previously noted, "what (content) biliterate learners and users read and write is as important as how (development), where and when (context), or by what means (media) they do so" (Hornberger & Link, 2012, p. 268).

Conclusion

Power and language ideologies play a role in the production of dual-edition texts, particularly in translated texts. Analysis of power and language ideologies visible in language, illustration, and design is therefore a critical component to text or text set selection for translation activities. Chapter 8 will broaden considerations of text selection to multimodality.

Translation Spotlight: Bilingual and Dual Editions of Children's Books

The spotlight will include a sample activity using bilingual or dual-edition children's books, including content-area and language objectives, to be applied according to the learning environment. The activity is based upon intermediate standards as they are representative of the cumulative nature of learning, that is, simplified versions will most likely have been presented prior and that expanded versions will be presented after. Of course, a content-area intermediate-grade standard does not necessarily align with an intermediate-level language standard; standards and objectives will need adjustment in both cases depending upon the learning context. Although many objectives could be applied to this activity, only a few are presented for brevity. Specific language objectives, such as vocabulary or verb tense, might be added to the general objectives.

Table 7.1 Translation Spotlight: Translation of Bilingual/Dual-Edition Children's Books

Sample intermediate lesson: Translation of bilingual/dual-edition children's books (Adapted from Colina & Albrecht, 2020)
Estimated time: 50-minute class period

Objective(s): Through translation of an excerpt from a bilingual children's book, I can:

CEFR (Council of Europe, 2020):
- *Produce a translation into (Language B) [English, in this lesson] which closely follows the sentence and paragraph structure of the original text in (Language A) [Spanish, in this lesson], conveying the main points of the source text accurately (p. 218).*
- *Use context cues to achieve the comprehension necessary to convey the main parts of a source text accurately through translation.*
- *Recognize cultural differences between the source and target text culture and how these might affect translation strategies.*

ACTFL (The National Standards Collaborative Board, 2015, pp. 4, 15):
- *Understand the main idea and key information in short straightforward fictional texts.*
- *Compare practices related to everyday life and personal interests or studies in my own and other cultures.*

CCSS (National Governors Association, 2010):
- *ELA-LITERACY.RL.7.1: Make logical inferences about what the text says and cite textual evidence in writing and speaking to support my inferences.*

Prior Skills:
- Content: For this lesson, students will be learning about making inferences from a text. Prior to the lesson, students should understand what it means to make inferences.
- Language: Intermediate mid-high (A2-B1) learners should be able to navigate past, present, and future tenses and conversations on familiar topics. They should have some knowledge of continuous and perfect tenses.
  ○ Learners should have some skill using a bilingual dictionary. You may need to distinguish between using a dictionary and translation of an entire text through AI or a tool like Google Translate. What skills will learners acquire through doing the translation themselves? What will they miss out on in the process if they use AI?

(continued)

Table 7.1 (continued)

Thematic alignment for text set: Cultural identity

Texts:	Cultural Contexts
Ada, A. F., & Campoy, I. (2013, 2014). *Yes! We Are Latinos!/¡Sí! ¡Somos Latinos!*	Multiple
Argueta, J. (2016). *Somos cómo las nubes/We Are Like the Clouds*	Salvadoran
Bowles, D. (2018, 2020) *They Call Me Güero/Me dicen Güero*	Mexican-American (borderlands)
Cisneros, S. (1983, 1994). *The House on Mango Street/La casa en Mango Street* (Anchor text)	Mexican-American (New York City)
Garza, C. L. (1996). *En mi familia/In My Family*	Mexican-American (borderlands)

Additional Materials:
- Enough copied and cut translation excerpts in English and Spanish from each of the texts in the set for collaborative groups of 3–4. Plan to distribute 4–5 brief matching excerpts in both languages to each group. Try to make excerpts from the same language look to be about the same length so that students must look at text and not length to re-match the sets. Choose excerpts based on your objectives.
- Electronic devices for students and teacher such as smartphones, tablets and/or computers

Projector
- If recommended technology is not available, use other note-taking materials for translations
- Electronic or paper copies of Spanish–English dictionaries
- Presentation, photos, or real hats used by different cultures, including the cultures of students in the class

Activate Prior Knowledge:
Show a variety of hats used by different cultures, including the cultures of students in the class. Ask about the types of activities the hats might be used for (Draggett et al., 2014). Have students infer: How do these activities represent a cultural perspective/cultural identity?
- Model: A baseball hat is commonly worn in the United States and represents the cultural value and attention placed upon sports.

Bilingual Editions of Children's Books Translation Activity
- Depending upon time for language arts or class periods for language instruction, this activity might be taught over multiple days.

- **Sample Activity #1**
  - Distribute excerpts to small groups.
  - Have groups match the sets. Depending upon the age, this can be a contest among groups. (3–5 minutes)
  - After sets are matched, discuss strategies used to match the sets. Possible answers: Recognition of cognates, translation of initial word or phrase, and so forth. (3–5 minutes)
  - Tell the class that in their groups, they will be translating one of the excerpts from (Language A) to (Language B). Remind them that literal translations often are not effective, and that they may need to translate functionally, or based on what the overall text is saying. Choose one excerpt to translate as a class and model literal versus functional translation, strategies for understanding new vocabulary or collocations, and so forth, such as context clues combined with dictionary use. Encourage groups to negotiate among themselves to come up with a translation that makes the most sense. (15–20 minutes)
  - Have groups choose (or assign) one of the excerpts to translate from (Language A) into (Language B). Translations can be written by hand, or, if technology is available, typed into a shared Google doc to project to the class so translations can be compared. (15–20 minutes)
  - After translations are complete, make some linguistic comparisons as a class. Depending upon the learning environment, these discussions might be in (Language A), (Language B), or both:
    - If some students translated the same excerpt, compare student translations and then the text's translation. This is most easily done through a projection. Otherwise, students could switch groups and compare, then share out with the class.
    - If students translated different excerpts, compare translations with the text's translation.
    - Ask how translations are similar or different. Do the differences matter?
  - After the discussion of linguistic comparisons, make some cultural comparisons:
    - What kinds of cultural perspectives did you find in your text? Were there products or practices that helped you to make an inference about cultural perspectives? Share first in small groups, then as a class.
    - What kinds of similarities and differences do you notice about cultural perspectives across the different texts and in the two languages? What kinds of inferences can you makesxzd based upon these comparisons?
- **Sample Activity #2:** Follow the same procedure, but use paired texts instead of the entire text set. Eliminate the matching activity.

(continued)

Table 7.1 (*continued*)

Materials:
- Text set (this may be larger than the one modeled here)
- Enough sets of copied, cut and mixed-up excerpts in English and Spanish from each set to distribute to small groups of 3-4 people in the class. Plan to distribute 4-5 brief matching excerpts in both languages to each group. Try to make excerpts from the same language look to be about the same length so that students must look at text and not length to re-match the sets. Choose excerpts based on your objectives.
- If available: Shared Google doc for class translations

Evaluation:
- **Formative:** Circulate among the students and listen to their conversations. Are they distinguishing between literal and functional translations? Are they using dictionaries and context clues? Are they negotiating for meaning as a group?
- **Summative:**
  - These will differ depending upon the standards-based objectives but should show mastery of the objective.
  - Possible products for evaluation might include:
    - The translation
    - A reflection about using inference to express the main idea while making a translation, citing textual evidence (written or an oral recording)
    - A reflection upon using inference to understand how cultural practices are based upon products and practices (written or an oral recording)
    - A Venn diagram, or a series of Venn diagrams, comparing cultural perspectives across languages and/or texts

Expansion:
For an online course, use digital copies of translation excerpts. Collaborative groups can work in real time or asynchronously.

8
Changing Modalities

As shown in Chapter 7, traditional texts play an important role in translation activities. However, given the wide range of visual media consumed in today's world, texts and text sets need to reflect diversity in modality (Dallacqua, 2022). De Oliveira and Smith (2019) noted that "Literacy practices have changed over the past several years to incorporate modes of representation much broader than language alone, in which the textual is also related to the visual, the audio, the spatial, etc." (p. vii). Whether in general pedagogy or in specific texts, multimodality combines varying modes of communication. Multimodal pedagogy or production of multimodal texts scaffolds students, in particular multilingual students in diverse classrooms, providing them with various ways to make meaning of the content and augmenting their capacity for learning (Kress, 2010).

This chapter will show that from a socially situated literacy perspective, traditional texts can be used in tandem with multimodal texts (Sembiante et al., 2019). The chapter begins by presenting translation from a multimodal design perspective (Kern, 2000; Smith et al., 2020). This is followed by an exploration of digital texts and the creation of multimodal text sets that include audio and video. This chapter ends with a multimodal Translation Spotlight on subtitling.

What is a Multimodal Text?

Texts may be oral or written, published or unpublished with varying social perceptions of what constitutes a legitimate text (Linares, 2022). The definition becomes more complex with the addition of multimedia and multimodality. *Multimedia* describes the tools or technology used to convey a message, although there tends to be confusion regarding where multimedia ends and where multimodality begins (Kress, 2010). In contrast, *multimodal* focuses on meaning making through "representations in many modes, each chosen from rhetorical aspects for its communicational potentials" (p. 22).

Multimodal texts may be as simple as the dual-language children's picture books discussed in Chapter 7, comics or graphic novels, or other illustrated texts in which a visual element contributes to the meaning of the text. They might also consist of a combination of oral and written elements and may be developed by language users. For example, students in Linares (2022) orally rewrote a written Catalan text, demonstrating their linguistic skill in a way that was typical of their language use but not ordinarily validated in the classroom. These students perceived legitimate text to consist only of oral expression or text messages, as opposed to the published, written text presented to them for a translation activity. Linares therefore proposed that "Students who may not have developed written practices in the language in question can be encouraged to produce translation in oral or multimodal mediums" (p. 65). Additional multimodal text forms range widely but might include advertisements, social media, songs, poetry readings, live drama performances, podcasts, or videos (Fois, 2020; Phipps & González, 2004).

According to Munday et al. (2022), researchers in general make four assumptions about multimodality. While considerations of multimodality in the context of this book are intended for practice rather than research, the assumptions are nevertheless useful as a guide in understanding the nature and use of multimodal texts. First, all communication is multimodal. Therefore, as texts are a means of communication, all texts are multimodal. How this is made explicit in teaching and learning becomes key, and leads to the second assumption: modes occur together, with each playing a specific role and the interaction of modes resulting in meaning making. For example, the reader's interpretation of the interplay of written text and illustrations in a children's picture book as discussed in Chapter 7 ultimately results in the meaning of the text. Botelho (2021) interpreted the use of simple watercolor illustrations in the Azorean Portuguese–English board book *Pretty Girl/Linda Menina* (citing Simões, 2016) as supporting the portrayal of the love between mother and child. On the other hand, the illustrations of Azoreans in the hybrid text *In Lucia's Neighborhood* (citing Shewchuk, 2013) stereotype the community. However, Botelho recommended that this type of multimodal text serves as a classroom model as students interview family and community members and then draw upon this cultural knowledge to write and illustrate a place-based narrative.

The third assumption is that each mode is characterized by affordances based upon its inherent nature as well as its historical and social use. The application of the mode is determined by these affordances. For example, an oral mode might consist of both drawing upon oral traditions in literature, such as myths, legends, songs, and proverbs used within many cultures, as well as the development of oral language skills that contribute to biliteracy (Escamilla et al., 2014). For example, in one of the author's bilingual teacher preparation courses on children's literature, students explore their community's oral tradition in literature by collecting examples from friends and family, then create multimodal presentations including text and photos to share their work.

The final assumption about multimodality is that "Language-focused analysis can only partially investigate complex meaning-making events in which different modes are employed" (Munday et al., 2022, p. 236). While this assumption is targeted toward research on multimodality, it highlights the complexity in meaning making through the practical application of multimodality as well, including through translation.

Multimodality and Multiliteracies

The inclusion of oral texts in translation returns to the broader definition of literacy presented in Chapter 2, that is, literacy that is socially situated and which moves beyond acquisition of skills in reading and writing. Indeed, one of the main arguments in discussions on new directions for literacy pedagogy noted by the New London Group (1996) was the ever-increasing proliferation of multimodality in today's world, namely, "the increasing multiplicity and integration of significant modes of meaning-making, where the textual is also related to the visual, the audio, the spatial, the behavioral, and so on" (p. 64). The resultant pedagogy of multiliteracies requires "understanding and competent control" (p. 61) of the interrelations of these many multimodal forms and socially situating language use within them (Warner & Dupuy, 2018).

The use of multiple modes can scaffold language learners in multiple ways. For example, visual, aural, textual, and spatial modes can scaffold language learning (Smith et al., 2020), and visual literacy can scaffold textual comprehension, especially for multilingual students reading in an additional language (Smith, 2019). Classroom use of multiple modes can also support identity development, consideration of different audiences, and interdisciplinarity (Smith et al., 2020). Some students may choose a nonverbal mode to express abstract ideas such as emotions, while others may prefer the organizational affordances of writing. Spanish–English bilingual students in a study by Cano and Ruiz (2020) demonstrated biliterate awareness through various multimodal writing activities in an after-school bilingual program. One student demonstrated orthographic awareness as she compared language structures while translating an English article in the school newsletter to Spanish, although she had not formally studied Spanish in school. Another student demonstrated biliterate audience awareness as he created a multimodal presentation for a pen pal in Mexico, introducing himself in Spanish because his audience would probably not understand English. However, he labeled a playground structure in English because he wasn't sure if his audience had been exposed to anything similar and wanted to be sure it was labeled. The Cano and Ruiz study also demonstrated the fluid movement between languages in a bilingual environment which incorporates multimodality, translanguaging and translation. In sum, multimodality creates space for language learners' voice and agency.

Laviosa (2018) described learners' development of translingual, transcultural skills in a graduate-level English language and translation course in Italy as they translated a poem from Italian to English. Learners noted that their bilingual practices "raise awareness of cross-cultural differences and enhance learners' sensitivity to nuances of vocabulary usage both in the source and the target language" (p. 195). However, Laviosa also suggested possible multimodal expansion of the assignment to include art or music that learners associated with the translated poem or the "animation" (p. 196) of the poem through audio and video elements incorporated into a slide presentation. While this activity was carried out in a translation course, Laviosa spoke of "moving boundaries" (p. 196) within both TS and educational linguistics, in which pedagogical translation might be encompassed, so that each field can inform the other as new best practices such as translation and multimodality are adopted and adapted.

Consumption and production of "moving, multilingual, and digitally mediated texts" (Keyes et al., 2014, p. 17), including digital gaming and social media (Warner & Dupuy, 2018), are ubiquitous among today's youth. This spread of digital media has been called the fourth industrial revolution, with the battle between page and screen being won by the screen (Cintas & Remael, 2020). In this new world, digitally mediated texts "accomplish a wide variety of social and cultural goals as they reflect, refract, and question youth identities and local conditions" (Keyes et al., 2014, p. 17). Youth in some environments have now spent their entire lives in a digitally mediated world, with multimodal communication a daily fact of life (Cintas & Remael, 2020). Digital communication can bring people together from different languages and cultures. In terms of language education, these practices can push educators to reconsider the integration of digital literacy and translingual pedagogies like translation which "encourage active, improvisational, and strategic mixing of linguistic codes" (David et al., 2019, p. 252; Warner & Dupuy, 2018) in their classrooms.

Importantly for the incorporation of pedagogical translation in multimodal pedagogy, Malova et al. (2019) equated the strategic classroom use of multiple languages, or "verbal modal resource[s]" (p. 24) to multimodality, describing studies which use vocabulary support in the home language to scaffold vocabulary acquisition in an additional language. Li (2022) connected these verbal modal resources to translanguaging, emphasizing the inherent multimodality of language and that translanguaging "embraces multimodality" (p. 409). For Li, translanguaging is about moving beyond the boundaries of named languages as well as the boundaries between language and other sign systems or modes. Consistent with socially situated literacy, translanguaging allows students "to utilize knowledge from their social worlds and express themselves through different language modes in order to increase their ability to convey meaning" (Rossato de Almeida, 2019, p. 74).

In the classroom, expression across language modes might take different forms. This could include writing assignments in which students draft in their home language and then translate for submission: "Allowing students to translate from their drafts enables them to think through and organize a text" (Rossato de Almeida, 2019, p. 77). Instructors might also model the use of translanguaging as a literary device in hybrid texts, after which bi- or multilingual students could be encouraged to deliberately translanguage in their texts to achieve desired literary effects, including in monolingual classrooms. Students could also be encouraged to engage in "multimodal codemeshing" (Smith et al., 2020), which involves "the use of multiple languages and modes in composing processes and products, where composers draw upon and mesh semiotic resources with varying degrees of intentionality and awareness to negotiate meaning with a reader" (p. 7) and emphasizes the integration of digital resources.

Malova et al. (2019) recommended scaffolding the acquisition of understanding and competent control of the relationships between various modes to aid in growth of EB depth of vocabulary, which in turn supports literacy acquisition. The following recommendations could be expanded to additional language–learning environments. They include using organizers, brief texts which contextualize the vocabulary, visuals, and actions such as gesture or acting which link oral vocabulary to the action. Pedagogical translation could be used for multimodal scaffolding as well. For example, the texts used to contextualize vocabulary could be translated using an activity like Escamilla et al.'s (2014) *Así se dice/That's How You Say It*. This translation activity uses "texts that are short and conceptually rich" (p. 75) to "scrutin[ize] language and emphasize[] the subtleties and nuances of communicating messages across cultures and languages" (p. 75). As students notice lexical similarities and differences while translating, they can add them to an organizer. When appropriate, they could draw their interpretations of synonyms which align well or which differ slightly, then explain the differences in the home or additional language, or translanguage, depending upon the language objectives. Keep in mind, however, that when students are using language to make meaning as opposed to producing work that must be evaluated in a named language, translanguaging should be assumed to be an appropriate practice (García, 2009).

Translation from a Multimodal Design Perspective

As with new conceptions of literacy, translation is founded upon making meaning in context (Adami & Ramos Pinto, 2020). When modes such as written and visual are present together in a text, it cannot be assumed that the visual elements can be automatically understood in the new context, nor that no new relationships between modes are introduced through the translation. Therefore, "it is imperative to recognize that neither mode can be completely isolated as a communicative event" (Smith, 2016, p. 3) as the sum total is greater than the sum of the parts. Historically, translation has run alongside communication trends; in recent years, this means that translation has followed the change from the page to the screen and the accompanying multiplicity of modes (Cintas & Remael, 2020).

It is useful at this point to return to conceptions of equivalence, as multimodal equivalence comes into play in translation of multimodal texts (Adami & Ramos Pinto, 2020). From a TS perspective, some continue to view only written text as part of a translation, with adaptation of other modes being considered as belonging to multimodal studies . However, others now consider multimodal equivalence to be part of a translation (Adami & Ramos Pinto, 2020), as will this chapter. Pedagogical translation activities may address multimodal equivalence in various ways. For published texts such as bilingual picture books, the effect of translation on the relationship between text and picture can be analyzed by the instructor when selecting the book and/or by students during translations, depending upon the objectives. Echauri Galván and Hernández (2020) studied reading comprehension through a multimodal, intersemiotic translation activity in which primary EFL students read a text in English and then demonstrated their understanding through drawing a picture that summarized what they had read. As an extension, students might retell the story in the additional language, using their illustration as a support. When considering the equivalence of images to translated text, images in published texts might be replaced in addition to the translation of text; Adami and Ramos Pinto (2019) note that consumers are accepting of "image manipulation" (p. 11) in advertising but not in film, leading to differing translation strategies between different types of media.

As digital means of communication become ever more popular for students as both consumers and producers, consideration of media types is essential in planning translation activities (Floros, 2021). Not only may students find digital media more relevant and engaging, but they may also "abandon the literal mode usually associated with pedagogical translation of fabricated texts or authentic text excerpts" (Floros, 2021, p. 284). This is an interesting commentary on achieving equivalence based upon the type of media. While many studies show the efficacy of authentic texts for pedagogical translation activities, Floros's comment speaks to the need for a range of resources, as might be evidenced in multimodal, multimedia text sets.

Floros (2021) notes that because of the ubiquity of digital media, the question has shifted from "if" it should be used pedagogically to "what" and "how" (p. 285). Beyond short films, documentaries, and sitcoms,

Floros recommended YouTube, comics, and social media pages, including the students' own, as potential resources for translation and resources and techniques used by professional translators such as software platforms, online dictionaries, and parallel texts in the home and additional language. As artificial intelligence becomes mainstream, students might also analyze machine translations of a text for accuracy and viability. As a distinct communication mode, the skill at comparison that arises from using these types of translation strategies may be considered a type of literacy within the multiliteracies framework: "The ability to compare and contrast, an ability explicitly cultivated by translation exercises, is more than essential in order for students ... to make meaning" (p. 286). Here Floros makes a key move from translation as a skill to translation as a literacy, therefore placing pedagogical translation not only as a strategy for other literacies but as a literacy in its own right.

Audiovisual translation (AVT) has attained a high level of social influence across consumers through a broad range of audiovisual genres (Cintas & Remael, 2021), which in turn makes it highly relevant as a pedagogical tool. For audiovisual translation, the instructor and students might use a similar process for analyzing video to dub or subtitle, in this case also including considerations such as gesture and aural elements such as background music or sound effects which correspond to meaning in the source language but may not in the target language. While only dubbing or subtitles may ultimately be added in, discussions regarding meaning making through the other semiotic elements could contribute to cultural understanding or the development of intercultural being (Phipps & González, 2004).

Most AVT research has been done at the university level. However, Fernández-Costales (2021) studied student perceptions of the potential of subtitling and dubbing English as a foreign language at the primary level, finding that students responded positively to both as language-learning tools. At the university level, Zengin (2019) studied the comparison of Turkish translations of English television and film scripts available online to help university students acquire "vocabulary chunks" (p. 955) such as collocations and other multi-word units. The author found that in the classroom, this was an effective language-learning strategy. The hope was that students would transfer this strategy to their independent learning by reviewing Turkish scripts prior to watching a television show or movie in English to increase aural comprehension, or, in other words, that they would make this a multimodal process. However, only a small number of students reported doing so. Nevertheless, this process has interesting potential as a multistep, multimodal activity that could be incorporated in the classroom and encouraged outside of it among learners of varying ages.

Talaván et al. (2016) found that collaborative reverse subtitling of two videos "substantially improved" (p. 57) Spanish university-students' first-year English writing skills. As this activity was completed in a distance learning class, collaboration was not synchronous. Students first prepared their own translation solutions, posted them to a group forum and then negotiated as a group regarding the final subtitles based upon linguistic and technical accuracy while instructors acted as consultants and project managers and scored the videos, uploading the top ten of sixty-eight submissions for group access. This multimodal translation activity demonstrates use of aural and written modes. There are multiple possible extensions. For example, as part of the project, collaborative groups could compare their own subtitles with some of the top submissions, noting similarities and differences and how these affected meaning (or not). Additionally, groups could analyze cultural elements in the visual mode and if these are affected through translation. Finally, the project could be adapted for different age groups and language-learning levels.

Digital Texts and Multimodal Text Sets

Digital literacies are complex, multimodal literacy practices that may be part of a multiliteracies approach (Ek et al., 2016). Traditional literacies like children's literature can be combined with digital literacies to create new spaces for students to engage with classroom material. Citing Luke's (1994) comparison of schools to a literacy marketplace which "favors the dominant cultural practices over those of language minority students" (p. 208), Ek et al. remind us that "literacy is a key site for societal power struggles" (p. 208). Within this literacy marketplace, digital literacies serve as "valuable currency" (p. 208) in a marketplace where access to technology may not always be equitable.

In a move toward developing digital literacies, Ek et al. (2016) offer multiple suggestions for the incorporation of digital storytelling in bilingual classrooms; these may be adapted by age and learning environment. Digital storytelling "combines the art of telling stories with multimedia ... As with traditional storytelling, digital stories can be designed as narratives to mirror ... rich oral tradition" (p. 210). Ek et al. use the context of Latino children in the United States, but oral tradition might be considered and integrated across cultures. In this sense, digital storytelling can be used to promote acquisition of linguistic skills through both process- and product-oriented activities, all of which create an intersection between cultural tradition and the classroom. This connection is illustrated in the dual-language book composing process outlined in Sneddon (2012). For this type of book, digital storytelling would be assumed to incorporate translation: that is, stories written in either the home or additional language would be translated into the other language as part of the digital storytelling process. Writing stories in the home language permits students to be more creative and opens the way for inclusion of language variety and fostering home–school connections (Ek et al., 2016).

Although the model text set in Chapter 7 can be considered multimodal due to the presence of illustrations in all of the texts, multimodal text sets here will be considered to also include elements beyond those present in traditional published texts, such as blogs; stand-alone art or photos; and audio or video recordings, including songs, podcasts, social media posts, and video clips. Individual elements may be considered multimodal or not, but as a whole, the set will be multimodal.

In keeping with a multiliteracies perspective on multimodality as a key element in today's literacies, Hoch et al. (2019) maintained that multimodal text sets are key to helping struggling readers in the home or additional language, or both, to navigate consumption of texts in today's digital world. In the context of an inquiry-based project, they proposed five principles for selecting digital and/or multimodal texts. First, attend to motivation and engagement. This principle addresses student voice and agency in engaging with texts which interest them or which they find relevant (see also Albrecht, 2024; David et al., 2019). Second, choose sources carefully in terms of scaffolding levels of complexity in the texts. Third, set up instruction as inquiry to encourage students to take part in generating their own questions regarding a topic. Fourth, provide means for students to synthesize the texts: "Reading across multiple multimodal texts makes the process of synthesis even more complex. A reader must create a mental model of the situation contained in each of the documents, then create a mental model of how the documents relate to one another ... and how this contributes to their understanding of the overall concept" (Hoch et al., 2019, p. 77). Because of this complexity, students will need scaffolding to support synthesis. While there is a research gap as far as translation supporting synthesis of multimodal text sets, an argument can be made in its favor due to research support for reading comprehension through pedagogical translation (Albrecht, 2024; Jiménez et al., 2015). These studies supported only comprehension of a single text, so additional activities such as the bilingual editions of children's books activity in Chapter 7 could be included to facilitate cross-text comparison. Hoch et al. (2019) also recommended use of graphic organizers like Venn diagrams or inquiry charts to help students with visual comparison of the texts. Translanguaging spaces should be created for these types of comparison activities, encouraging students to work with their entire linguistic repertoires as they make meaning across texts, languages, and cultures (Li, 2010).

Fifth, and finally, the audience and purpose for whom students write should be authentic. In Hoch et al.'s study (2019), students wrote on an educational blog site about an inquiry project carried out through the multimodal text set. On this site, students could write multimodally, including graphics, charts, and hyperlinks. Because students could also read about and respond to each other's work, they were able to aim their writing toward a clear, authentic audience and purpose. An extension of this activity might be to translate one's own or a peer's work in order to reach a broader audience linguistically and culturally, as in Manyak's (2008) class news or Sneddon's (2012) multilingual book project.

Using the same theme of *Cultural Identity*, the text set presented in Chapter 7 might be expanded multimodally in the following ways:

1. Add a brief video which introduces the topic and captures students' attention. Depending upon the language-learning environment, this might be in the home or additional language. Translation extension: Subtitle the video.
2. Add an audiobook version or a recording of one of the texts excerpted for translation. Translation extension: In small groups, collaboratively translate one of the texts excerpted for translation. Compare translations among groups and make changes as needed. Record the translation for a class audio library. Have parents or community members add recordings.
3. Add a comic or graphic novel. For this set, Hernandez's *The Dragonslayer/La Matadragones* (2018) might be included. Text pairing: Have students choose a legend shared in their homes or communities and compare it with one of the legends in the comic book. Translation extension: Write the legend in the home and additional language by hand or digitally and illustrate, potentially in the same format. Digital platforms could include a presentation like Google Slides or PowerPoint, a comic book generator, and so forth. Make a bi- or multilingual class book of family oral traditions. Record the legend in the home and additional language and add it to the classroom audio library.
4. Add a captioned photo or a set of captioned photos. Thinking back to the discussion on baseball caps as products representative of practices and perspectives in the United States (Translation Spotlight, Chapter 6), a set of photos of hats representing differing cultures within the additional language community might be added to the model set. Students can discuss how these products might represent practices and perspectives in the respective cultures. Translation extension: Translate the captions.
5. Add a popular or traditional song related to the theme. For this set, the traditional birthday song *Las mañanitas* might be included. Translation extension: Translate stanzas in groups; compare translations. Discuss: What are the cultural practices represented in this song? How are these representative of cultural perspectives or values? How do these practices and perspectives relate to your own practices and perspectives? As applicable, discuss the birthday song used in English or another language. Does translation of the birthday song in one language translate culturally into the second language? If there is no birthday song, what are the other cultural products, practices, and perspectives?

Production of Multimodal Texts

Students can be encouraged to create multilingual, multimodal texts. Multimodality leaves open space for both instructor and student creativity in the selection and application of modes. In Manyak (2008), for example, primary multilingual students contributed collaboratively and orally to their classes' daily news in multiple languages, which were then written on a large sheet of paper in front of the class which served as the "newspaper." Bilingual peers helped with translations. In this activity, students' linguistic and cultural resources were valued as the class worked together in constructing this multimodal text. In another multilingual primary classroom, students wrote, illustrated, and translated their own stories, then added written translations in their own languages to their peers' texts (Rowe, 2019). Students also made audio recordings in multiple languages of the texts to share with friends and families and to add to the classroom library. This multimodal translation activity thus included written, visual, and aural modes. Students might also translate short texts in globalized advertisements, keeping in mind the corresponding adaptations that may need to be made in the visual mode (Butzkamm & Caldwell, 2009; Colina & Albrecht, 2020), create a class blog with translations for parents or publish their own videos in the home language (Ek et al., 2016) and reverse subtitle to the additional language, or vice versa.

Beyond written texts, texts that may be used for translation also include "audio-medial texts, such as films and visual and spoken advertisements" (Munday et al., 2022, p. 101). These provide audio and visual augmentation to written or oral texts. Experts in the field of AVT note that the field has entered an "educational turn" (Fernández-Costales, 2021, p. 282), with consistent research results showing its benefits in language teaching and learning. A translation activity might involve subtitling; dubbing; creative subtitling, in which the original is reinterpreted rather than directly translated (Talaván & Lertola, 2022); audio description or intersemiotic translation of visuals for the visually impaired (Incalcaterra McLoughlin & Lertola, 2014); or voice narration (Incalcaterra McLoughlin & Lertola, 2014). These tasks require receptive or productive language use, and benefits include "vocabulary retention, intercultural awareness, fluency and production skills" (Fernández-Costales, 2021, pp. 281–282); critical thinking; multimedia literacy; and validation of multilingualism in areas with multiple indigenous languages, such as India or South Africa (Incalcaterra McLoughlin & Lertola, 2014). After reviewing the state of AVT in language teaching and learning, Incalcaterra McLoughlin & Lertola (2014) recommended its mainstream incorporation to maximize these learning benefits.

When planning an AVT activity, Talaván and Lertola (2022) identified six options for subtitling. These include intralingual, in which additional language subtitles are added to an additional language video. Filling in blank keywords is an introductory option. The second is also intralingual subtitling; however, students complete the subtitles themselves. For intralingual creative subtitling, students may add creative subtitles based upon their interpretations of the video clip with or without technical support. Interlingual standard subtitling involves a more linguistically complex video, and students produce home language subtitles for an additional language video. Interlingual reverse subtitling is a common approach, with the language of the subtitles being in the home language (Talaván et al., 2016; Talaván & Lertola, 2022). The following translation subtitling activity will model interlingual reverse subtitling, as research has shown this to be the most beneficial subtitling activity, particularly for beginners (Incalcaterra McLoughlin & Lertola, 2014).

Translation Spotlight: Subtitling

Before You Start

As with incorporation of any new activity or pedagogy, including those requiring technology, incorporation of a subtitling activity will take some advanced preparation. The steps are as follows:

1. Choose a subtitling platform that will be accessible for your students. Possible platforms may be specialized, like Subtitling Workshop, or more general, like YouTube. The European Union has also developed ClipFair, a platform designed for subtitling in language teaching which does not require downloading (Incalcaterra McLoughlin & Lertola, 2014).
2. Upload a short video clip that incorporates cultural elements (Talaván & Lertola, 2022) to the platform, making sure not to violate copyright restrictions. Practice subtitling. Depending upon your students' level, you might choose video clips from short ads, animated cartoons, movie trailers or TED talks.
3. You will need to decide how to address other modes in the video, such as background music, prior explanatory subtitles, and environmental text. They may merit an initial discussion of how multiple modes contribute to meaning making.
4. Practice watching for cultural elements in the language, visuals, or audio. Think about whether these will merit discussion and/or how students might address them. What might be some of the effects if there are elements that are not translatable?
5. This practice will also give you an idea of the level of difficulty your students will be dealing with, how long of a video clip to choose and whether to separate it into scenes to assign to collaborative groups. Fernández-Costales (2021) used clips that were less than one minute.

6   Once you have experimented with the technology, find or make a tutorial for your students.
7   Think about how you want student groupings to work. Research has shown collaborative translation to be highly effective (Fernández-Costales, 2021; see also Chapter 9).

While it may seem overwhelming to learn to use new technology and to create new assignments (Talaván et al., 2016), the research showing AVT to be a highly effective instructional tool argues in its favor. Working with an instructional team to learn the required technology and to design lessons could help mitigate some of these issues. Similarly, in primary and secondary environments with school- or system-wide content-area leadership, these leadership teams could help with the design and implementation of AVT activities at the level of curriculum planning. To maximize the time spent on training and planning, as well as the benefits of AVT use, leaders or instructors may consider incorporating multiple AVT activities into the curriculum. For example, Talaván and Lertola (2022) proposed didactic sequences for five different AVT modes that might be taught over a semester, or for one AVT mode that might be taught over one and a half months.

For the following lesson plan, a prior lesson will be necessary in which students also learn how to use subtitling software. Depending upon the learners, this might be initiated in class or through a flipped lesson in which students watch a video tutorial at home to prepare for subtitling in class. Students will then need to become familiar with reverse subtitling, including understanding the main idea of a video text and shortening it for a subtitle in the new language. This might be through a model subtitling lesson in which the instructor walks students through identifying the key material in a frame that needs to be translated, discussing how to shorten it if possible, and discussing strategies for working with new vocabulary. In the video clip in the lesson plan that follows, at times multiple characters talk simultaneously. This can be handled through the subtitling software but is complex. Students might instead be given the option to creatively subtitle (Fernández-Costales, 2021). In this case, they could summarize.

Note taking strategies for beginning interpreters could be utilized in subtitling activities. In interpreter training, taking notes while listening to an oral text is a skill taught over time. Students have repeated opportunities for practice until the skill becomes automated, freeing up mental capacity for the act of interpretation (Gillies, 2005). Unless practice activities are incorporated to this degree in the language classroom, it is assumed that automation will not occur. Nevertheless, language learners may learn to take and practice taking notes in a systematized way that aids them in the process, as these notes will represent both the lexical and overall structure of the oral text. A key note-taking strategy is to identify the main idea of the message through identifying the subject–verb–object (SVO) if starting from

English for each sentence, thus eliminating the need to interpret superfluous text. A less grammar-oriented way to approach this same strategy is to identify "who does what to whom" (Gillies, 2005, p. 41). For example, applying this strategy to the sentence, "Students have repeated opportunities to practice, freeing up mental capacity for the act of interpretation" would become the following:

Subject (who): Students

Verb (does what): have

Object (to whom, combining direct and indirect for simplicity): opportunities to practice.

Thus, the text is simplified, yet the core idea is preserved. Note takers in general prefer to abbreviate, and for character-based scripts often prefer to develop their own note-taking styles, which may include bilingual notes, symbols and/or simplified characters to be able to write faster (Chen, 2017). Instructors may find it beneficial to introduce and practice note-taking strategies prior to an actual subtitling activity, again with the caveat that this is a skill that requires extensive practice to reach a level of automation.

Standards and Objectives

Prior to a review of the sample AVT lesson, several advance considerations regarding standards and objectives for an AVT activity need to be made. First, the CEFR descriptors for translation provide for translation from text to speech but not the reverse. For the sample lesson on subtitling, the descriptors have therefore been modified accordingly. As with Chapter 7, the objectives for both language and content are intermediate, which may reflect competence or grade level, or both, depending upon the learning environment. Starting at an intermediate-language level will require that translation move from the home language into the additional language, as intermediate learners may be unable to understand speech in the new language. However, directionality could again be modified depending upon language level. In the interest of space, ACTFL benchmarks are abbreviated. ACTFL objectives are based upon performance indicators. Standard, proficiency benchmarks or descriptors and objectives can all be adapted by language level.

Conclusion

Texts and text sets need to reflect diversity in modality given the wide range of visual media consumed in today's world and the resultant changes in literacy practices (Dallacqua, 2022; De Oliveira and Smith, 2019). Multimodal translation combines varying modes of communication, which diverse language learners can leverage as they make meaning of the content (Kress, 2010). Chapter 9 adds considerations on collaboration for translation activities.

Table 8.1 Translation Spotlight: Video Subtitling

Sample translation lesson: Video subtitling

Objective(s)

CEFR (*Council of Europe, 2020*):
Processing Text in Writing:
- I can summarize [through subtitles in my new language] the main content of complex spoken and written texts in my own language on subjects related to my fields of interest and specialization (p. 99).

ACTFL (2017, p. 4):
- I can understand the main idea and key information in a short straightforward fictional or informational video [as indicated through my ability to subtitle a scene].

CCSS (National Governors Association, 2010):
- CCSS.ELA-Literacy.RL.7.4: [Through an AVT activity,] I can determine the meaning of words and phrases as they are used in an oral text, including figurative and connotative meanings.

Prior Skills:
- Content: Prior to the activity, students should be familiar with identifying the main idea in text and with the subtitling software being used.
- Language: Intermediate mid-high (A2-B1) learners should be able to navigate past, present, and future tenses and conversations on familiar topics. They should have some knowledge of continuous and perfect tenses.
  - Students should have some skill using a bilingual dictionary. You may need to distinguish between using a dictionary and translation of an entire text through AI or a tool like Google Translate. What skills will learners acquire through doing the translation themselves? What will they miss out on in the process if they use AI?
  - If language conventions are going to be discussed and/or graded, these should have already been taught and should be added into the standards and objectives.

Materials:
- Video clip for translation: *The Sandlot 25th Anniversary* (Fathom Events, 2018). In advance, divide the clip into segments of about thirty seconds and post segments on a course website for students to view. Different groups will translate individual segments. Depending upon the number of groups and the number of segments, some segments may be translated more than once.
- Subtitling software (for example, Movavi, Subtitle Workshop)
- Instructor and student electronic devices such as smartphones, tablets and/or computers

AVT Reverse Subtitling Activity
Activate prior knowledge (Before watching):
- Ask students what they know about baseball. What is the object of the game? What are some well-known teams? What vocabulary is used to talk about the game? What is some of the equipment used to play? How does the game of baseball represent cultural identity?

- Ask if anyone has seen the movie *The Sandlot*. After students respond, tell them they will be reverse subtitling a brief trailer from this movie about baseball. In particular, introduce the term 'heater' as a very fast pitch. Tell them to take notes about key vocabulary and/or cultural elements while they watch.

While you watch:
- Watch the video as a class, with students taking notes about key vocabulary they will need to translate the video, as well as of cultural elements. Students may need to view the video more than once.

After watching:
- Discuss students' notes, making a group list on a projected document or on a whiteboard of key vocabulary they will need to translate. Were there any words that might be hard to translate? Model strategies for finding appropriate functional translations.
- Divide students into cooperative groups of 3 or 4 and assign each group a segment from the video to subtitle, using the SVO note-taking strategy. Depending upon class length, this activity may need to be divided across more than one class period.
- As a class, watch each group's subtitled segments in order. Discuss areas that were hard to translate, and share class input on the effectiveness of translations. This could be done orally or in writing.

Evaluation:
- **Formative:** Circulate among students and listen to their conversations. Are they able to identify the main idea? Are they distinguishing between literal and functional translations? Are the translations they are choosing from dictionaries appropriate to the context?
- **Summative:** The subtitled segment will be the product for evaluation. For this lesson, the objectives focused only on meaning making, so the evaluation would focus on equivalence in meaning, including figurative and connotative meanings. If you are going to evaluate linguistic features, be sure to add these to the objectives.

Expansion/Modification:
- Earlier learners could fill in the blanks for partially completed subtitles.
- More advanced students can try standard interlingual translation from the additional into the home language.
- Videos representative of either the home or additional culture may be selected, with questions and discussions modified accordingly.
- Add in cultural standards and objectives, then include discussion regarding multimodal cultural elements in the video and how these may or may not be addressed in translation.
- Add in content objectives if you are doing CBLI and are tying the activity to a content area.
- Add in specific linguistic objectives if specific linguistic features are to be graded.

Part III: Considerations in Teaching Translation

9
The Benefits of Collaboration

Collaboration has always been in play in the field of translation. According to Cordingley and Manning (2016), "From Antiquity to the Renaissance, translation was frequently practiced by groups comprised of specialists of different languages and with varied skills. At the center of translation teams, experts from various cultures came together to find solutions to translation problems" (p. 1). This continues to be the case today (Washbourne, 2010). For translator trainees, collaboration can contribute to translation quality through peer feedback; pooling varied perspectives, knowledge and expertise to negotiate the meaning of the text; and motivation through shared responsibility (Kenny, 2008; Kiraly, 2012; Prieto-Velasco & Fuentes Luque, 2016). Similarly, collaboration is a key element in pedagogical translation as it provides opportunities for negotiation or mediation for meaning (Axelrod & Cole, 2018; Barnes, 2018; Cano & Ruíz, 2020; CEFR, 2020; Keyes et al., 2014). For some language learners, collaborative translation can also contribute to positive affect, and, hence, motivation to learn (Albrecht, 2024; Beauvais & Ryland, 2021). This chapter, therefore, takes a look at theoretical and practical foundations for collaboration and then moves to considerations for incorporating collaborative translation activities, looking at teacher–student and peer-to-peer collaboration structures in the classroom and then at school-to-home collaborations in which students with another home language can involve parents or other family members in their work (Sneddon, 2012). The chapter will present a Translation Spotlight on a school-to-family collaboration.

Purposes of Collaboration

Collaboration serves multiple purposes in translation. In professional translation, collaborations may be formed between the various stakeholders such as translators and clients, and teams of translators may also work together on a single translation project, thus challenging the conception of "one author, one translator" professionally and pedagogically (Alfer, 2017). Team pedagogical translations may therefore function to mirror authentic professional contexts and may be designed for in-person or online synchronous or asynchronous instruction utilizing document sharing tools like Google Docs (Prieto-Velasco & Fuentes Luque, 2016). In terms of designing collaborative translation activities or projects to meet learning objectives, objectives, and assessments must be carefully considered given their collaborative nature (see Chapter 10) and keeping in mind the possibility of group assessment (Prieto-Velasco & Fuentes Luque, 2016).

Translation can also serve as an aid in negotiating for meaning. Based upon the social constructivist view that learning is socially situated (Lave & Wenger, 1991; Vygotsky, 1978), it has been proposed that translation is also inherently social and hence translators construct meaning through interaction (Kiraly, 2000). Because of its socially situated nature, Kiraly (2005) argues in favor of authentic translation tasks and contexts (i.e., collaborative contexts) for translators in training. This proposal for socially situated learning applies to translation in the language classroom as well (González-Davies, 2017) and connects theoretically to socially situated literacy as social interaction is foundational to both (Street, 1984; Vygotsky, 1978). For example, collaboration can be used to negotiate for meaning as a bilingual reading comprehension and writing strategy. During a collaborative translation strategy in Cano and Ruiz (2020), "When the group came to a line that they wanted to translate, the students collaboratively produced their own Spanish translation, which, when negotiated among the group, they could later compare to the one in the book" (p. 166). Translation from a translanguaging stance is often assumed in these types of environments as students use their entire linguistic repertoire among themselves for sense making (García & Leiva, 2014). In linguistic contact zones where more than one language is used in proximity to another, and where diverse classrooms are often a result, Carreira and Kagan (2018) refer to this process as "pooling linguistic repertoires" (p. 158), or "distributed competence where communication results from collaborative capacities of groups" (Stoof et al., 2002, p. 354). Collaboration may therefore be deliberately used to develop the competencies of an entire class as students pool their linguistic or other repertoires, highlighting the key role of the instructor in establishing collaborative structures.

Thinking is socially mediated and thinking activities, including tasks, are often collaborative, thus requiring language to complete the tasks (Council of Europe, 2020; Puzio et al., 2013). Collaboration can be approached through sociocultural theory, in which learning is social and a more-knowledgeable person scaffolds another's learning (Vygotsky, 1978). Scaffolding can be considered to be a type of mediation, as it is "the division of labor between participants in an activity, where the teacher (or another more-experienced participant) simplifies tasks, poses questions, manages frustration, and offers suggestions ... thus making this process inherently dialogical in nature" (Kultti & Pramling, 2018, p. 208). Using sociocultural theory as a framework, Frawley and Lantolf (1985) first connected scaffolding and language learning, with subsequent researchers and theorists supporting this approach. Phipps and González (2004), for example, maintain that "collaboration in language-learning can be used to make explicit the journey to understanding how language works in making the world meaningful" (p. 85).

In collaborative, scaffolding structures, the more knowledgeable person may be the instructor. For example, Jidai et al. (2017) focused on teacher–student scaffolding at a bilingual preschool. Through oral translation, or interpretation, of preschool-age songs from English to Finnish, teachers played an active role in meaning making, both through their own questioning and through facilitating peer-to-peer collaboration of tasks that were in their zone of proximal development, that is, tasks that would otherwise have been beyond the students' current abilities. During the translation activity, instructors rephrased and simplified questions as needed based upon student responses so that students could successfully complete the activity. For example, instructors offered lines from the song *Twinkle, Twinkle Little Star* in English, then asked students if word order as well as meaning in the Finnish version would be the same, prompting students to think metalinguistically.

The more knowledgeable person may also be a peer, supporting the implementation of collaborative structures in the classroom and directing considerations in group formation (Pacheco et al., 2015; Rogoff, 1990). Additionally, students can be positioned as experts informing the instructor, including regarding their home languages (Pacheco et al., 2015). Within collaborative group structures, peers may alternate in this role (Puzio et al., 2013). Alternating expert roles may be thought of in terms of distributed expertise, in which thinking is shared among group members and the "explicit knowledge that group members bring unique and different forms of expertise" (p. 333) is recognized. Puzio et al. found that through a pedagogical translation activity, students demonstrated varying forms of "linguistic, cognitive and sociocultural knowledge" (p. 336) which was joined in completing the activity. For example, one student led his group through his oral translation expertise as all participated in negotiation for a translation acceptable to the group. However, he declined to write in Spanish, feeling that was beyond his expertise, so another student took on that role.

The CEFR, ACTFL, and CCSS frameworks incorporated in this book all address collaboration. For those following the CEFR (Council of Europe, 2020), this framework clearly outlines the importance and role of collaboration. The CEFR proposes an action-oriented approach with learners as social agents with the primary goal of communication, rather than language as an object of study. Collaboration of any type can encourage community through student–student and teacher–student interaction and validate various ways of knowing (Keyes et al., 2014). According to the CEFR (Council of Europe, 2020), teacher–student and student–student collaborative interactions mediate to structure collaborative endeavors and facilitate student relationships and access to knowledge. In the CEFR, collaboration is presented as a mediating concept. Mediating concepts facilitate in "constructing and elaborating meaning and ... facilitating and stimulating situations that are conducive to conceptual exchange and development" (Council of Europe, 2020, p. 91). Collaborative tasks should be designed such that learners share and explain different input and work together to achieve a goal.

In alignment with standards focused on communication, learner motivation must also be considered. For example, in the EFL context, Fois (2020) noted that post-secondary learners must consider the activities in which they engage as fostering the ability to communicate in English; if they do not, they will not consider it to be useful. Hence, the dialog involved in translation is an additional argument in favor of collaborative translation activities. Similarly, in secondary Modern Foreign Languages workshops in Great Britain, Beauvais and Ryland (2021) found that collaborative translation contributed to participants' literary and language skills. Within an action-oriented approach, the need for structured collaboration on tasks with a focus other than language is inherent, with co-construction of meaning being central. How collaboration is structured will be determined by the learning context and learner proficiency.

Collaboration is incorporated into the ACTFL proficiency standards as well. As noted in *The keys to strategies for language instruction: ACTFL guide for professional language educators* (Grahn & McAlpine, 2017), collaboration is an activity which promotes communication, flexibility, engagement, and the ability to work with a diverse team and share responsibility for a final product. Within the Can–Do Statements (The National Standards Collaborative Board, 2015), the interpersonal communication mode incorporates negotiation of meaning "in spoken, signed or written conversations to share information, reactions, feelings, and opinions" (n.p.), which would assume collaboration in some of these activities. Some proficiency benchmarks mention collaboration as well, including for online projects.

Similarly, the CCSS for collaboration and comprehension link collaboration among diverse partners with comprehension of topics and texts (National Governors Association, 2010). Wolsey et al. (2014) aligned this collaborative process toward comprehension with "concept development and the associated vocabulary and language structures at all levels" (p. 2). In other words, the social, cooperative nature of language can be leveraged toward learning objectives (García & Flores, 2014). Nevertheless, the CCSS for collaboration are designed from a monolingual perspective. This requires that they be adapted for bilingual environments through a translanguaging stance and through activities such as pedagogical translation which contribute to the development of concepts, vocabulary, and language structures (García & Flores, 2013; Jiménez et al., 2015). In a mixed-methods study on the use of translation in a mixed secondary heritage–additional language Spanish class, Albrecht (2024) found that both groups of learners benefitted from collaborative group structures, although HLLs focused more on engagement with peers and additional language learners focused on co-construction of meaning. While the number of participants was too small to generalize findings, the findings nevertheless point to the varying benefits of collaborative translation for different learners.

Collaboration in Pedagogical Translation

Just as collaboration has always been in play in the field of translation, it is also key in pedagogical translation. From a socially situated literacy perspective, collaboration, language and literacy have been connected (Rajendram, 2015). Adding in translation, González-Davies (2017) found that novice-to-intermediate primary and secondary student participants linked CEFR descriptors for *plurilingual comprehension, plurilingual repertoire, spoken translation of written text* and *facilitating collaborative interaction with peers*, demonstrating the interconnection of translation, linguistic learning, literacy learning and collaboration. Pedagogically, collaborative translations may be teacher–student, as in whole-group discussion or the "we do" phase of direct instruction. They may also be peer–peer; and/or home–school, where all parties involved work together to support a learner or learners. The following sections focus on peer-to-peer and home–school collaboration.

Peer-to-Peer Collaborative Translation

Peer-to-peer collaborative translation can include multiple benefits. These include comprehension checks through peer-to-peer scaffolding; production of more complex and accurate texts in EFL writing; improved reading comprehension; enhanced participation for bilingual students; opportunities to negotiate for meaning; and noticing of grammatical and lexical features of the new language, including academic vocabulary (Källkvist, 2013; Linares, 2022). Benefits of peer-to-peer collaborative translation will be more fully described across multiple language-learning environments in the next paragraphs, with commentary and suggestions for how these approaches might be adapted.

According to Linares (2022), "Translation as a collaborative endeavor can bolster solidarity among minority students as readers and translators equipped with the multilingual resources to make sense of a source text"

(p. 58). A pedagogical translation task certainly would be described as a collaborative effort to achieve a goal or a translation. Keyes et al. (2014) developed a specific collaborative translation protocol characterized by students "reading an academic text, translating key passages, and evaluating these translations" (p. 17). In the activity, EB secondary students collaborated to produce oral and written translations of texts selected for thematic relevance and translatability. During these activities, students negotiated for meaning, participating more than in other activities as they argued about "right" and "best" translations (p. 20). Contrary to the authors' initial predictions, students were able to produce their translations with little instructor intervention. Similarly, Jiménez et al. (2015) found that through application of their Teaching Reading and New Strategic Language Approaches to English learners (TRANSLATE) protocol applied in collaborative groups, EB students vocalized comparison of linguistic features and were able to deepen their comprehension of texts.

In a study designed to support middle-grade reading comprehension through collaborative translation of short excerpts of text, Puzio et al. (2013) found that "collaborative translation made an array of student expertise visible" (p. 337). As learners negotiated for meaning, they demonstrated skill in translation and metalinguistic awareness through pragmatic competence; evaluation of lexical equivalence and social context. The skill they demonstrated led to a willingness to move beyond negotiation to argue for their choices and to recognize the strengths that individual members of the group were able to contribute to the translation. Puzio et al.'s findings may be particularly valuable across EB learning environments in which students do not always have the opportunity to express opinions or demonstrate their knowledge due to linguistic and cultural barriers.

Collaborative translation may be used for translation of literary texts. Beauvais and Ryland (2021) studied the benefits of collaboration in secondary literary translation workshops in Great Britain, finding that through collaborative translation of a literary text, students mobilized literary and language skills, including "reflections spanning literary style and mood, and linguistic, metalinguistic and cultural questions" (p. 300). However, the authors found some negative affect when the activity was positioned as a linguistic one, recommending that a literary translation activity instead be positioned as exploratory. An exploratory activity may help to gain student buy-in for translation, but in classrooms where instructors are expected to meet certain objectives, including language or content, instructors wanting to implement literary translation activities might consider a scaffolding process or didactic sequence starting with very brief passages in order to build students' linguistic confidence and capacity (see *Así se dice* in Escamilla et al., 2014; Corcoll, 2013; and/or González-Davies & Soler Ortínez, 2021, for sample primary and secondary didactic sequences).

Additionally, collaborative translation activities may be designed to foster critical thinking. Källkvist (2013) designed a university-level study to help determine when to use L1–L2 translation activities in learning difficult structures in an additional language, in this case, English. One of her conclusions was that collaborative dialog during a translation activity led to higher levels of student- rather than teacher-led questioning, demonstrating higher order thinking and benefits for acquisition of academic language. This is an interesting potential objective for incorporating collaborative translation across language-learning environments, including in monolingual classes with bilingual students where all learners are expected to have opportunities to generate their own higher-order questions as required by the CCSS (National Governors Association, 2010) or other content-area standards.

In a bilingual post-secondary translation class, Postlewate and Roesler (2022) assigned dyads of native French and native English speakers to translate book reviews into each language, respectively, which were then submitted for publication in academic journals. This authentic task caused students to take care to craft accurate, well-informed translations and to see the applicability of translation as a skill. While this activity was designed for a translation course, it could be adapted for language instruction. For example, in a dual-language classroom where half of the students speak English and half speak Spanish, learners could support each other in translating a text into the other language, with the goal of publication for the class, the school, or the larger community. Similarly, world language learners could be paired with heritage speakers of the language they are learning. Texts for translation could range from student-generated texts, thus incorporating writing (see e.g., Cummins, 2019, or Sneddon, 2012); to class or school newsletters, also with the potential for incorporating writing (see e.g., Cano & Ruiz, 2020, or Manyak, 2008); to more advanced literary texts (Beauvais & Ryland, 2021).

However, several caveats must be made when considering peer-to-peer collaborative structures for translation activities. First, collaborative translation is *not* concurrent translation on the part of the instructor. That is, it is not "collaborative" in the sense that the instructor speaks in the additional language and either simultaneously translates for learners or translates when learners appear to not understand. Concurrent translation may be detrimental to student learning as the learner tends to tune out the new language and pay attention only to the known language (Ulanoff & Pucci, 1993). Additionally, collaborative structures are not set up for EBs or heritage speakers to translate for native English-speakers or speakers of another dominant language (Cano & Ruiz, 2020). In mixed Spanish as a world language classes in the United States, for example, world language learners may rely upon the HLLs in their midst to translate for them. While this type of negotiation for meaning may happen in mixed groups, this should not be the purpose of the grouping strategy, and instructors may want to consider differentiating group formation between heritage and world language speakers (Albrecht, 2024; Henshaw, 2015).

Henshaw (2015), for example, studied the learning gains of mixed HL–L2 dyads in a university-level Spanish course. She found that the direction of benefits depended upon the task. That is, for vocabulary learning, HLLs helped new language learners more, while for form-focused, grammatical tasks like accent placement, new language learners helped HLLs more. Overall, new language learners applied information from HLLs correctly more often than the other way around. Henshaw proposed that this might have been due to HLL perception of new language learners' lower proficiency and subsequent assumptions of inaccurate information. On the other hand, additional language learners trusted HLLs' information more and were willing to trust their judgment, even when it was incorrect. In sum, while each type of learner had skills that could benefit the other, this case illustrates the complexity of mixed groups and the need for considering differentiation.

Given the potential pitfalls of collaboration in mixed groups of language speakers, recommendations from TS should be considered. In examining directionality, or whether a translator is translating into their home language ("Language A," and generally the standard for professional translators) or their additional language ("Language B"), Washbourne (2010) recommended that translators collaborate in pairs, with one dominant speaker of each language supporting the other. Not all language classrooms will support this structure, but it can serve as a potential tool in some dual-language, multilingual, or heritage–world language classrooms. Additionally, it may be helpful for pairs to establish their collaborative roles (Washbourne, 2010).

Similarly, collaborative groups at times reflect hierarchical, marginalizing structures for some students, and at others may be dominated by friend groups, gender, or bossy students (Keyes et al., 2014; Puzio et al., 2013). Collaborative work may have better outcomes when instructors have students discuss how they might best work together and then develop team norms prior to beginning collaborative work (Kochis et al., 2021), and some standards, such as CCSS ELA-Literacy.Sl.9-10.1.B in the United States, include working with peers "to set rules for collegial discussions and decision-making ... clear goals and deadlines, and individual roles" (National Governors Association, 2010). A specific teaching strategy to promote turn taking is the use of talking chips, in which each student has a given number of "chips," or small tokens representing a turn to speak. Each student must have a chance to use a token before another student who has already used one may speak again, or, alternatively, a student who has used all of their chips may not speak again until everyone else has used up theirs. This might be a strategy to implement only if turn taking appears to be an issue, given the dynamic and fluid conversations that often take place during collaborative translations.

Finally, students in collaboration may come up with an incorrect conclusion which is then transferred to incorrect language use on the part of the individual (Källkvist, 2013). To avoid this issue, learners should take part in instructor-scaffolded learning in addition to student-led discourse. To determine what, if any, misunderstandings may be arising, the instructor may use strategies such as circulating around the classroom during a translation activity and listening to student conversations; collecting and reviewing student works in process for an informal assessment, including shared documents for in-person or online courses; and/or have students complete an exit ticket after the activity in which students list what they learned as well as any questions or wonderings that came up during the collaborative activity.

Home–School Collaboration

Through school-to-home collaborations, students with another home language can involve parents or other family members in their work. The likelihood that early learners will become biliterate increases as they are able to read and write in both languages at home, at school and in the community, so parent or extended family involvement is key (Reyes et al., 2012). For example, when studying "the border-crossing biliteracies of Latinx families living in the Midwest" (Nuñez, 2023, p. 275) of the United States, Nuñez (2023) found that these families were using collaborative strategies with local and transnational family members to help their children complete their homework. For an assignment similar to the dual-language family story in this chapter's Translation Spotlight, a mother and child wrote collaboratively, translanguaging and using Google translate as a tool to support their translation process, with the child analyzing whether the translation made sense for their monolingual English-speaking audience (Sneddon, 2009). Although this study took place in the United Kingdom, instructors across learning contexts might consider how they can incorporate transnational family resources into collaborative assignments when designing translation activities. While these studies focused on primary-aged students, they might be modified for secondary or post-secondary courses such that learners draw upon their family and community funds of knowledge while writing in two languages (Moll et al., 1992).

Translation Spotlight: Dual-Language Family Story Writing Activity

This Translation Spotlight presents suggestions for establishing collaborative structures at school and at home, followed by a sample school–home collaborative translation activity.

Setting up a Peer-to-Peer Collaborative Structure at School

Although the CEFR (Council of Europe, 2018) recommends flexibility based upon language-learning context and regional pedagogical traditions, a sample structure for setting up collaborative structures will be provided here with the assumption that this structure can be adapted by context. Grahn and McAlpine (2017) recommend six steps for setting up successful collaborative group structures. First, groups should be no larger than 4–5 people, balanced by gender and varied by talent. Second, groups should have a goal for the task at hand and a structure for individual responsibility so that all members will contribute to the task. The goal will be based upon the translation assignment (or, following TS, upon translation briefs), and cooperative group roles can help structure these activities (Center for Teaching and Learning, 2024). For a translation activity, each member could have a role such as "facilitator," who gets the group started and makes sure everyone's voice is heard; "reporter," who will report on the group's final work to the class; "recorder," who writes down group members' ideas on a shared document, whiteboard, and so forth as participants suggest varying terms or structures; and "time keeper," who keeps everyone on task and reports the amount of time remaining halfway through and almost through the activity. These roles and responsibilities should be reviewed prior to beginning an activity. Despite the presence of a recorder, the instructor may want all group members to submit a translation to help ensure that all have been actively engaged.

Roles may change by educational environment. In a professional translator simulation, Prieto-Velasco and Fuentes-Luque (2016) assigned post-secondary translation students the roles of documentalist, translator, reviser/layout designer and project manager. These are described and simplified for pedagogical translation tasks as follows. The documentalist's job was careful reading of the source text and identification of key terms, including in parallel texts, and creation of a glossary of terms to be used by team members. Translators determined the function of the text and then translated, paying attention to cultural considerations. Revisers, clearly, revised, looking in particular for inconsistencies while comparing source and target texts, and set up the publication layout for the final project, speaking to the goal for the cooperative task. Project managers set up a timeline and deadlines for task completion and assigned tasks to group members. As an important aside, online asynchronous groups of translators in training have been shown to have more difficulty reaching consensus regarding collaborative translations, pointing to the potential need for scheduling periodic synchronous meetings (Kenny, 2008), including for asynchronous pedagogical translation collaborative projects.

Third, establish group norms. This helps encourage open communication and trust among group members and the instructor. Norms might include turn taking to talk, respectful disagreement, how to move forward or backward when addressing the topic and when to ask for the instructor's help. Fourth, the task should be divided so that all members of the group are responsible for part of the final product. For a translation activity, all group members might work together on a translation, with each member responsible for the final product of a given section prior to submitting it. A jigsaw activity is another way to encourage responsibility (Halley et al., 2013). For a jigsaw translation activity, each group translates one section, for example, a stanza from a poem, and then groups reform so that one person from each prior group is a member of the new group and is responsible for sharing their group's translation. Norms and procedures for this type of activity need to be carefully established in order for it to be successful, as do a means for assessing individual contributions in the second set of jigsaw groups so that some participants do not arrive to the new group with nothing to share. The fifth step is to implement pre- and post-tests to demonstrate learning; this might be done through a check for background knowledge and a final reflection, in addition to the group's translation. Albrecht (2024) used this methodology in order to identify the individual learning experienced by each student during a translation activity, as well as their perceptions regarding the efficacy of the task. Finally, both instructor and participants should informally assess the efficacy of group interactions while they are underway and after the fact; this could also be a part of the final reflection.

Setting up a Home-School Collaborative Activity

A home–school collaborative translation activity is presented in what follows, with several modifications to the structure recommended by Grahn and McAlpine (2017), namely: First, establish who will be involved in this collaborative activity. Beyond the student, this could be a family or community member or, depending upon the context, one or more friends. Second, establish a goal for the task and clearly defined roles such that neither participant takes over the other's work. For students and parents or older siblings, for example, who will do the writing? This may depend upon the student's level of skill, for example, and if they are familiar with the script of the home language. Once the story is written, who will correct for conventions? This may again depend upon the student's level of knowledge. Will this be during the drafting stage? A checklist for conventions in both languages may be helpful. Third, group norms should again be established, such as for turn taking, disagreeing, or moving forward or backward on the translation. The fourth step, division of the product for individual responsibility, may largely remain the same. For the fifth step, the student could complete a pre- and post-test at home or at school. Pre- and post-tests might be an interesting way to assess learning of parties involved beyond the student in order to hone future iterations of the assignment. For the sixth step, instructor and participant reflection on group interactions, participants could submit reflections on the activity to the instructor.

Dual-Language Family Story Writing Activity

Socially situated literacy expands beyond traditional, skills-based instruction in reading and writing of the standardized language to include broader communities and cultures representative of diverse students. The development of biliteracy within this framework can therefore be scaffolded by family and community members (Ek et al., 2016). Research has shown that including family in reading and in producing dual-language texts can contribute to biliteracy and cultural validation for both students and family members (Louie & Davis-Welton, 2016; Sneddon, 2009). However, in keeping with a socially situated literacy approach, it is important to recognize family literacy practices (Rowe & Fain, 2013). This translation activity, therefore, focuses on recording a family story in the home and target languages through narrative. Narrative assignments can be designed to validate and maintain students' home cultures (Ek et al., 2016) and may be assigned in homogeneous bilingual or diverse multilingual groups (Louie & Davis-Welton, 2016).

Based upon your student population, you may need to include other narrative options. These could range from an imaginary experience to family or cultural traditions and customs to recording a well-known legend or folktale (Louie & Davis-Welton, 2016; Sneddon, 2009; 2012). Sneddon (2009), for example, reviewed various home–school dual-language book projects, including mother–child workshops which produced online bilingual texts at a school with a significant Somali population in which students wrote, illustrated and published a traditional Somali folktale in dual-language format. Similarly, two students who had been taught to read in Albanian by their mothers co-authored a fictional story in English and Albanian. Through the process, they negotiated for an equivalent meaning in the translation, including for idioms that had no literal translation (Sneddon, 2012). Throughout the research study, both students and mothers were interviewed about the process. This partnership contributed not only to the students' linguistic skills and cultural identity but also resulted in increased parent involvement at the school.

This activity could be completed and published through traditional book format but has many options for multimodality, including for adding photos, drawings, voice recordings, maps, and so forth. Dual-language books may be published in hard or digital format and made available for classroom libraries, validating students' languages and cultures; serving as a resource for students learning a new language and teachers to discuss the books with students without knowing the home languages; and acting as a bridge between home and school as parents may participate in their students' literacy acquisition. Additionally, if the classroom is multilingual, students may become familiar with each other's languages (Sneddon, 2009).

Vertical alignments of the CEFR, ACTFL proficiency standards and CCSS all provide indicators for the age range, writing and language-learning levels at which students may be ready for the sample dual-language family story writing lesson. For the CEFR, learners may write "straightforward connected texts on a range of familiar subjects" (Council of Europe, 2020, p. 66) by the B1 level; however, they should probably be at a B2 to complete the assignment. As students generally start learning a second language in Europe by the mid-primary level, they may be ready for this narrative assignment by early secondary. Learners in other contexts may be able to complete the assignment by the fourth year of instruction. For world language learners in the United States, it is also expected that students be at the novice-mid level after four years of instruction. For many students, this would be during their final year of secondary instruction.

Students who are second language learners may be expected to be meeting both content and language standards through a CBLI approach. In the United States, for example, students are expected to be meeting CCSS for content and ELD standards simultaneously (Fenner, 2023) and may therefore be able to complete a dual-language story at a much earlier stage. Narrative, for example, is introduced in the CCSS halfway through the primary grades and is built upon each subsequent year through secondary school. A consideration of the different frameworks for language learning illustrates how standards may need to be combined and/or adapted across global language-learning environments.

Conclusion

Collaboration is a key element to consider when designing translation activities as it can contribute to student learning and positive affect. Collaborative translation activities can be designed as teacher–class, peer-to-peer, or home-school. For all, it is important to design collaborative structures with care, including attention to group dynamics and the establishing of norms for participation so that all group members have a voice and feel safe in contributing. Effective collaborative structures can then mediate for student learning through translation.

Table 9.1 Translation Spotlight: Family Story Writing

Objective(s): Through a dual-language family story writing activity, I can:

CEFR (Council of Europe, 2020):
- *Write a clear, detailed narrative of a family story in two languages, marking the relationship between ideas in clear connected text and following established written and narrative conventions (p. 188).*
- *Produce a clearly organized translation of a narrative in my home language into my new language that reflects normal language usage (p. 218).*

ACTFL (The National Standards Collaborative Board, 2015)
- *Write a story about my life, activities, events, and other social experiences [in two languages], using sentences and a series of connected sentences.*

CCSS (National Governors Association, 2010)
- *ELS-LITERACY.W.7.3. Through writing a narrative [in two languages], I can engage and orient the reader by establishing a context and point of view and introducing a narrator and/or characters; organize an event sequence that unfolds naturally and logically through transition words; use descriptive words as a narrative technique; and provide a conclusion that follows from and reflects on the narrated experiences or events.*

Prior Skills:
- Language:
  - Intermediate mid-high (A2-B1) learners should be able to navigate past, present, and future tenses and conversations on familiar topics. They should have some knowledge of continuous and perfect tenses.
  - Students should have some skill using a bilingual dictionary. You may need to distinguish between using a dictionary and translation of an entire text through AI or a tool like Google Translate. What skills will learners acquire through doing the translation themselves? What will they miss out on in the process if they use AI?
- Writing:
  - This assignment assumes developing written literacy in the home and additional languages, probably at differing levels.
  - This lesson assumes that students will have already been introduced to the components of narrative writing, including beginning, middle, and end; setting; point of view; description; and vocabulary that indicates sequence. For the translation component, students could be given a list of transition words or sequence words in advance.
  - Writing: Students should already have a personal writing checklist to be used when revising their work. They can use this for work in both languages.

Materials
- Writing Checklist to be sent home with students
- Sample Writing Checklist

Writing Checklist
- Did I write my story in my home language?
- Does my story illustrate something about my home culture?

- Is it 300–500 words long?
- Does it have a beginning, middle, and end? Is there a conflict that is resolved?
- Is there a clear setting?
- Did I use descriptive words to describe the people and places in my story? (think of words that describe what you see, hear, smell, taste, and touch/feel)
- Did I use words that show sequence? (first, next, last, then, after)
- Are my writing conventions accurate?

Family Story Writing Activity

Consider modeling each phase of the activity with students prior to having them do it independently. For example, before your translation activity, model options for looking up words or collocations that students don't know. This might include standard dictionaries and online dictionaries. However, multilingual students might also look up the same word in multiple languages in order to gain a fuller depth of understanding of nuance in its meaning; they might also do a search for the word in context in the target language to make sure they are using it correctly.

Instructions for Students

Choose from the following activities:
Before you write:
Draw a map of your neighborhood or another significant place where you have spent time. Mark three places on your map where notable events happened. Choose one event that you would like to write about.

OR

Discuss some family stories with a family member. These could be stories about a parent or other family member or they could be stories that a family member has traditionally told, like myths or legends. Choose one that you would be interested in writing down.

Write:
With a parent or other family member who can assist you, in your home language, write a draft of the story that you have chosen. Be sure to include narrative elements like beginning, middle, and end; descriptive words; and transition words that show the sequence of events.

Translate:
Bring your work to class, where you and a classmate will work together to translate each other's stories.

Publish:
For your final product, decide how you would like to design your translated book. Will the two languages be together on one page, or will you create two books with the same story, one in each language? Will you write on paper or type on a computer? What kinds of illustrations would contribute to the meaning of your story? Will you draw these or find photos online?

(continued)

Table 9.1 (*continued*)

Evaluation
- Informal evaluation: Collect and review students' (and parents') ideas about the story they plan to use prior to having them start writing. If ideas seem unclear, have students talk their ideas through with you and/or with peers.
- Formal evaluation: Use the final hard or digital copy of the dual-language book for the formal evaluation. Be sure to align what you evaluate with your objectives, which will probably be broader than those modeled in this lesson. If you find that you are evaluating something not in the objectives, change the objectives or the evaluation so that they are aligned.

Expansion/Modification
- Objectives may be modified to include expectations for interpersonal communication during the translation activity
- Objectives may be modified to include linguistic expectations for written communication
- Add dates to the parent instruction page to clarify the project timeline.
- In second language environments, consider whether you will allow written translanguaging during the translation process.
- Have students record their bilingual stories (Sneddon, 2012) on a site like YouTube. They could include reverse subtitles.
- In the author's experience, post-secondary students have still benefited from collecting family stories. The translation process should include collaboration with peers.
- Create a printed or digital anthology of stories for the class to use.
- You may need to modify the family event in which stories are shared in small groups (Short 1996) for online and/or older students, but students should be given the opportunity to present or 'publish' their work as authors.
- Audio or video record your instructions if there are parents who are not able to read.
- If parents or family members speak the new language, have them and the students work together on the translation of the story.
- Add more advanced requirements for literary elements like simile and metaphor or hybrid text for literary effect; and plot structure, including conflict and resolution, as needed

Instructions for Parents/Family Members/Guardians:
Your student has been learning about writing narratives or stories. This is a collaborative writing project between you and your student to practice writing a narrative in the form of a family story. Your role will be to collaborate with your student in recording a family story, with your child doing the writing. The story could be an event that happened in your family or a story frequently told in your family, like a myth or legend.
The project will be completed in the following phases:
1 Decide upon the story you will write together. Send your idea back to class with your student along with any questions you may have.

2 With your student, draft the story in your home language in 300–500 words. Make sure your student is doing the writing. Don't worry about corrections until the draft is written.
   a. The first draft should be handwritten.
   b. Make sure the story includes the following:
      i. A clear point of view (Who is telling the story, a character or a narrator?)
      ii. A beginning, middle and end
      iii. A setting (Where does the story take place?)
      iv. Descriptive words (words that show what the character(s) are seeing, hearing, tasting, smelling, and feeling)
      v. Words that show sequence (first, next, then, finally, at last, etc.)
3 After the first draft of the story is written, review the writing checklist with your student. Together, decide on any changes that might be needed and make them.
4 Send the draft back to school with your student.
5 Your student will translate the story at school.
6 Your student will create the final, illustrated product on paper or digitally.
7 Please plan to attend our author's event to share stories with other members of the class and their families.

10

Literacy Objectives and Measuring Learning

Chapter 10 addresses the application of standards and development of objectives and assessments for pedagogical translation activities, building upon the proposal that all language learning, whether world or bilingual, be viewed through a bilingual lens (Turnbull, 2018). The implications of this proposition on outcomes for the acquisition of biliteracy will therefore be considered. This will be followed by steps for the development of content and language objectives for translation activities across language learners and language-learning environments, together with potential frameworks for objectives and assessment, such as TS (Colina, 2008); the CEFR (Council of Europe, 2020); the ACTFL World-Readiness Standards (The National Standards Collaborative Board, 2015); the CCSS (National Governors Association, 2010); and biliteracy (Escamilla et al., 2014). Differentiation and informal and formal assessments of Translation Spotlights will then be discussed. Assessments might range from informally checking for understanding to production of a translated product or a product in two languages to be formally evaluated. The chapter will end with a Translation Spotlight modeling alignment of standards, objectives, activities, and assessment.

Key Terms: Standards, Objectives, Assessment, and Evaluation

Standards

In education, standards broadly define what students should be able to know and do at varying levels and are commonly implemented to provide consistency in expectations. Given the interdisciplinarity of pedagogical translation, standards may be language- or content-based and will be selected according to the learning context. For example, world language standards in the United States will be based upon the ACTFL World-Readiness Standards, which are also applied on standard language exams used globally; world and second language standards in Europe and many other countries throughout the world will be based upon the CEFR. Another term for *standards* is *framework,* as in the *Common European Frame of Reference for Languages: Learning, Teaching, Assessment.* One of the primary goals of the CEFR "is the promotion of the positive formulation of educational aims [objectives] and outcomes [through assessment] at all levels" (Council of Europe, 2018, p. 25). Similarly, shortly after the publication of the ACTFL *Standards for Foreign Language in the 21st Century,* Troyan (2012) stated that "it is apparent that the National Standards embody what the profession believes is important in assessment, instruction, and learning; in other words, the National Standards represent the inherent values of our professional community" (p. 118).

The CCSS in the United States will serve as a model of content-area standards; other applicable content-area standards should be substituted in according to learning context. The CCSS are designed to "provide clear and consistent learning goals (Read the Standards, 2021) and to "clearly demonstrate what students are expected to learn at every level" (para. 1) to achieve mastery, which is demonstrated through high-stakes testing. However, monolingual ideology raises its head within the standards: With one in five students in the United States being bilingual, the CCSS do not address bilingualism or bilingual practices (García and Flores, 2013), which impacts these students' performance on standardized exams as they are required to "deactivate" (p. 156) all of their linguistic repertoires except for English.

Additionally, according to García and Flores (2013), while the standards have moved from autonomous views of literacy, they "have ignored the ideological framework of New Literacy Studies–the fact that social, cultural, political, and economic factors influence literacy practices" (p. 153), leaving instructors to the complex navigation process of applying high-stakes standards that do not match their learners. Multiple states and other institutional entities have developed corresponding Native Language Arts standards to help address this issue, and each state has its own English language proficiency standards which describe the "knowledge, skills and abilities students who are learning English as a new language need to access… grade-level academic content" (California English Language Standards, 2023, p. 8; Lafond, S., 2023), illustrating the complexity of finding the combination of standards needed for diverse groups of learners and then applying appropriate instructional strategies to maximize their learning. García and Flores (2013) argue that if translanguaging is not acknowledged as a bilingual practice and pedagogy, "the CCSS may further contribute to the stigmatization of the language practices of bilinguals and doom them to academic failure" (p. 155).

Translation from a translanguaging perspective can be implemented to help bilingual learners meet monolingual standards as students can develop needed skills in both languages. For example, in terms of connecting standards between language and content-area frameworks, the English Language Arts (ELA) standards for the CCSS are structured around monolingual listening, speaking, reading, and writing (García & Flores, 2013). However, as these are also key skills in any additional language-learning standards, this would be a key jumping off point for developing translation objectives and assessments for bilingual learners. Work is being done to align ELD standards with the CCSS (Fenner & Segota, 2023). While different content-area standards are applied in other global contexts, it is important to keep in mind the minoritization of the home languages of native and migrant students which is commonplace across educational environments.

The elements of goals or objectives; learning; and outcomes or assessment are evident in all of these frameworks. Frameworks such as the CEFR, the World-Readiness Standards, or the CCSS will guide the development of translation objectives, activities, and assessment, and translation quality, language, and content-area standards may be used in tandem if appropriate to the learning context.

Objectives

As with standards, learning objectives describe "what students are *expected to know and do*" (Orr et al., 2022, para. 3, emphasis in original) to achieve a given outcome. However, objectives are applied to a specific learning environment. They may be broad, applying to course outcomes, or narrow, applying to unit or lesson outcomes. The outcomes of objectives should be measured through assessment (Orr et al., 2022) as defined in the next subsection, Assessment and Evaluation. This chapter will only address lesson objectives. Objectives should be aligned with standards. For translation activities, objectives will align with standards in the area(s) in which they are being used such as the CEFR, ACTFL, CCSS in the United States or similar standards in other global contexts, such as ELD. Because the achievement of a given outcome specified by the objectives is measured through assessment, formal assessment of translation activities should also align with objectives.

Teaching and learning must of course also align with standards, objectives, and assessments. For example, Biggs (2003) described a rhetoric course in which objectives stated that by the end of the course students should have developed critical thinking skills. However, course material was delivered through lecture and tested by multiple choice, neither of which supported development of critical thinking and was therefore not aligned with course objectives. The decision about whether to incorporate pedagogical translation should also be based upon alignment with standards and objectives; when translation is used as a formal assessment, the form of assessment should align with the objectives. This process will be expanded upon throughout the chapter.

Assessment and Evaluation

This chapter deals with individual, rather than program, assessment, and evaluation. The terms *assessment* and *evaluation* are differentiated by some but not by others (Cook, 2010; Kern, 2000). According to some, assessment provides data which can be drawn upon to improved teaching and learning but is not graded (Angelo & Cross, 1993). Within this definition, assessment is formative. In contrast, evaluation of content mastery is graded, or summative. Evaluations may include course components beyond content, such as social–emotional learning or intercultural competence (Dewi, 2015). Kern (2000) describes evaluation as analysis of the data, which in this sense may overlap with summative assessment in which student work is evaluated for a grade. For clarity, *assessment* in this chapter and throughout the book will be used as an umbrella term which includes both formative and summative assessment, or evaluation.

Translation can be assessed in and of itself, or it can serve as an assessment tool for many content- and language-area objectives. Indeed, according to Butzkamm and Caldwell (2009), "As an assessment of an individual's broad language awareness, [translation] is arguably unrivaled" (p. 198). In addition to language awareness, translation can be used to assess reading comprehension because it offers insight into the reader's thinking as opposed to simply showing that comprehension happened through assessment tools like multiple choice questions (Linares, 2022). In Albrecht (2024), for example, a comprehension post-test demonstrated whether secondary world and heritage language learners had understood the poem they had translated, while errors in actual student translations demonstrated gaps in understanding the poem's meaning. However, it is important to keep in mind that when translations are assessed, there should not be one "correct" (Phipps & González, 2004, p. 153) translation to which student work is compared, as has traditionally been the case in post-secondary language courses. Similarly, high stakes, standardized exams aligned with the CCSS may require students to answer multiple choice or short answer reading comprehension questions. Pedagogical translation activities may therefore prepare students with the higher-order thinking required for questions which ask for meaning to be inferred.

Planning Pedagogical Translation Through a Biliteracy Lens

Kern (2000) proposed three elements for assessing literacy-based language learning. First, language and learning should be broad-based, with objectives beyond language learning including social, cognitive, and cultural elements, thus demonstrating not just literacy but also socially situated literacy. Second, assessment needs to be approached from multiple dimensions: "What is needed is an aggregate measure involving analysis of a student's reading across a variety of contexts" (p. 272), including genre, difficulty, and manner of selection, and the writing should be similarly broad-based. Collaborative and individual work in and out of school should also be assessed. It is interesting to consider translation activities from this multidimensional perspective. For example, the texts—or text sets—for translation can represent this multidimensionality, as can writing assignments in and out of class (see e.g., the family story assignment, Chapter 9). Finally, assessment must be aligned with teaching and learning, as illustrated in the translation spotlight.

Planning for instruction and assessment through a biliteracy lens means that while an additional language is being learned, the home language is being maintained and/or developed. In other words, Kern's (2000) three elements for literacy-based learning can be simultaneously applied to home and additional languages. Application might look different across language-learning environments, with more specific attention being placed upon objectives for home language maintenance and development for second or heritage language learners, especially given the tendency for language loss among migrants and its subsequent individual and social effects (Educational Research Institute, 2024). However, translation will generally require attention to literacy in home and additional languages given that translation activities require learners to draw upon texts in both languages. This assumption requires a caveat among multilingual learners, particularly in an environment where two dominant languages are being used for translation activities and the learner uses an additional language at home. For example, in Kultti and Pramling (2018) most learners' home language was Finnish and English was the additional language. However, some learners spoke an additional language at home. These were not utilized in the translation activity, which involved cross-linguistic comparison to develop metalinguistic awareness. To have incorporated home languages, instructors would have needed to ask learners for comparative examples from their home languages, possibly collaborating with parents in advance as well, and then incorporated home languages into the objectives and assessment.

Approaching language teaching and learning with a biliteracy lens will impact the development of objectives. While only products in the new language may be evaluated in world language environments, through a biliteracy perspective, home language maintenance and growth is nevertheless assumed. In a world language environment, attention to the home language might be addressed through including translation objectives in which linguistic and cultural elements are compared or through dual-language writing. In second language environments, bilingual or EB students may be required to be assessed through high-stakes testing in the dominant language. Thus, bilingual strategies for textual comprehension developed through pedagogical translation may transfer to high-stakes testing and play a significant role in learner performance.

Although reading and writing tend to be a default focus for the development of literacy, the additional language skills of listening and speaking are also in play. Escamilla et al. (2014) combined listening and speaking under the umbrella concept of *oracy*, which is the ability to express oneself in and understand spoken language. Citing research that oracy positively impacts reading achievement in two languages, they maintained that oracy development is a key objective in biliteracy development. Therefore, it must be included in biliteracy objectives (Escamilla et al., 2014).

Oracy objectives should be deliberate and structured. For bilingual environments, they should also reflect different proficiency levels between languages. To plan oracy objectives, Escamilla et al. (2014) recommended asking what type of language skills are needed to complete a given task and what type of structures and vocabulary students must have to be able to express themselves. Oracy objectives should include "language structures, vocabulary and dialogue" (Escamilla et al., 2014, p. 21). These should serve to expand students' ability to express themselves using a broader range of grammar and vocabulary when participating in literacy-related discussions. Oracy development is not unplanned and random, nor is it based upon correct and incorrect answers, rote response, repetition of language that is too advanced or decontextualized, copying dictionary definitions, or writing disconnected sentences to practice vocabulary.

A series of bilingual preschool studies in Finland which was prompted by the need to study strategies appropriate to teaching linguistically and culturally diverse groups illustrates oracy development through a translation activity. These studies examined how children developed and expressed metalinguistic awareness and negotiated meaning while orally translating a children's song. The translation involved dialog and co-construction of meaning between students and instructors, with results showing that the activity contributed to language learning and comprehension, including figurative language (Jidai & Kultti, 2017; Kultti & Pramling, 2017; 2018). The language development, metalinguistic awareness and comprehension developed through oracy would in turn be expected to contribute to biliteracy development (Escamilla et al., 2014).

Turning to writing objectives, in dual-language writing it is important to remember that writing in the home language may be stronger than writing in the new language, again necessitating discussion of functional rather than word-for-word translation which is not attainable at the same level when the work is assigned and throughout the composition process. Encouragement of circumlocution and metalinguistic strategies may be required. In the author's experience (through formative and summative assessments), attempts to translate from the home language at a higher level to the new language at a lower level of proficiency may lead to frustration and uninformed mechanical translator use. These are important considerations to make in presenting a dual-language assignment and in formative assessment of student work, for example, in the dual-language family story project (Chapter 9).

While a biliteracy lens may be applied to world or second language learning environments, assessment approaches will differ. That is, while in a world language class the new language will of course be assessed, in second language environments home languages may be assessed as well (see e.g., the family story project, Chapter 9). Escamilla et al. (2014) highlighted the importance of assessing bilingual writing holistically rather than from a parallel monolingual perspective. That is, students' bilingual strategies and the influence of the home language must be taken into account when assessing writing in the new language rather than viewing writing in each language as separate and independent, or as the home language interfering with acquisition of the new language. Identifying student language levels in both languages is key in assessing more than one language (Escamilla et al., 2014), although bilingual translation strategies such as guided writing (see Translation Spotlight, Chapter 5) may require assessment in only one language. However, from a biliteracy perspective, translation assumes that both languages are in play in the process and the product. Ultimately, in practice, bilingual educators must determine in which language students will be assessed for high stakes testing, keeping in mind which translation strategies might contribute to mastery of the standards in more than one language.

Overview of Models and Frameworks for Standards, Objectives, and Assessment

Multiple frameworks from varying disciplines may be applied in the development of objectives and assessments for translation in language and content learning. We start with Colina's (2008) model for assessing translation quality, which may be overlaid with other language or content frameworks. The CEFR and ACTFL frameworks will be described next, followed by heritage language and content-area standards.

Translation Studies

Within the field of TS, assessment approaches vary but have some commonalities which may be utilized in assessing translations in the language classroom (see e.g., Angelelli, 2009; Colina, 2008; House, 2015; Waddington, 2001). Rubrics can provide structure for consistent grading of identified translation criteria (Angelelli, 2009). A simplified, holistic list of potential criteria which might be included in a rubric for a translation activity is as follows:

1. Linguistic accuracy: Spelling, grammar, vocabulary, clarity
2. Functional adequacy: The translation meets the intended "goals, purpose, audience and function of the text" (Colina, 2008, p. 129) and conveys the source text message without unneeded changes
3. Pragmatic competence: Consideration of context and cultural nuance
4. Cohesion and coherence: Ideas are organized logically, including through cohesive devices

This range of categories draws attention to the need in pedagogical translation for assessment elements beyond linguistic form, as assessment focused only on form might otherwise result in word- or sentence-level evaluation reminiscent of grammar translation. It also aligns with a literacy-based approach to language learning. For example, linguistic accuracy demonstrates the effective use of language, and functional adequacy requires that the translator understand audience and purpose. Pragmatic competence requires that students recognize the role of context for meaning making, and cohesion and coherence are essential writing skills. These criteria can therefore be overlaid with the language and content standards which follow.

Language Standards

The CEFR and ACTFL language standards are utilized globally and are proficiency-based, which "can do" statements emphasize in performance descriptors for both (Council of Europe, 2018; The National Standards Collaborative Board, 2015). The CEFR defines proficiency as "the glimpse of someone's underlying competence derived from a specific performance" (Council of Europe, 2018, p. 32). Similarly, ACTFL defines proficiency as "a range and measures what a language user can do regardless of where, when, or how they learned the language" (ACTFL Proficiency Scale, 2024). How, then, does a socially situated literacy approach to language learning relate to language proficiency standards? In other words, which approach falls within the other? According to Kern (2000), a literacy-based approach provides "the larger context of evaluating how learners create and interpret meanings – drawing not just on their language skills but also on the full breadth of their experience and knowledge" (p. 268), recalling the multilingual and social turns in second language acquisition theory which place language learning within larger contexts. Objectives and assessments based upon proficiency-based standards should therefore be considered part of learners' larger, socially contextualized process for meaning making.

The teaching of grammar is an additional consideration in creating objectives and assessments for translation activities. Even within proficiency-based approaches, grammar instruction has been, and continues to be, a common approach to language teaching. For this reason, grammar instruction will be discussed prior to practically addressing objectives and assessments. Traditional grammar instruction has been incorporated in language teaching as the foundation upon which later skills are built, often with the result that language learners know about a language but are unable to use it to actually communicate. Indeed, the grammar translation method discussed in Chapter 2 was utilized to teach discrete grammar points with the objective that students would be able to read in the additional language but not communicate. In contrast, communicative language teaching of the twentieth century swung in the other direction, with little focus on grammar and students often lacking structural control (Cook, 2010).

As objectives and assessment in language assessment frameworks are today largely based upon proficiency, how is grammar taught within proficiency-based frameworks? The answer, according to ACTFL, is again found in a communicative context (Teach Grammar, 2024). Byram (2020) pointed out that progression in language teaching, such as that required in teaching grammar, is like putting the corners of a puzzle together to give shape to the whole endeavor in the early stages. After this point, there is not necessarily an organized progression but cyclical attention to varying elements which only all come together in the advanced stages. These considerations in sequencing will impact the nature—and sequencing—of grammar and other objectives depending upon learner level. Similarly, the CEFR offers language profiles of what grammatical features learners tend to know at each level (Brun-Mercer, 2021).

How does grammar fit within literacy-based language instruction? Kern's (2000) discussion on literacy-based language teaching applies to grammar instruction as well: in literacy-based teaching, we are certainly interested in assessing students' knowledge of syntax and vocabulary as well as their ability to use language to fulfill particular communicative functions, but within larger considerations of how learners are making meaning. In other words, grammar, or structural control, must be assessed within the context of how students make meaning of a text, again keeping in mind that a text may be written or oral. In a translation activity, grammar might be assessed by how structural control or lack of it reflects the meaning students have brought across from the text in the source to the target language. It might also be assessed by how use of form affects the functionality of the translated text.

Common European Frame of Reference for World and Second Language Learning

The CEFR describes what world and second language learners generally know at a given level. That is, it provides "common descriptive metalanguage to talk about language proficiency" (Council of Europe, 2018, p. 29). The assumption is that the CEFR descriptors are for adult learners but can be applied to young learners, that is, students from ages 7–15. An overlay of Colina's (2008) four assessment categories fits neatly with the CEFR descriptors as translation standards are included within the *CEFR Companion Volume* (2020). The *Companion Volume* also includes standards for literacy and ICC.

American Council on the Teaching of Foreign Languages World-Readiness Standards

The ACTFL World-Readiness Standards (The National Standards Collaborative Board, 2015) are based upon the five Cs of communication, cultures, connections, comparisons, and communities. These are expected to be used in an integrated fashion and are designed to be overlaid with the CCSS. This points to their use in content-based language teaching, particularly for second language learners. While readers of this book may be in contexts using other standards, the objective in this chapter is to model the overlay of two sets of standards in complex language-learning environments.

The World-Readiness Standards are designed to apply from primary through post-secondary levels; and to world, native, heritage, and second language learners. The ACTFL Proficiency Guidelines (2024) are based upon novice, intermediate and advanced performance; interpersonal, interpretive and presentational communication; and performance parameters consisting of functions and tasks, accuracy, context, content and text type (i.e., FACT performance parameters). Accuracy falls within the parameter of comprehension and comprehensibility, with four sub-parameters including language control, vocabulary, communication strategies, and cultural awareness. Language control is taught and assessed in terms of conceptual, partial, and full. In terms of grammar instruction, according to ACTFL (2024), "instead of focusing on grammar rules and diagramming sentences, teachers should guide students towards an understanding of how grammar functions. Students learn how to use the form rather than memorized conjugations that may not be applicable across contexts" (n.p.).

In contrast to the CEFR, neither the ACTFL World-Readiness Standards nor the Proficiency Guidelines directly include translation. However, translation as a means and as an end might be incorporated in objectives and assessments in multiple ways, including being overlaid with Colina's

Table 10.1 Sample Alignment of Translation Quality Assessment and ACTFL Proficiency Standards, Translation of Proverbs Activity

ACTFL Standard(s)	ACTFL Proficiency Benchmark(s)	ACTFL Can-Do Statement(s), Modified	Assessment of Translation Quality
Interpretive Communication: What can I understand, interpret, or analyze in authentic informational texts that I hear, read, or view (ACTFL 2017, p.1)?	I can understand the main idea and some pieces of information on familiar topics from sentences and series of connected sentences within texts that are spoken, written, or signed (ACTFL 2017, p.1).	Through a translation of proverbs activity, I can: - Identify the underlying message in a written proverb in another language, including through recognition of grammar structures and vocabulary.	Functional adequacy; meaning Linguistic form (conceptual)
Intercultural Communication: Investigate Products And Practices To Understand Cultural Perspectives (ACTFL 2017, p.1)	In my own and other cultures, I can make comparisons between products and practices to help me understand perspectives (ACTFL 2017, p.1).	Through a translation of proverbs activity, I can: - In my own and other cultures, explain how proverbs are related to cultural perspectives.	Functional adequacy; meaning

(2008) translation assessment quality. Subject-specific vocabulary may not always be relevant, particularly at lower levels. For the translation of proverbs activity, ACTFL and translation quality assessment might align as demonstrated in Table 10.1.

To clarify, functional adequacy of a translated proverb would be demonstrated through meeting the function and audience of the target text in the translation. To do this, the translator (student) must understand the main idea of connected sentences within a written (or oral) proverb. As proverbs are generally tied to cultural traditions (Bradeanu, 2007), some understanding of the source and target audience must also be assumed to successfully identify the main idea as well as to capture the meaning in translation. As proverbs must often be translated as a whole piece of text to capture the meaning, addressing meaning in a translated proverb may entail matching proverbs with similar meanings but without textual equivalence.

That is, wholesale alteration may be required. In the translation of proverbs activity (Chapter 6), for example, functionally equivalent translations in the additional language are matched to proverbs in the home language. This fosters cultural comparison and requires attention to linguistic form in the source text, although it might forgo linguistic comparison in the translation.

Heritage Language Standards

In a multilingual, multicultural world, the growing diversity of language classrooms must be assumed and the needs of immigrant students or children of immigrant parents addressed (Educational Research Institute, 2024). In dominant language environments, heritage language loss is common, as its speakers begin to lose "functions, registers and domains of use" (Mattheoudakis et al., 2020, p. 1021), particularly in writing. According to the Educational Research Institute (2024), "the right to study one's heritage language [is] universal" (para. 2) and, on the macro level, should be a fundamental element in language policy. On the micro level, standards for teaching and assessing HLLs must be in place. Subsequent paragraphs in this section will examine application of the CEFR, ACTFL, and CCSS to heritage language learning.

The CEFR (Council of Europe, 2001) was designed for implementation across formal and informal learning environments as well as for different language learners. Many environments implementing the CEFR assume heritage language maintenance and development to be the responsibility of families or communities as opposed to educational institutions (Mattheoudakis et al., 2020), leaving a paucity of research on the application of the CEFR to heritage language assessment. Indeed, criticism of the CEFR has indicated that it has been implemented primarily for dominant language learning toward employability and skill acquisition, with home or minoritized languages being backgrounded, as in the case of Thailand and Malaysia (Savski, 2020). Piccardo (2017) analyzed the intersection of migrant languages and cultures with host country languages and cultures through the CEFR's plurilingual lens; it can be assumed that heritage speakers will be found within migrant communities. Because plurilingualism focuses "on the relationships between the languages an individual speaks, the underlying linguistic mechanisms and cultural connotations, the personal linguistic and cultural trajectory as well as the persons' attitude toward language diversity, stressing openness, curiosity, and flexibility" (Piccardo, 2017, p. 2), there seems to be space to apply it to heritage language teaching and assessment.

In terms of ACTFL standards, the question arises of whether different standards should be used for HLLs. The ACTFL actively supports research on and teaching of heritage language. Although the World-Readiness Standards indicate that they are designed for heritage language environments, in a systematic review of the literature on HLL assessment, Son (2017) found studies both supporting and opposing use of the ACTFL standards to assess post-secondary HLLs. Those supporting use of the ACTFL standards found that they "take into consideration multiple aspects of language use, including function, context, and accuracy" (p. 374). As previously mentioned, these can be used to measure proficiency. However, those opposing their use argued that as the standards were designed for world language learners, they do not reflect the language development trajectory of HLLs. Son concluded that not enough research has been done to determine the efficacy of ACTFL proficiency standards for HLLs. Nevertheless, this book will work within the ACTFL standards, proposing options for the development of HLL-specific objectives and assessments; indeed, the Center for Applied Linguistics (n.d.) recommended that in mixed classrooms, differentiated assessments may need to be available for heritage and non-heritage learners, which would of course require differentiated objectives.

Content Standards

CBLI is an approach used in world and second language learning (Genesee, 1994; Swain, 1996). The terminology *bilingual* or *second language learner* tends to shift to *heritage language learner* in dedicated language-learning environments. As terminology shifts with the learning environment, so do learning standards. As previously indicated, in the United States, CCSS are one framework for teaching and assessing content such as language arts, math, social studies, and science. In other learning contexts, different standards will be applied.

A literacy-based approach to language learning requires incorporation of CBLI, with learning objectives designed prior to implementation of a translation activity. In David et al. (2019), for example, two teachers spent most of their reflections on a translation activity focusing on student-centered linguistic problem solving and only began thinking about learning objectives for pedagogical translation activities in exit interviews. However, by the end of the translation lesson, one of the teachers "was able to leverage students' reflections on these translation challenges to connect to the reading skill of inferring information about a character from details in the text" (p. 270). According to this teacher, translation needed to be considered as the means toward a learning objective, not the end (however, note that the CEFR includes acquisition of translation as a skill toward an end). In her case, the goal was interpretation of poetry through "routinizing student production of metacognitive statements about their work" (p. 271) as they translated.

Similarly, the translation activity in Jidai et al. (2017) was designed to familiarize preschool students of ages 6–7 with metaphor, synonyms, and syntax through increased metalinguistic awareness. As students translated, negotiation occurred through "changed word order, unchanged word order, and word order vs. ways of expressing meaning" (p. 208). Objectives in other studies have included language learning, such as depth of vocabulary, including homonyms (Kultti & Pramling, 2018) and cross-linguistic connections (Escamilla et al., 2014). They also included content, such as reading comprehension (Cano & Ruiz, 2020) through components such as text-level themes which became evident as students negotiated for meaning through translation (Cano & Ruiz, 2020; Keyes et al., 2014). In all cases, the objectives were set in advance.

The texts selected for a translation activity should align with standards-based objectives, as in Pacheco et al.'s (2015) study of intermediate-grade EBs: "Teachers not only selected sentences that were linguistically challenging and/or important for comprehending an important aspect of the story (including plot, characterization, or major themes), but that also aligned with long-term curricular aims" (p. 52). This translation activity aligned with content and language standards. For reading standards for literature, students used the TRANSLATE protocol to be able to cite textual evidence to defend their translation choices; for speaking and listening standards, students used textual evidence to logically support their arguments about character; and for language standards, they learned about active and passive voice and verb tenses.

Development of Learning Objectives and Assessments for Translation Spotlights

This section draws upon the Translation Spotlights in Chapters 5 and 9 to model development of language and content objectives, focusing on differentiating objectives among diverse learners and on formal and informal assessments.

Differentiating Objectives

Translation as a pedagogy can be used across language learner types (Cano & Ruiz, 2020; Gasca Jiménez, 2019; González-Davies, 2017). It might be argued, then, that translation as an assessment could also be used across language learner types while integrating Colina's (2008) four standards for translation translation quality assessment, although skills being taught and assessed might differ based upon learner needs. For example, objectives for linguistic assessment for HLLs might focus on "vulnerable grammar topics identified by formal studies" (Carreira & Kagan, 2018, p. 156) as opposed to "starting with grammar explanations and vocabulary lists" (p. 156) typically used in world language instruction. Heritage and world language learners might be taught differentiated mini-lessons prior to a translation

Table 10.2 Sample Differentiated World and Heritage Language Objectives

World Language Objective	Spanish Heritage Language Objective
I can understand the main idea and some pieces of information within a written text on a familiar topic, including through attention to vocabulary and syntax in translation.	*Through attention to vocabulary, syntax and accuracy in a guided writing translation activity, I can improve my accuracy in written expression through recognizing the silent h at the beginning of a word.*

activity, with HLLs focusing on Carreira and Kagan's vulnerable topics or on connecting oral language to reading comprehension (Albrecht, 2024). Differentiated language objectives for world and heritage language learners might look like the expanded example in Table 10.2 from the guided writing translation spotlight in Chapter 5.

In the context of post-secondary Spanish heritage language programs, Beaudrie (2016) recommended differentiated assessment which "complements differentiated instruction, seeking to provide all students with multiple opportunities to demonstrate their learning and progress" (p. 152) and which reflects the varying skill levels often present in heritage language classrooms. Differentiated assessments might include varying the length of a writing assignment, for example. Translation assessments would, of course, also be differentiated in alignment with objectives.

Formal and Informal Assessments

As illustrated in the translation spotlights throughout this book, formal translation assessments may take multiple forms but should align with standards and objectives in order to determine the level of student mastery. Translations may be used to formally assess language or content objectives or may be assessed as an end product. Informal or formative assessments are used to check for student understanding during the instructional cycle prior to formal assessment in order to modify instruction as needed (Kern, 2000). Kern (2000) noted that assessment in language teaching has traditionally been summative. However, literacy-based language teaching must incorporate formative assessment due to its process orientation. These can be backward designed to help meet the vocabulary and rigor of summative assessments (Richards, 2013).

Types of formative assessment of translation activities might include class discussion, written comments on a translation draft, administering pre- and post-tests before and after an activity (Grahn & McAlpine, 2017; Kern, 2000) or the instructor circulating among students to check for understanding while they work. For translation activities, this would include whether students have moved beyond word-for-word to functional translation and whether students appear to be working toward mastery of content and language objectives. The author has found this type of assessment to be an essential component of intermediate translation activities to make sure that students are on track, particularly with their equivalence strategies. Additionally, students may often feel more comfortable with asking questions or to point out "aha" moments as the instructor circulates than to speak with the whole class listening. During data collection for Albrecht (2024), for example, multiple students pointed out collocations that they were having difficulty with as the author circulated. During the translation of an ad campaign activity (see Chapter 6 Translation Spotlight) in another intermediate class, the author noticed that some of the groups were making cultural assumptions which caused misalignment between the text and the new graphic. When multiple students or groups appear to have similar issues, the instructor can stop the activity and address the issue to the whole class or in small groups based upon students' needs. Comments or answers to questions during whole-class discussion of a translation activity can also serve as informal assessment of student mastery of language, culture, and/or content objectives.

Students can also engage in self- and informal peer assessment. For example, in Keyes et al. (2014), prior to a translation activity, the instructors modeled asking the question "Does it make sense?" (p. 21). Students subsequently used this strategy to assess each other's work: "Some of the best student translators evaluated to determine if a translation 'made sense' because students often constructed word-for-word translations that were nonsensical at the sentence level" (p. 21). These student analyses led to peer discussions about the nuanced appropriateness of translations, including with voice and word choice. The type of formative assessment or assessments used will depend upon the activity, objectives, and proficiency level.

From a TS perspective, evaluation of the approach used by the student should depend upon the objectives. That is, for example, if the translation includes syntactic difference that does not adversely affect meaning, this change should not affect the grade (Colina, 2002).

Translation Spotlight: Designing Language and Content Translation Assessments to Align with Standards and Objectives

Designing Translation Objectives

Translation activities may be designed and incorporated into existing content based upon applicable standards and objectives which are then modified to reflect the translation activity. The following steps are recommended for writing literacy-based translation activity objectives:

1. Identify content which a translation activity would work well to teach, whether language or other subject areas.
2. Make sure to select relevant standards and proficiency benchmarks/descriptors and that objectives exist and are aligned.
3. Modify or write new objectives to include what will be taught in the translation activity. This may include language, content, cultural or other objectives. Objectives should be specific and measurable, and content standards may need to be linked with English language proficiency or other relevant standards (Focus on learning, 2015).

These steps are modeled as follows, using the Chapter 9 dual-language family story project.

Identify content in which a translation activity would work well: Narrative.

The collaborative dual-language family story project in Chapter 9 works well to teach narrative because it takes into account diverse linguistic and cultural backgrounds.

Standards, proficiency benchmarks/descriptors and objectives should be aligned.

CEFR, Creative Writing (Council of Europe, 2020). *"Involves imaginative personal expression in a variety of text types"* is already written to align with the B2 descriptor *"Can write clear, detailed descriptions of real or imaginary events and experiences, marking the relationship between ideas in clear connected text, and following established conventions of the genre concerned"* (pp. 187–188).

ACTFL (The National Standards Collaborative Board, 2015). *"I can present information to narrate about my life"* (p. 11) is already written to align with the proficiency benchmark *"I can … express my thoughts about familiar topics, using [a] series of connected sentences through written language"* (p. 1).

CCSS (National Governors Association, 2010): CCSS.ELA-Literacy.W.7.3 *"Write narratives to develop real or imagined experiences or events using effective technique, relevant descriptive details, and well-structured event sequences"* is written to align with the CCSS proficiency benchmarks included in the Chapter 9 Translation Spotlight, including CCSS.ELA-Literacy.W.7.3.C, "*Use a variety of transition words, phrases, and clauses to convey sequence and signal shifts from one time frame or setting to another.*"

Within your course, objectives may have already been written for these standards and descriptors. If so, they would need to be modified to reflect the element of translation in the activity. If not, new aligned objectives would need to be written.

CEFR: For the model lesson, the CEFR descriptor was modified to align with the translation activity: *I can write a clear, detailed narrative of a family story in two languages, marking the relationship between ideas in clear connected text, and following established narrative and written conventions.*

The following elements of the objective will be measured in two languages and should be included in the rubric as illustrated in the following sample: Clarity (written conventions, accuracy), detail (descriptive vocabulary), clear connected text (transition words or phrases), and established narrative conventions (beginning, middle, and end; setting; characters; logical sequence of events).

ACTFL: For the model lesson, the proficiency benchmark was modified to reflect the assignment: *In two languages, I can write a story about my life, activities, events and other social experiences, using sentences and a series of connected sentences.* Specific narrative elements and written conventions that will be formally assessed should be included in the rubric, as illustrated in the following sample.

CCSS: For the model lesson, the proficiency benchmark was modified to reflect the assignment: *Through writing a narrative in two languages, I can engage and orient the reader by establishing a context and point of view and introducing a narrator and/or characters; organize an event sequence that unfolds naturally and logically through transition words; use descriptive words as a narrative technique; and provide a conclusion that follows from and reflects on the narrated experiences or events.* Written conventions that will be formally assessed should be included in the rubric, as illustrated in the following sample.

Some instructors prefer to use backward design (Richards, 2013). Through this approach, think about what learners should show mastery of through summative assessment after completing the translation activity. This is what they will be assessed on and what the objectives should reflect.

Assessing Translation Objectives

The rubric in Table 10.3 for the dual-language family story (Chapter 9 translation spotlight) demonstrates the alignment between objectives and assessment, keeping in mind that for the dual-language story, the story is the object of the summative assessment which might receive a grade. The rubric is worded for the additional language to reflect the analytical process and critical thinking required for a translation; for a home-language rubric, the "additional language" and "translation" wording could be removed under Description. Keep in mind that "can-do" descriptors are written for instructors to assess student work and for students to assess their own progress.

Conclusion

Multiple frameworks for translation standards, objectives, and assessment may be applied across language- and content-area-learning environments. It is the standards and objectives which place translation activities within a larger curriculum. Additionally, it is key that the translation activity selected aligns with standards, objectives and formal assessment. Objectives, activities, and assessments may need to be differentiated to most successfully meet the needs of linguistically and culturally diverse groups of learners.

Table 10.3 Rubric: I Can Write a Narrative in My Additional Language

Narrative element	My narrative in my additional language:			
	4	3	2	1
Clarity	Is clear because it follows the conventions in my writing checklist with accuracy	Is mostly clear but does not accurately follow 1–2 of the conventions in my writing checklist	Is somewhat unclear because it does not accurately follow 3–4 of the conventions in my writing checklist	Is unclear because it does not follow the conventions in my writing checklist
Description	Uses rich, descriptive precise vocabulary to convey meaning for my intended audience in the additional language. I have considered how meaning might change in my translation based upon cultural difference and my word choice.	Uses some descriptive vocabulary, but it may not always convey meaning for my intended audience in the additional language	Uses very little descriptive vocabulary, which affects how successfully I convey meaning for my intended audience in the additional language	Does not use descriptive vocabulary, or the vocabulary I use does not convey meaning for my intended audience.
Connected text	Demonstrates connected text and sequence through consistent use of transitions	Mostly demonstrates connected text and sequence, although a few transitions could be added	Is missing transitions, making some of the text seem disconnected or hard to follow, although a few transitions connect the text and indicate sequence.	Does not include transitions to connect the text or indicate sequence.

Narrative conventions	Follows clear narrative conventions because I have a clear beginning, middle, and end; a setting; characters.	Mostly follows clear narrative conventions, but is missing or has incompletely developed one of the following: a clear beginning, middle, and end; a setting; characters.	Irregularly follows narrative conventions and is missing or has incompletely developed two of the following: a clear beginning, middle, and end; a setting; characters.	Does not follow narrative conventions because it is missing all of the following: a clear beginning, middle, and end; a setting; characters.
Written conventions	Uses accurate written conventions in spelling, punctuation, and grammar. Infrequent errors do not distract from meaning.	Reflects some inaccuracy in written conventions in spelling, punctuation, and grammar. Errors occasionally distract from meaning.	Reflects frequent inaccuracy in written conventions in spelling, punctuation, and grammar. Errors frequently distract from meaning.	Is unclear because of dominant inaccuracy in written conventions in spelling, punctuation, and grammar. Errors completely distract from meaning.
TOTAL:				

11
Considerations for Literacy-Based Language Teacher Preparation

Although pedagogical translation is a strategy that can be incorporated in any environment with bi- or multilingual learners, its successful implementation has been resoundingly connected to teacher preparation from scholars in TS, education, and applied linguistics (González-Davies, 2017; Jidai et al., 2017; Laufer & Girsai, 2008; Pacheco et al., 2015). Despite this connection, translation is still generally not included in teacher preparation or professional development programs (Fois, 2020). This chapter therefore outlines key considerations in preparing pre- and in-service teachers to implement translation for literacy learning. It will start with a general overview of who language and literacy teachers are. This will be followed by recommendations for incorporating translation into existing classroom structures, then move to recommendations for including translation into in-service teacher professional development and teacher preparation programs. The chapter will end with a Translation Spotlight on unit planning.

Who Are Language Teachers? Who Are Literacy Teachers?

Who are language teachers and who are literacy teachers? The simple answer might be that language teachers teach in world or second language programs, and literacy teachers teach reading and writing. However, an extension for language teaching might include language for specific purposes; heritage language instruction; and bilingual education, in which two languages are used to teach content, including language arts. More broadly speaking, some claim that all teachers are—or ought to be—language teachers, especially given the high number of bi- or multilingual learners within content-area courses (Walton et al., 2002). From the perspective of the CCSS in the United States, for example, teachers across content areas are responsible for English language and literacy development (García & Flores, 2014). This intersection of language and content involves "discourse, complex text, explanation, argumentation, purpose, structure of text, sentence structures, and vocabulary practice" (p. 152). Language is therefore "action and practice" (p. 152).

The reasoning process involved in the conclusion that all teachers are language teachers can be applied to literacy instruction. When considering the unique skills required to read within discrete content areas, some claim that all teachers are also—or ought to be—literacy teachers (Kirsten, 2019). Literacy-based language pedagogies may be considered at all levels and in all content areas. According to Kern (2000), "The single most important factor in attaining the goals of a literacy-based curriculum is highly qualified language teachers" (p. 316). To be highly qualified, language teachers need a high level of competence in spoken and written language; cultural knowledge; familiarity with literature; ability to mediate between multiple perspectives and meanings, learners' cultures and target language culture; and academic coursework and mentoring. Additionally, language teaching must align with Available Designs, as described in a pedagogy of multiliteracies, and teachers should be aware of broader sociocultural contexts in which communication is taking place (Kern, 2000).

Key Considerations in Implementing Translation for Literacy-based Learning

When implementing pedagogical translation, instructors may draw upon multiple existing skills, plan for vulnerability while making changes, and learn and implement new skills and strategies.

Drawing on Existing Skills

Although instructors or program directors wishing to incorporate translation may feel uncomfortable doing so, drawing upon existing skills and knowledge can be helpful in implementing translation as a new strategy (David et al., 2019). Existing skills might include providing scaffolding, differentiated instruction, and language and literacy expertise (Kultti & Pramling, 2018; Pacheco et al., 2015; Puzio et al., 2013). For example, an instructor already skilled at scaffolding student learning could deliberately apply this framework to translation as a new pedagogical strategy across multiple age and language-learning levels. Kultti and Pramling (2018) observed that the scaffolding provided to students directly impacted the skills acquired through translation of children's songs in a bilingual preschool. They found that instructors scaffolded student learning by introducing antonyms and synonyms prior to the translation activities. Student comprehension might also be scaffolded prior to beginning a translation activity by activating prior knowledge or schema (Kern, 2000).

Similarly, teachers already differentiating instruction by learning level and type of learner could differentiate in a translation activity. Taking the translation of a medical intake form as an example (Colina & Albrecht, 2020), for older primary students (for example, bilingual students who are already translating for their families, see Welch 2015), secondary or post-secondary students, translation of the form could incorporate the following differentiated approaches:

- Choose targeted vocabulary from a word bank to fill in the blanks, OR
- Choose from a selection of vocabulary words to fill in each blank (for example, an informal term used in common speech versus the formal medical term, thus requiring distinction in register), OR
- Translate terms by using an online dictionary (again requiring recognition of and distinction between informal and formal vocabulary), OR
- Work with syntactic considerations in tense, word order, and so forth, OR
- Work with pragmatic considerations regarding patient response to the translated form

Depending upon the learners in a given environment, one or a variety of these approaches could be utilized.

Differentiated instruction might also be determined by the range of languages spoken in the classroom, with the instructor speaking some or none of the languages (Puzio et al., 2013; Sneddon et al., 2012). In this case, translation activities could be differentiated as follows:

- Students speaking the same home language could work on a translation from the home language into the target language, or vice versa. In Sneddon et al. (2012), for example, two primary student speakers of Albanian wrote a bilingual Albanian–English children's story together, with parents supporting writing in the home language.

- Students could start with a text in the target language and translate into their home language, independently or collaboratively if possible. In (Rowe, 2018), primary students added their peers' translations of their own stories, generating multilingual texts and positioning each other as experts. While this activity was targeted toward primary-aged learners, it demonstrates the flexibility of translation as a strategy, as the complexity of the text could be modified to apply to a broad range of ages and language levels.
- Students could write a story in their home language and translate it to the target language individually or collaboratively (see e.g. Celic & Seltzer, 2013).

Instructors might also capitalize on their own target language and/or literacy expertise in discussions of the source text or of student translations. An instructor in Pacheco et al. (2015), for example, questioned students about their home-language vocabulary choice after noticing that students speaking the same home language had chosen different words in translation for the same word in English, initiating a rich conversation regarding nuance of meaning and character, and requiring in-depth comprehension of the source text. Target language discussions might also include elements of the source author's craft, comprehension strategies like inference, or the linguistic and cultural meaning of idiomatic expressions which students might have difficulty understanding (Pacheco et al., 2015).

Colina and Albrecht (2020) described five steps for incorporating translation activities into existing world language content. These may also be applied in other language-teaching environments. The steps include:

1. Determine what your students are linguistically ready to do so that objectives and activities may be designed around student capability
2. Determine standards and goals/objectives, as applicable (see this book, Chapter 10)
3. Determine what content you might build a translation activity around
4. Plan the activity, including considerations regarding what prior knowledge your students need; advance preparation of materials; and procedures for the activity, including already-existing structures for introducing new material
5. Plan for formative and/or summative assessment to align with objectives, and reflect upon the success of the activity, including with students. For example, did students demonstrate mastery of the objectives? What went well? What could be improved? Were the instructions clear? Were there any surprising outcomes?

Instructors may find that several, if not all, of the steps align with planning structures that they are already implementing, or, in other words, that they can draw on existing pedagogical expertise in incorporating translation strategies.

Vulnerability and Change

Multiple factors can affect teachers' approaches to literacy-based language teaching and learning. Monolingual or standard language ideologies and policies can affect teachers' approaches to language teaching and learning, and, as a result, many instructors are socialized into monolingual practices in which first language use by either instructor or student is never acceptable (Cummins, 2019). This might include community language school or post-secondary world language instructors who are teaching assistants and who have had little to no instruction in pedagogy beyond their own experience as students. Regarding a plurilingual teaching approach, Esteve (2020) noted that "…adopting a plurilingual approach certainly involves deeply reconceptualizing teachers' current–mostly monolingual–classroom practices" (p. 417). Language teacher education should therefore "first challenge teachers' own beliefs about language and the way they teach it" (p. 417). While Esteve spoke from a plurilingual perspective, it could be argued that any approach moving beyond monolingualism would require a similar self-examination.

Teachers may also believe that incorporating home languages is not their job, as in primary and secondary language arts classrooms in Pacheco et al. (2015). Consequently, the implementation of bilingual strategies such as pedagogical translation may require recognition of institutional and personal language ideologies and the need for a change in teaching stance—as well as the acquisition of new skills (Linares, 2022). Indeed, "Teachers have tremendous power in choosing how to enact language policy within their classrooms, and with the right instructional tools they can wield this power to learn about students' linguistic strengths and leverage these strengths in instruction" (Pacheco et al., 2015, p. 51).

Exercising agency in enacting language policy may entail a shift from perception of learner deficiency to strength (Moll et al., 1992), including as bilingual speakers. From a monolingual SLA perspective, the language being taught is that of a monolingual native speaker, which positions learners as deficient with an impossibly high standard to reach (Widdowson, 2003). Indeed, "The ideas about how a foreign language should be taught, or what generally constitutes adequate achievement, do not generally come from an experience of foreignness" (p. 156). In the French region of Alsace, for example, French and German are the languages of instruction, with complete separation between the two. The goal of this separation is to avoid learner mixing of languages, as "language mixing is still considered an obstacle for the acquisition of normative academic language" (Hartmann & Hélot, 2020, p. 97). As instructors and institutions tend to be initiated into this approach both socially and politically, a shift to a bilingual teaching stance can be difficult and must be deliberate and explicit. As instructors undergo a shift from monolingual to bilingual teaching, however, the curricula becomes more relevant and accessible to students, and it becomes the norm to draw upon multiple languages for teaching and learning, with students positioned as bilingual subjects who can draw upon all of their linguistic resources to communicate and make meaning (Keyes et al., 2014; Kultti & Pramling, 2018). This shift, then, becomes a shift from monolingual toward bilingual teaching and language learning as bilingualization.

A shift toward bilingual teaching may also require that instructors recognize underlying assumptions about language and identity (Hartmann & Hélot, 2020; Linares, 2022). Many world language and bilingual programs continue to approach language teaching from a monolingual perspective, with the assumption that languages are to be taught and learnt separately. According to Linares (2022), "Instructors may become aware of erroneous assumptions that they previously held about their students' linguistic and cultural identity when language instruction was confined to the target language" (p. 52). Erroneous assumptions may include positioning students as deficient in both their home language and the language of schooling and therefore in need of remediation, particularly for the acquisition of academic language. Efforts toward linguistic remediation then mask underlying raciolinguistic ideology "that frames the home language practices of racialized communities as inherently deficient" (Flores, 2020, p. 24). Recognition of discourses of languagelessness or deficiency should result in the aforementioned shift toward bilingual teaching, with bilingual learners positioned as language experts able to draw upon all of their linguistic resources or as language architects who use their agency to make linguistic choices in their design of meaning (Flores, 2020; Pacheco et al., 2015). As students are taught from a bilingual stance, their identities as bilingual speakers are therefore recognized and valued (Hartmann & Hélot, 2020).

The implementation of pedagogical translation may also require instructors at all levels to recognize and work with their own vulnerability as they implement this new strategy. According to Linares (2022), this vulnerability stems from the fact that instructors may "no longer consider themselves as linguistic experts in all classroom languages" (p. 68). Moreover, beyond questions of linguistic competence, language instructors who have taught monolingually may feel they lack the skill to implement bilingual strategies such as translation. This may be in world language instruction, in which monolingual ideology is in play and instructors teach only in the target language, or in a monolingual classroom in which second language learners are present, again with monolingual ideology in play.

Nevertheless, if the overarching goals of language instruction are bilingualization and the development of biliteracy (Carreira, 2020; Widdowson, 2003), then bilingual strategies like pedagogical translation may be most appropriate, regardless of whether the instructor and/or other students in the class are monolingual. For example, young sequential bilinguals, or students learning a second language after acquiring a first, "are able to achieve biliteracy only if educators use their repertoires to leverage these children's participation in meaningful learning and literacy experiences" (Reyes et al., 2012, p. 309). This may require, for example, that instructors recognize their role as gatekeepers of student classroom use of home language varieties. Recognition of this privileged role may lead instructors to allow students to translate from source texts which the instructor does not understand and which the students would need to explain (Linares, 2022).

However, instructors must also be aware of students' cultural positioning toward these texts, as an outsider assumption that students are relating culturally to a text may be incorrect (David et al., 2019). In a study of two intermediate, secondary mixed heritage–additional language Spanish courses, the author selected the poem *Wheels/Ruedas* for translation from David Bowles's volume *They Call Me Güero/Me dicen Güero,* given the cultural and linguistic authenticity of the text, including a much more informal register than is typically taught in language classrooms and that is more reminiscent of casual speech. However, some HLLs did not perceive value in the activity as they thought the vocabulary they did not know was only related to ranching, which they did not find relevant to their lives. This led to the recommendation that HLLs be included in text selection in order to find texts they relate to (Albrecht, 2024).

Although recognition and utilization of student language variety positions students as experts, instructors may feel their authority is being challenged and therefore deny students the opportunity to use their home languages (Widdowson, 2003). However, rather than basing decisions on instructional approach on feeling their authority is being challenged, instructors may instead deliberately position themselves as learners, collaborators, or experts depending upon the learning context (Linares, 2022). According to Pacheco et al. (2015), "As teachers interact with students, they have the opportunity to learn more about students' heritage languages, expertise, and background knowledge. As students interact with the teacher and their peers, they have the opportunity to learn more about the text, language, and the tools needed for comprehending both" (p. 53). Instructors therefore must recognize and determine the instructional role they will play in a given translation activity.

World language or content-area classes with both mono- and bilingual students are complex learning environments which require a higher level of differentiation. Pacheco et al. (2015) recommended that in content-area classes with both mono- and bilingual students, instructors have monolingual students translate between dialects or registers of their own language while emergent bilingual students translate into their home language. In mixed heritage–world language classes, the question of linguistic and/or cultural authenticity arises for heritage speakers of the language, returning to the potential need for involving students in text selection. This might include providing a thematic text set (including multimodal, see Chapter 9) from which students could choose their own texts (Albrecht, 2022), then comparing both translations and thematic approaches in the different texts, all of which require higher-order thinking. Depending upon the course, the standards and objectives, these conversations might take place in the home language, the additional language, or both.

As instructors shift their conception of the role they are playing in literacy-based translation activities, a shift in conception of professional identity may also occur (McLaughlin, 2022). That is, their role may shift from that of instructor to facilitator of cross-linguistic mediation: "It is incumbent upon us to reflect with our students on the complex search for approximation between languages, considering such features as the sounds, word choice, and cultural milieu of a text. By incorporating translation as process in language education, within K–12 and higher education settings alike, educators can model translingual and transcultural competence as a perpetual work-in-progress" (Linares, 2022, p. 110). Instructors may not only need to change their stance regarding language instruction, but also acquire the skills needed to implement pedagogical translation. Speaking about world language classrooms, Pintado-Gutiérrez (2022) placed the responsibility for acquiring research-based pedagogical tools such as translation on teachers so that they can best meet the expected language-learning outcomes for their students.

Studies across ages and language learner type therefore point to the need for change in teaching stances based upon monolingual or standard language ideologies or policies in order for acquisition and implementation of new, research-based pedagogies like pedagogical translation to take place. As Lippi-Green (2011) pointed out, it is in schools that standard language ideology is introduced. While instructors may effect these changes individually based upon their own practice, changes may also be implemented at the institutional level through curricular changes as well as professional training (Linares et al., 2022). Because "the local context dramatically impacts the take up of new pedagogical practices" (David et al., 2019, p. 271), this may be an argument in favor of considering implementation of translation at the institutional level, as well as for its long-term sustainability within a given locale. David et al. (2019) recommended a combination of design elements of the translation strategy used in their study, combined with design elements based on local context. Their strategy was part of the larger Project TRANSLATE, designed specifically to develop reading comprehension and "positive literacy outcomes" (p. 258). TRANSLATE instructional theory consists of implementing the TRANSLATE protocol, in which students engage in problem solving across languages, and teachers observe and integrate students' metalinguistic knowledge in a move toward student content-area learning.

The study itself described how teachers adapted the new strategy to their existing instructional practices, finding that "the local and sometimes unpredictable nature of the student practices that are the focus of these pedagogies make it challenging to specify for teachers exactly how to do it in an a priori way" (David et al., 2019, p. 271). The authors concluded that certain elements of an instructional practice may be designed in advance, while teachers must be guided in other aspects to make design choices that are appropriate to their context. Because of the fluid nature of this pedagogy, the authors recommended that instructors have space within professional development to share their experiences and understandings as they implement new pedagogies. Additionally, in the interest of maintaining an equal instructor–student power balance, the authors highlighted the importance of seeking student reflections on their own practices as new instructional approaches are designed and implemented.

Learning and Implementing New Skills

Instructors might need to acquire a variety of new skills when implementing pedagogical translation. For example, in a literacy-based language-learning program, teachers must set "appropriate literacy goals" (David et al., 2019, p. 265), with translation being the strategy used toward meeting these goals (see Chapter 10 of this book for setting objectives to be met through translation activities).

Metalinguistic Awareness

Because of the important role played by metalinguistic awareness in translation, instructors will need to expect, recognize, and cultivate statements pointing to student metalinguistic awareness or understanding of how language works (Beauvais & Ryland, 2021). They will therefore need to understand characteristics of metalinguistic awareness, such as lexical or syntactic reflection. According to Kultti and Pramling (2018), it is challenging for students to develop linguistic and metalinguistic skills, and instructors must therefore deliberately plan for the development of these skills through scaffolding. Similarly, Beauvais and Ryland (2021) demonstrated the important role of instructor cultivation of metalinguistic awareness after studying the implementation of literary translation in a series of British secondary world language workshops. They argued that during literary translation activities, student use of metalinguistic skills positively impacted the development of linguistic and literary skills, provided that the metalinguistic skills were recognized and drawn upon by the instructor. Literary awareness was an awareness of "what makes language aesthetically pleasing" (Beauvais & Ryland, 2021, p. 293) and tended to combine positively with metalinguistic awareness. On the other hand, linguistic awareness by itself, described as an awareness of how English and/or another language works, was often couched negatively by students in terms of similarity and difference. The authors found that "questions from the workshop leaders that required pupils to call upon existing *linguistic* skills, rather than guesswork from metalinguistic insight, were often met with silence or even distress" (pp. 295–96, emphasis in original), therefore recommending that instructors select literary texts likely to encourage metalinguistic discussion.

Translation and Equivalence

Returning to the application of TS theory to pedagogical translation, instructors incorporating pedagogical translation should have some awareness of the role of equivalence in translation, whether or not they speak another language. The approach to equivalence may be determined by both content and language learning objectives if translation is being used as a means. Equivalence may be addressed at the phonological, lexical, semantic, syntactic, and pragmatic levels, as well as at the levels of register, genre, and discourse. At any level of equivalence, cultural difference may come into play and should be considered as should the function of the translation.

Literacy Teaching and Pedagogical Translation

Several approaches to incorporating pedagogical translation in language learning are available through the pedagogy of multiliteracies. First, students might respond to the Available Designs in a source language text, namely, their knowledge of language and vocabulary, register, genre, and so forth. For example, in investigative reporting in English, students might expect to find answers to the five W's of who, what, where, when, and why, and the H, how. They might also expect to find short sentences and vocabulary such as "alleged" if the article is reporting a crime.

According to Kern (2000), literacy-based language teaching includes the three elements of Responding, Revising, and Reflecting. Each will be discussed in turn and connected to pedagogical translation. Depending upon the language and learning objectives, translation may be incorporated at any of the three phases but will not necessarily be incorporated at every phase, particularly when there is some overlap in the process, as will be seen in what follows. First, for Responding, readers cannot understand a text without some type of response, so students must first have the opportunity to respond to a text. From the lens of Rosenblatt's (1978) Reader Response Theory, reading is student- rather than text-centered, and student response involves making meaning from the text. Many monolingual activities have been developed to encourage this type of reader response, such as mapping characters' "hearts," or values and motivations, within a heart-shaped map; tracing the outline of a student's body and then charting characters' cultural values within the outline; and drawing a response to a scene in a text (Short, 2024). Monolingual activities such as these could be modified, with students being encouraged to draw upon their full linguistic repertoires or to translanguage, as part of their meaning-making processes. Similarly, in language classrooms, students might also be given the option to translanguage orally while responding in writing in the target language. Activities such as these might be incorporated for Responding, followed by a translation activity at the Revising or Reflection step.

Bilingual strategies such as pedagogical translation might also be considered as means of reader response. For example, students could translate a short bilingual text like a poem or an excerpt from a bilingual text and compare their translations to the professional translation. They could then evaluate similarities and differences between translations, determining if, how and why these differences matter. Instructor strategies for selection of texts for translation then also come into play. Beyond questions of textual authenticity discussed in Chapter 7, texts must also be considered in terms of their potential for discussion. Keyes et al. (2014) found that "Choosing shorter excerpts from a text with rich, figurative language yielded the most thoughtful debate and discussion" (p. 22). Similarly, Escamilla et al. (2014) and Kultti and Pramling (2018) recommended short texts that are rich in meaning and figurative language use even for very young EB learners, as these types of texts encourage students to move from a focus on lexical or semantic meaning to narrative structure or meaning-centered translations.

The second element of literacy-based language instruction is Revising. This includes placing a text within a different contextual frame and requires in-depth reading. Because translation includes attention to cultural difference, it may be considered by definition as placing a text within a different contextual frame and hearkens to Venuti's (2018) domestication and foreignization of texts. Intermediate or advanced students could be encouraged to decide whether their "revision" would best be domesticated or foreignized in the target language context, to defend their decision and to identify what elements of their revision reflect their choice.

The third element of literacy-based language teaching is Reflecting. At this phase, students reflect upon the author's possible intentions and how the meaning might change if the text were written differently, reflection that is inherent in the act of translation. In this sense, students may reflect upon how lexical or syntactic choice, among others, might change the meaning of the text. Based upon Lefevere's (2017) conception of translation as an act of rewriting which makes plain not only the author's intention but also ideologies, students may also reflect upon how the act of translation might make plain or obscure the author's original intent and ideological perspective, as well as represent their own. For older intermediate or advanced learners, this is a case in which post-colonial translation theory might be used to frame the process, as it requires translators to pay attention to the historic influences and dominant-culture influence on the texts chosen for translation and subsequently translated (Niranjana, 1992). Because translation is always considered an attempt at bridging the source and target culture (Venuti, 2017), instructors should plan to encourage learners to reflect upon the cultural elements present in the text and how their own cultural schema might affect their approach to translation. Because of the cultural reflection required, it is important for instructors to explicitly teach that culture is mediated through language.

In-Service Professional Development for Translation

While needed shifts in teaching stance and pedagogy may take place individually among in-service teachers, they should also take place institutionally. Processes proposed by translator trainers (see e.g., Kelly, 2014, and Orlando, 2019) might be utilized in professional development for language teachers, to be modified by educational contexts such as primary, secondary, or post-secondary education; bilingual, heritage, second, or world language; and by other local needs and contexts as determined by the various stakeholders, such as institutions, instructors, and students (Orlando, 2019). This type of professional development might require interdisciplinary cooperation between translation and education professionals, with translation professionals interested in pedagogical uses of translation providing expertise (see e.g., Center for Educational Resources in Culture, Language and Literacy, 2021).

While additional steps are more fully developed elsewhere in this volume, they are briefly described here. Professional development should include needs assessment based upon context (as discussed previously), clearly delineated learning outcomes, varied pedagogical approaches, program and learner assessment, and collaboration. Kelly (2014) recommends that professional development should include clear, assessable objectives based upon Bloom's taxonomy (see also Chapter 10). When considering objectives, curriculum for translator trainers might focus on alignment with professional translator standards (Kelly, 2014); language educator professional development could focus on standards alignment (see Chapter 10). Mellinger (2021) and Orlando (2019) recommend varied pedagogical approaches and highlight balancing teacher- and student-centered approaches along with incorporation of relevant technology (see Chapter 8; see also the following Translation in Teacher Preparation Programs) and experiential learning. Professional development should include program assessment through participant feedback opportunities such as surveys as well as learner assessment (see Chapter 10). These approaches may, of course, be used to model instructional strategies that participants might use in their own classrooms.

Translation in Teacher Preparation Programs

Bilingual teaching strategies like pedagogical translation must also be incorporated into teacher preparation programs. However, as discussed in Chapter 1, an approach to introducing innovative pedagogies like pedagogical translation in language teacher preparation rests upon the multilingual and social turns in SLA because of dominant monolingual societal and institutional norms. According to Keyes et al. (2014), as of the turn of the twenty-first century, "Nearly 40% of the world's population receives an education that minimally uses, neglects or avoids a student's heritage language ... This continuity presents a profound pedagogical problem" (p. 17). This problem has resulted in gross instructional inequities (Flores, 2020; García, 2014). As noted by Kramsch (2022), "Pity the language teacher in our multilingual times!" (p. 467).

To address these inequities and the reality of bi- or multilingual student populations, Keyes et al. (2014) recommended "innovative instructional approaches that leverage the strengths of bilingual students" (p. 17). If taught in programs which prepare instructors for any type of language teaching, innovative instructional approaches such as pedagogical translation might not only disrupt monolingual and standard language ideologies affecting approaches to language teaching, but provide instructors with strategies that meet the needs of the world's multilingual language learners. As the world's population is increasingly bi- or multilingual, it makes sense to approach language teacher preparation through a bi- or multilingual approach to language and literacy, rather than a monolingual approach, across language-learning environments.

These shifts should be tied to the multilingual and social turns in SLA, especially as even multilingual instructors tend to teach monolingually given the high symbolic capital of the dominant language (Kramsch, 2022). Kramsch suggests that instructors open to a multilingual approach in SLA also have a translanguaging stance within translingual practices. Translingual practices involve fluid, social language use by multilingual speakers, often within zones of language contact, to make meaning in and outside of educational environments. These practices are linked to multiliteracies, which move beyond conceptions of literacy as reading and writing in a single language to communication in multiple modes and languages (Canagarajah, 2013).

Communication in multiple languages by definition involves language hierarchy, although this is often implicit. Explicit attention to decolonization as a part of preparation for multilingual instruction is therefore also key, and, interestingly, can be related to decolonization in professional translation practices, allowing marginalized voices to be heard. However, "Featuring diverse vocabularies in a class syllabus or in an edited volume on multilingualism is no guarantee of a decolonized mindset. It only transforms multilingualism into multiple monolingualisms in a hierarchical relationship to one another" (Kramsch, 2022, p. 469). According to Kramsch (2022), a multilingual teaching approach focuses on language diversity and involves "multimodality, translation, and translanguaging…untranslatabilities and incompatibilities of meaning" (p. 470), all of which again tie to multiliteracies. Within teacher educator programs, then, instructors must be aware of their own approach to multilingual language instruction and the relationship of their instructional practices to that approach. They can then make explicit the need for a shift to a multilingual stance in order to incorporate innovative strategies.

Carreres and Noriega-Sánchez (2021) recommended that strategies used in translator training might inform approaches to world language teaching, particularly in terms of communicative, task-based activities. Similarly, Carreira (2016) recommended top-down activities for bilingual or heritage language learners as these strategies focus more on discourse and teach grammar and vocabulary as determined by context. Translation may function as a communicative, task-based, top-down activity in many learning environments, and it may also function as a bottom-up activity focused on grammar and vocabulary typically used with world language learners. While this flexible array of possibilities shows the benefit of using translation in language teaching, its range also points to the need for training within teacher preparation programs and beyond.

Conclusion

Successful implementation of pedagogical translation requires preparation, both in teacher preparation and in-service professional development. Multiple areas may be addressed, including identifying one's language-teaching stance, drawing on existing skills, teaching translation without speaking all students' languages, and strategies for incorporating translation into existing or new programs. With intentionality, translation can be incorporated into language and literacy teaching across diverse learning environments and student demographics.

Translation Spotlight: Sample Thematic Unit, Cultural Identity

This sample thematic unit will be assumed to span two weeks and to be modifiable according to context. It will include the following:

- A sampling of prior translation activities that might be incorporated into larger thematic units, including paired texts and standard and multimodal text sets for translation
- Suggestions for modification of units by grade, skill level, language learning environment, and translation stance
- Possible linguistic and cultural learning outcomes for the unit, which would drive formulation of learning objectives in the classroom

Table 11.1 Translation Spotlight: Sample Thematic Unit

Sample Thematic Unit: Cultural Identity
Learning level: Intermediate mid
Estimated time: Two weeks (the unit may take longer if the instructor chooses to take time to evaluate and offer feedback on student work in between assignments)
Key questions:
- What are some of my cultural practices? How do these practices affect my identity? How do cultural practices affect others' identities?
- How can I use my own and others' narrative writing to identify and express cultural perspectives?
- How can I use translation to identify and compare cultural practices and perspectives?
- How can I use translation to recognize and apply linguistic norms in my home and an additional language?

Unit Objectives: By the end of this unit, I will be able to use translation to:

CEFR (Council of Europe, 2020):
- *Produce clearly organized translations from (Language A) into (Language B) that reflect normal language usage but may be over-influenced by the order, paragraphing, punctuation, and particular formulations of the original (p. 218).*
- *Produce translations into (Language B), which closely follow the sentence and paragraph structure of the original text in (Language A), conveying the main points of the source text accurately, though the translation may read awkwardly (p. 218).*
- *Write clear, detailed descriptions of real or imaginary events and experiences marking the relationship between ideas in clear connected text, and following established conventions of the genre concerned in my home and an additional language (p. 188).*

ACTFL (2017):
- *Compare cultural products and practices to help me understand perspectives.*
- *Understand the main idea and key information in short fictional and informational texts that I read.*
- *Tell a story about my life, activities, events, and other social experiences, using sentences and series of connected sentences.*

(continued)

Table 11.1 (continued)

CCSS (National Governors Association, 2010):
- CCSS.ELA-Literacy.RL.7.4: *Determine the meaning of words and phrases as they are used in a text, including figurative and connotative meanings; analyze the impact of rhymes and other repetitions of sounds (e.g., alliteration) on a specific verse or stanza of a poem or section of a story or drama.*
- CCSS.ELA-Literacy.L.7.1: *Demonstrate command of the conventions of standard English grammar and usage when writing or speaking.*
- CCSS.ELA-Literacy.W.7.3: *Write a narrative to develop real or imagined experiences or events using effective technique, relevant descriptive details and well-structured event sequences.*

Prior Skills:
- Students will need to know how to review each other's writing for content, in this case, narrative elements. If they have not done this before, they will need this to be modeled. If they have done this before, they will need a refresher.

Day 1 (Monday): Introduction of thematic unit, *Cultural Identity*
- Key questions: *What are some of my cultural practices? How do these practices affect my identity? How do cultural practices affect others' identities?*
- Translation lesson: Translation of proverbs (Chapter 6)

Day 2 (Tuesday): Thematic unit, *Cultural Identity*
- Key questions: *What are some of my cultural practices? How do these practices affect my identity? How do cultural practices affect others' identities?*
- Translation activity: Translation of an advertisement (Chapter 6)

Day 3 (Wednesday): Thematic unit, *Cultural Identity*
- Key questions: *How can I use my own and others' narrative writing to identify and express cultural perspectives?*
- Translation activity: Guided writing through translation of a vignette
- Homework: Talk to family member(s) about topics for a bilingual family story

Day 4 (Thursday): Thematic unit, *Cultural Identity*
- Key questions: *How can I use my own and others' narrative writing to identify and express cultural perspectives?*
- Additional activity: Write a narrative vignette about a memorable family event or tradition in the new language, following the narrative structure of the translated text.
- Evaluation: Narrative vignette. This should be evaluated for the narrative elements present in the objectives. Linguistic elements may be graded if they are present in the objectives.
- Additional activity: Finish narrative vignette as needed in class.
- Translation activity: Introduce the family story writing activity (Chapter 9).
- Homework: Begin drafting the collaborative family story.

Day 5 (Friday): Thematic unit, *Cultural Identity*
- Key question: *How can I use my own narrative writing to identify and express cultural perspectives?*
- Formative assessment: Have students share their work as partners or in small groups; circulate and check on student work.
- Additional activity (multimodal): Begin illustrations for the dual-language family story writing activity.

Day 6 (Monday): Thematic unit, *Cultural Identity*
Formative evaluation: Dual-language family story, home language draft due. Additional revisions and illustrations will be finished in class during the week.
- Students will peer-review each other's work for narrative content, using the writer's checklist (Chapter 9).
- At this point, the instructor may want to take the rest of the week to review and comment on student work prior to resuming the activity, provided that the instructor speaks the home language. If not, the story will serve as the basis for translation into the new language, which will be evaluated, and the translation activity can move forward.

Day 7 (Tuesday): Thematic unit, *Cultural Identity*
Translation activity: Students will do the following:
- Translate the home language version of their story into the additional language
- Use their writing checklist to check for required narrative and linguistic elements, including conventions

Evaluation:
- Students will peer review a classmate's work for narrative elements only, using the writing checklist.
- Formative assessment: Translation into the additional language due. At this point, the instructor may want to take time to review and comment on student work prior to resuming the activity.

Day 8 (Wednesday): Thematic unit, *Cultural Identity*
- Activity: Students will work on the design of their story, including adding title page and illustrations. If they are working digitally, they may also consider adding audio in both languages.

Day 9 (Thursday): Thematic unit, *Cultural Identity*
- Activity: Students will work on the design of their story, including adding title page and illustrations. If they are working digitally, they may also consider adding audio in both languages.

Day 10 (Friday): Authors' celebration (Thematic unit, *Cultural Identity*)
Activity: Host an authors' celebration, including family members, so that students and their family members can share each other's work.
Unit evaluation: The dual-language family story will be assessed according to the unit objectives.

Table 11.1 (continued)

Expansion/Modification:
- Include Language Arts standards in other languages
  - Change the focus throughout the unit from narrative to another genre
- Include content-area standards in the home and new languages
- Include oral objectives for the collaborative interactions in class

Conclusion: Moving Toward Equitable Outcomes in Language Learning

Language teaching and learning can be fraught with systemic inequities. Dominant languages may be taught at the expense of minoritized languages. Dominant pedagogies may be applied when culturally sustaining pedagogies would be more appropriate. And monolingual ideologies can smother bi- or multilingual students' experiences and abilities, leading to inequitable instructional practices and learning outcomes. Additionally, language teaching environments are increasingly diverse, with EBs learning content in monolingually instructed classrooms, heritage speakers of the language being taught in world language classrooms or in dedicated after-school programs, and second language learners in pull-out classes. The good news is that pedagogical translation can be highly effective for language and socially situated literacy learning while addressing these inequities and complex learning environments.

Pedagogical translation moves us from the grammar translation focus on teaching discrete grammar points and translation use at the policy level that perpetuate and sustain social inequities to linguistic and cultural learning and to equitable outcomes for diverse learners because it is a way to "recenter...pedagogy around a multilingual experience" (McLaughlin et al., 2022, p. 113). Linares (2022) pointed out that "Disparities in education begin long before individuals enter higher education programs, making pedagogical projects such as [pedagogical translation] paramount in fostering equity from early years of schooling" (p. 70). Similarly, McLaughlin et al. (2022) noted, "Translation is an invaluable tool for developing more equitable pedagogies in higher education" (p. 113). The conclusion will therefore summarize the benefits of incorporating translation into language and content-area learning while looking forward to its contribution to more equitable learning environments and literacy-based language acquisition.

Most initial studies on pedagogical translation focused on language-learning benefits. However, with the passage of time, studies began to shift to plurilingual, pluricultural, or translanguaging foci, reflecting the social and multilingual turns in SLA theory and the need for socially contextualized language learning, and coinciding with socially situating literacy within New Literacy Studies. Overall, socially situated literacy instruction within language teaching focuses on discourse rather than only linguistic structure or only communication (Kern, 2000). In this way, the social and cultural contexts in which language is and will be used drive the language-learning process through authentic literacy events. This process, particularly in the move toward bilingualization and biliteracy (Hornberger & Skilton-Sylvester, 2000; Widdowson, 2003), may also be used to challenge dominant power norms evident in language and literacy practices.

Pedagogical translation can be used across language levels and language-learning environments for linguistic, cultural, and literacy learning. Linguistic objectives ranging from morphology to syntax may be addressed in a translation activity, as may content-area objectives such as narrative structure. However, from a plurilingual or translanguaging stance, translation activities should also be designed to draw upon students' linguistic and cultural backgrounds and to build intercultural competence, ICC (Byram, 2020; González-Davies, 2017; Pym, 2018), and/or intercultural being (Phipps & González, 2004). Inclusion of these components aligns with a socially situated literacy approach to language teaching.

To select texts for pedagogical translation activities, text types may be wide ranging, from oral to written and from advertisements to the literary canon. However, texts must be carefully selected to align with learners' linguistic abilities, to reflect the source culture, and to be relevant to learners. To represent multiple perspectives on a single theme, as well as to expand the pedagogical ways in which translation activities might be used to support other objectives, texts might be paired or grouped in sets, including multimodal sets. Given the daily exposure many students have to today's digital world, they will find digital multimodal texts and translation activities relevant and engaging.

Both professional and pedagogical translation are fundamentally collaborative endeavors (Carreres & Noriega-Sánchez, 2021). Collaboration may involve extensive discussion and negotiation for meaning among peers, often giving students learning a language in an unfamiliar or new environment agency and voice. It may also involve learners' families or communities in sharing linguistic and cultural knowledge and in dual-language writing, thus bridging the gap between school and home. Collaboration may be highly engaging to learners, thus affecting motivation. However, collaborative structures need to be carefully designed in advance in order to maximize the effectiveness of collaborative work.

Finally, successful incorporation of pedagogical translation requires careful teacher preparation. Preparation might include assessment of institutional, personal, or learner language ideologies and how these might affect the use of a bilingual strategy in the classroom; or professional development opportunities hosted by institutions which have made the decision to utilize translation. Preparation might also include assessment of areas of strength which could be drawn upon in designing and implementing translation activities, as well as areas of reluctance or growth which need to be recognized and addressed.

For those thinking about incorporating translation with a focus on developing socially situated literacy into their language-learning environments, consider using the following questions which span the prior chapters in this book as a template for your planning:

1 What are the governmental or institutional approaches to teaching language and to biliteracy development? Are monolingual ideologies in play? How can I position the use of translation in order to gain support?
2 Do I have monolingual or standard language ideologies, and have my students and/or their families internalized monolingual ideologies which might impact the incorporation of translation in my teaching?
3 Can translation be incorporated into a larger curriculum, or will it need to be piloted at the individual classroom level?
4 What type of translation activities are my students developmentally and linguistically ready for? How can translation activities support my students' linguistic development?
5 How can the use of translation in my language-learning environment support the development of my students' biliteracy?
6 How can my students' diverse linguistic and cultural backgrounds be drawn upon in translation activities?
7 How can intercultural competence, ICC, or intercultural being be developed through translation activities?
8 Am I already using texts that could be incorporated into a translation activity? What other texts might I use? Do they meet the criteria for authenticity?
9 Should I develop a text set specifically for translation? Am I already using a text set or text sets from which I can draw translation activities?
10 How can I incorporate multimodality into translation activities that support literacy development? Do I have the knowledge and materials needed to do so? If not, how can I acquire them?

11. How will I use collaborative structures for translation activities? What types of norms need to be established for collaboration to be successful?
12. How can I involve students' families or communities in translation activities?
13. What types of existing linguistic, cultural, and literacy objectives might be addressed through translation activities? For new courses, how can I incorporate translation to meet linguistic, cultural, and literacy objectives?
14. What types of activities presented in this volume might be used to meet these objectives? Will the activities I am considering need to be adapted to meet students' needs? Will students find the activities useful and/or authentic?
15. How will these activities be informally assessed?
16. How will they be formally assessed? Will the assessments align with objectives and activities?
17. What teaching skills and content mastery do I already have that I can draw upon to support the incorporation of translation into my teaching repertoire?
18. What types of activities am I already using in my teaching environment that might be adapted into or supported by translation activities?
19. For mixed groups of mono- and bi/multilingual speakers, should I consider intralinguistic as well as interlinguistic translation?
20. How can I plan to incorporate student feedback and my own reflection to improve activities I have used?

In the introduction, I expressed the hope that educators across language levels and teaching environments might benefit from the literacy-based pedagogical translation strategies presented in this book. Ultimately, however, the greatest hope is that diverse learners might find their own and other languages and cultures validated and their worlds bridged and broadened through engaging in pedagogical translation.

REFERENCES

ACTFL. (2017). *ACTFL Can-Do statements: Performance indicators for language learners*. ACTFL. Retrieved June 7, 2025 from https://www.actfl.org/uploads/files/general/Resources-Publications/Can-Do_Benchmarks_Indicators.pdf.

ACTFL. (2024). *Teach grammar as a concept in context*. ACTFL Language Connects. Retrieved June 5, 2025 from https://www.actfl.org/educator-resources/guiding-principles-for-language-learning/teach-grammar-as-a-concept-in-context.

ACTFL. (2024). *ACTFL proficiency guidelines*. Retrieved from https://www.actfl.org/uploads/files/general/Resources-Publications Retrieved June 5, 2025 from ACTFL_Proficiency_Guidelines_2024.pdf.

Ada, A. F. & Campoy, F. I. (2014). *¡Sí! Somos latinos*. Santillana USA.

Adab, B. J. & Schäffner, C. (2000). *Developing translation competence* (1st ed.). J. Benjamins.

Adami, E. & Ramos Pinto, S. (2020). Meaning-(re)making in a world of untranslated signs: Towards a research agenda in multimodality, culture and translation. In M. Tomalin, M. Boria, A. Carerres & M. Noriega-Sánchez (Eds), *Beyond Words: Translation and Multimodality* (pp. 104–30). Routledge.

Adamson, A. & Jenson, V. (Directors). (2001). *Shrek I* [Film]. DreamWorks Distribution.

Adichie, C. N. (2009, July). *The danger of a single story* [Video]. TED Conferences. https://www.ted.com/talks/chimamanda_ngozi_adichie_the_danger_of_a_single_story?utm_campaign=tedspread&utm_medium=referral&utm_source=tedcomshare.

Agirdag, O. (2010). Exploring bilingualism in a monolingual school system: Insights from Turkish and native students from Belgian schools. *British Journal of Sociology of Education*, 31(3), 307–21.

Alamillo, L. (2007). Selecting Chicano children's literature in a bilingual classroom: Investigating issues of cultural authenticity and avoiding stereotypes. *Association of Mexican American Educators Journal*, 1(1), 53–62.

Alarcón, F. X. (2005). *Angels ride bikes: And other fall poems/Los ángeles andan en bicicleta: Y otros poemas de otoño*. Children's Book Press.

Albrecht, S. (2022). *The mediation of translation for K-12 biliteracy acquisition in bilingual and heritage language learning environments* [Doctoral dissertation, The University of Arizona].

Albrecht, S. (2024). Pedagogical translation for reading comprehension in mixed HL–L2 secondary classrooms. *Foreign Language Annals*, 58(1), 90–110.

Albrecht, S., Hill, C. & Smith, K. J. (2023). Pedagogical translation as a culturally sustaining pedagogy in bilingual language environments. *English in Texas*, 53(2), 42–9.

Albrecht, S. & Navarrete-Burks, L. (2025). My favorite field trip: Creating a translanguaging space for urban explorers in a state park. *Science Scope*, 48(4), 40–6.

Albury, N. J. (2015). Your language or ours? Inclusion and exclusion of non-indigenous majorities in Māori and Sámi language revitalization policy. *Current Issues in Language Planning*, 16(3), 315–34. https://doi: 10.1080/14664 208.2015.984581.

Álfaro, C. (2019). Preparing critically conscious dual-language teachers: Recognizing and interrupting dominant ideologies. *Theory into Practice*, 58(2), 194–203. https://doi.org/10.1080/00405841.2019.1569400.

Alfer, A. (2017). Entering the translab: Translation as collaboration, collaboration as translation, and the third space of 'translaboration'. *Translation and Translanguaging in Multilingual Contexts*, 3(3), 275–90.

Amanti, C. (2019). The (invisible) work of dual language bilingual education teachers. *Bilingual Research Journal*, 42(4), 455–70.

Angelelli, C. V. (2009). Using a rubric to assess translation ability: Defining the construct. In A. Pym & Torres- Simón (Eds), *Testing and Assessment in Translation and Interpreting Studies*. John Benjamins.

Angelo, T. & Cross, K. P. (1993). *Classroom assessment techniques: A handbook for college teachers*. Jossey-Bass A Wiley Imprint.

Argueta, J. (2016). *Somos como las nubes/We are like the clouds*. Groundwood Books Ltd.

Arreguín-Anderson, M. G. & Ruiz-Escalante, J. (2016). Dichos y adivinanzas: Literary resources that enhance science learning and teaching in the bilingual classroom. *Multicultural Literature for Latino Bilingual Children: Their Words, Their Worlds*, 167–82.

Arriba García, C. D. (1996). *Introducción a la traducción pedagógica*. Universidad de Oviedo.

Augustyn, P. (2013). Translation and bilingual practice for German vocabulary teaching and learning. *Die Unterrichtspraxis/Teaching German*, 46(1), 27–43.

Axelrod, Y. & Cole, M. W. (2018). 'The pumpkins are coming... vienen las calabazas... that sounds funny': Translanguaging practices of young emergent bilinguals. *Journal of Early Childhood Literacy*, 18(1), 129–53.

Babino, A. & Stewart, M. A. (2018). Remodeling dual language programs: Teachers enact agency as critically conscious language policy makers. *Bilingual Research Journal*, 41(3), 272–97. https://doi.org/10.1080/15235882.2018.1489313.

Baer, B. J. & Koby, G. S. (2003). *Beyond the ivory tower: Rethinking translation pedagogy* (1st ed.). John Benjamins.

Barnes, K. (2018). Reviving pedagogical translation: An investigation into UK learners' perceptions of translation for use with their GCSE Spanish studies and beyond. *Translation and Translanguaging in Multilingual Contexts*, 4(2), 248–81.

Baker, M. (2018a). *In other words: A coursebook on translation*. Routledge.

Baker, M. (2018b). Translation and the Production of Knowledge(s). *Alif: Journal of Comparative Poetics*, (38), n.p. https://link-gale-com.uhd.idm.oclc.org/apps/doc/A592785826/AONE?u=txshracd2590&sid=bookmark-AONE&xid=bd5bd336.

Barrera, R. B. & Quiroa, R. E. (2003). The use of Spanish in Latino children's literature in English: What makes for cultural authenticity? In D. L. Fox and

K. G. Short (Eds), *Stories matter: The complexity of cultural authenticity in children's literature* (pp. 247–65). National Council of the Teachers of English.

Barton, D., Hamilton, M. & Ivanič, R. (Eds). (2000). *Situated literacies: Reading and writing in context.* Psychology Press.

Bartlett, L. (2007). To seem and to feel: Situated identities and literacy practices. *Teachers College Record 109*(1), 51–69.

Bassnett, S. (2014). *Translation.* Routledge.

Beaudrie, S. M. (2016). Advances in Spanish heritage language assessment. *Advances in Spanish as a Heritage Language*, 143–58.

Beaudrie, S., Ducar, C. & Potowski, K. (2014). *Heritage language teaching: Research and practice.* McGraw-Hill.

Beauvais, C. & Ryland, C. (2021). 'We actually created a good mood!': Metalinguistic and literary engagement through collaborative translation in the secondary classroom. *Language, Culture and Curriculum*, 34(3), 288–306.

Beeman, K. & Urow, C. (2013). *Teaching for biliteracy: Strengthening bridges between languages.* Caslon Publishing.

Belpoliti, F. & Plascencia-Vela, A. (2013). Translation techniques in Spanish for heritage learners' classroom: Promoting lexical development. In D. Tsagari & G. Floros (Eds), *Translation in language teaching and assessment* (pp. 59–90). Cambridge Scholars Publishing.

Benjamin, W. (1968). *The task of the translator* (H. Zohn, Trans.). In H. Arendt (Ed.), *Illuminations* (pp. 69–82). Schocken Books.

Bialystok, E. (2001). Metalinguistic aspects of bilingual processing. *Annual Review of Applied Linguistics, 21*, 169–81.

Biggs, J. (2003). Aligning teaching and assessing to course objectives. *Teaching and Learning in Higher Education: New Trends and Innovations*, 2(4), 13–17.

Bintz, W. P. & Ciecierski-Madara, L. M. (2022). Middle grades readings: Where are the picture books? *Middle School Journal, 53*(3), 22–30.

Bishop, R. S. (1990). Mirrors, windows, and sliding glass doors. *Perspectives: Choosing and Using Books for the Classroom*, 6(3), ix–xi.

Block, D. (2003). *The social turn in second language acquisition.* Georgetown University Press.

Blommaert, J. (2015). Language, asylum, and the national order. In J. Blommaert and B. Rampton (Eds), *Language and superdiversity* (pp. 31–58). Routledge.

Botelho, M. J. (2021). Reframing mirrors, windows, and doors: A critical analysis of the metaphors for multicultural children's literature. *Journal of Children's Literature, 47*(1), 119–26.

Bourdieu, P. (1991). *Language and symbolic power.* Harvard University Press.

Bowles, D. (2020). *Me dicen Güero.* Vintage Español.

Bowles, D. (2018). *They Call Me Güero.* Cinco Puntos Press.

Bowles, D. (2014). Translating "An Otomi song of spring" from the Nahuatl codex songs of Mexico. *Translation Review, 88*(1), 37–44. https://doi:10.1080/07374836.2014.887342.

Bradeanu, L. (2007). From centre to margins: Multicultural aspects of the origins of proverbs. *Culture, 52*, 22–6.

Brochin, C. & Medina, C. L. (2017). Critical fictions of transnationalism in Latinx children's literature. *Bookbird: A Journal of International Children's Literature*, 55(3), 4–11.

Brun-Mercer, N. (2021, June 23). Understanding (and using) CEFR criterial features for grammar instruction. *World of Better Learning*. Retrieved from: https://www.cambridge.org/elt/blog/2021/06/23/using-cefr-criterial-features-for-grammar-instruction/.

Burgo, C. (2018). Meeting student needs: Integrating Spanish heritage language learners into the second language classroom. *Hispania, 100*(5), 45–50.

Butzkamm, W. & Caldwell, J. A. (2009). *The bilingual reform: A paradigm shift in foreign language teaching*. Gunter Narr Verlag Tübingen.

Byram, M. (2020). *Teaching and assessing intercultural communicative competence: Revisited*. Multilingual matters.

Cai, C. & Eisenstein Ebsworth, M. (2018). Chinese language varieties: Pre- and in-service teachers' voices. *Journal of Multilingual and Multicultural Development, 39*(6), 511–25.

California English language development standards (Electronic edition): Kindergarten through grade 12 (2023). Common Core State Standards California. California Department of Education. Retrieved from https://www.cde.ca.gov/sp/ml/documents/eldstndspublication14.pdf.

Canagarajah, A. S. (Ed.). (2013). *Literacy as translingual practice: Between communities and classrooms*. Routledge.

Canga-Alonso, A. & Rubio-Goitia, A. (2016). Students' reflections on pedagogical translation in Spanish as a foreign language/Reflexiones sobre la traducción pedagógica de estudiantes de español como lengua extranjera. *TEJUELO. Didáctica de la Lengua y la Literatura. Educación, 23*, 132–57.

Cano, J. & Ruiz, N. T. (2020). "Wait! I don't get it! Can we translate?": Explicit collaborative translation to support emergent bilinguals' reading comprehension in the intermediate grades. *Bilingual Research Journal, 43*(2), 157–77.

Carreira, M. (2016). Innovative strategies for heritage language learners through macro based teaching: Pedagogical principles and implementation strategies for heritage language and mixed classes. In M. Fairclough and S. M. Beaudrie (Eds.), *Innovative Strategies for Heritage Language Teaching: A Practical Guide for the Classroom* (pp. 162–183). Georgetown University Press. https://ebookcentral-proquest-com.uhd.idm.oclc.org/lib/uhdowntown/detail.action?docID=4713650

Carreira, M. & Kagan, O. (2018). Heritage language education: A proposal for the next 50 years. *Foreign Language Annals, 51*(1), 152–68.

Carreira, M., Garrett-Rucks, P., Kemp, J. A., & Randolph, L. J. (2020). Introduction to heritage language learning: An interview with María Carreira. In P. Garrett-Rucks & L. J. Randolph (Eds.), *Southern Conference on Language Teaching: Dimension 2020*. Southern Conference on Language Teaching.

Carreres, Á. (2014). Translation as a means and as an end: Reassessing the divide. *The Interpreter and Translator Trainer, 8*(1), 123–35.

Carreres, Á. & Noriega-Sánchez, M. (2018). *Mundos en palabras: Learning advanced Spanish through translation*. Routledge

Carreres, Á. & Noriega-Sánchez, M. (2021). The translation turn: A communicative approach to translation in the language classroom. *Research-publishing*.

Cazden, C. B. (1974). Teaching as a linguistic process in a cultural setting. In N. L. Gage (Ed.), *The Conference on Studies in Teaching: Report of Panel 5*. National Institute of Education.

REFERENCES

Celic, C. & Seltzer, K. (2013). Translanguaging: A CUNY-NYSIEB Guide for Educators. https://www.cuny-nysieb.org/wp-content/uploads/2016/04/Translanguaging-Guide-March-2013.pdf. Retrived June 5, 2025, from https://www.cuny-nysieb.org/wp-content/uploads/2016/04/Translanguaging-Guide-March-2013.pdf

Center for Applied Linguistics. (n.d.). *Heritage language assessment module.* Retrieved from https://www.cal.org/flad/heritage-language-assessment-module/.

Center for Educational Resources in Culture, Language and Literacy. (2021). *Cross-cultural thinking through translation and interpretation.* The University of Arizona. https://cercll.arizona.edu/project/tandi/.

Center for Teaching and Learning. (2024). *Using roles in group work.* Retrieved from https://ctl.wustl.edu/resources/using-roles-in-group-work/.

Chappell, S. & Faltis, C. (2007). Spanglish, bilingualism, culture and identity in Latino children's literature. *Children's Literature in Education, 38,* 253–62.

Chen, S. (2017). Note-taking in consecutive interpreting: New data from pen recording. *Translation & Interpreting: The International Journal of Translation and Interpreting Research, 9*(1), 4–23.

Chen, X. (2019). Selecting and using dual language books in classrooms and beyond. *NABE Journal of Research and Practice, 9*(3–4), 191–197.

Cisneros, S. (1994). *La casa en Mango Street.* Vintage Español.

Cisneros, S. (1983). *The House on Mango Street.* Bloomsbury.

Cintas, J. D. & Remael, A. (2021). *Subtitling: Concepts and practices.* Routledge.

Colina, S. (2015). *Fundamentals of Translation.* Cambridge University Press.

Colina, S. (2002). Second language acquisition, language teaching and translation studies. *The Translator, 8*(1), 1–24.

Colina, S. (2008). Translation quality evaluation: Empirical evidence for a functionalist approach. *The translator, 14*(1), 97–134.

Colina, S. & Albrecht, S. (2020). *Incorporating translation in the world language classroom.* Pressbooks. https://opentextbooks.library.arizona.edu/scolina/

Colina, S. & Angelelli, C. V. (Eds). (2017). *Translation and interpreting pedagogy in dialogue with other disciplines.* John Benjamins.

Colina, S. & Lafford, B. A. (2017). Translation in Spanish language teaching: The integration of a "fifth skill" in the second language curriculum. *Journal of Spanish Language Teaching, 4*(2), 110–23.

Conteh, J. & Meier, G. (Eds). (2014). *The multilingual turn in languages education: Opportunities and challenges.* De Gruyter.

Cook, G. (2010). *Translation in language teaching: An argument for reassessment.* Oxford University Press.

Cook, V. (1992). *Linguistics and second language acquisition.* St. Martin's Press.

Cope, B. & Kalantzis, M. (2013). "Multiliteracies": New literacies, new learning. In M. R. Hawkins (Ed.), *Framing languages and literacies* (pp. 105–35). Routledge.

Corcoll, C. (2013). Developing children's language awareness: Switching codes in the language classroom. *International Journal of Multilingualism, 10*(1), 27–45. https://doi.org/10.1080/14790718.2011.628023.

Cordingley, A. & Manning, C. F. (2016). What is collaborative translation? In A. Cordingley and C. F. Manning (Eds), *Collaborative translation: From the Renaissance to the digital age* (pp. 1–30). Bloomsbury.

Coste, D., Moore, D. & Zarate, G. (2009) *Plurilingual, pluricultural competence.* Council of Europe. https://rm.coe.int/168069d29b.

Council of Europe (2001). *Common European framework of reference for languages: Learning, teaching, assessment—Companion volume*. Council of Europe Publishing.

Council of Europe (2018). *Common European framework of reference for languages: Learning, teaching, assessment—Companion volume*. Council of Europe Publishing.

Council of Europe (2020). *Common European framework of reference for languages: Learning, teaching, assessment—Companion volume*. Council of Europe Publishing. https://www.coe.int/en/web/common-european-framework-reference-languages.

Cummins, J. (1979). Linguistic interdependence and the educational development of bilingual children. *Bilingual Education Paper Series*, 3(2), 222–51. California State University.

Cummins, J. (2007). Rethinking monolingual instructional strategies in multilingual classrooms. *Canadian Journal of Applied Linguistics*, 10(2), 221–40.

Cummins, J. (1980, 2016). The cross-lingual dimensions of language proficiency: Implications for bilingual education and the optimal age issue. *TESOL Quarterly*, 50(4), 940–44. http://www.jstor.org/stable/44984725

Cummins, J. (2019). The emergence of translanguaging pedagogy: A dialogue between theory and practice. *Journal of Multilingual Education Research*, 9(13), 19–36.

Cummins, J. (1981). The role of primary language development in promoting educational success for language minority students. In California State Department of Education (Ed.), *Schooling and language minority students: A theoretical framework* (pp. 3-50). California State University.

Dagilienė, I. (2012). Translation as a learning method in English language teaching. *Studies About Languages*, 21, 124–129.

Dallacqua, A. K. (2022). Reading when the world is on fire: Teaching with comics and other multimodal text sets. *Study & Scrutiny: Research on Young Adult Literature*, 5(2), 38–63.

Daly, N. (2018). The linguistic landscape of English–Spanish dual language picture books. *Journal of Multilingual and Multicultural Development*, 39(6), 556–6.

David, S. S., Pacheco, M. B. & Jiménez, R. T. (2019). Designing translingual pedagogies: Exploring pedagogical translation through a classroom teaching experiment. *Cognition and Instruction*, 37(2), 252–75.

Davin, K. J. & Heineke, A. J. (2017). The Seal of Biliteracy: Variations in policy and outcomes. *Foreign Language Annals*, 50(3), 477–632.

De Oliveira, L. C. & Smith, B. E. (2019). Preface. In L. C. De Oliveira & B. E. Smith (Eds), *Expanding literacy practices across multiple modes and languages for multilingual students* (pp. vii-ix). Information Age Publishing.

Dewi, H. D. (2015). *Comparing two translation assessment models: Correlating student revisions and perspectives* [Dissertation, Kent State University].

Dougherty, J. (2021). Translanguaging in action: Pedagogy that elevates. *ORTESOL Journal*, 38, 19–32. https://files.eric.ed.gov/fulltext/EJ1305313.pdf.

Draggett, P., Conlin, C., Ehrsam, M., & Millán, E. (2014). *Temas: AP Spanish Language and Culture*. Vista Higher Learning.

Duolingo (n.d.). *How does Duolingo work?* Duolingo for Schools. https://duolingoschools.zendesk.com/hc/en-us/articles/6830287021581-How-does-Duoli

ngo-work-#:~:text=Duolingo%20works%20along%20this%20framew
ork,our%20users%20through%20translation%20exercises.
Edwards, V. (2015). Literacy in bilingual and multilingual education. In W. E. Wright, S. Boun, & O. García, O. (Eds.), *The Handbook of bilingual and multilingual education* (First Edition) (pp. 75–91). Wiley-Blackwell.
Echauri Galván, B. & García Hernández, S. (2020). Traducir en colores: la traducción como herramienta de evaluación de la comprensión lectora en inglés como lengua extranjera/ Translating in colours: Translation as an assessment tool for reading comprehension in English as a second language. *Revista Española de Pedagogía*, 78(276), 327–46. https://doi.org/10.22550/REP78-2-2020-07.
Educational Research Institute. (2024, February 21). *The global call to action for heritage language education*. https://menntavisindastofnun.hi.is/is/global-call-hle.
Ek, L. D., Sánchez, S. N. & Guerra, M. J. (2016). Cultural multiliteracies: Integrating technology with Latino children's literature. In E. R. Clark, B. B. Flores, H. L. Smith, & D. A. González (Eds.), *Multicultural literature for Latino bilingual children: Their words, their worlds* (pp. 207–22). Rowman & Littlefield.
Ellis, R. (2003). *Task-based language learning and teaching*. Oxford University Press.
Equipboard. (2019). *The muffin man in 10 different languages* [Video]. https://youtu.be/r996xvCDhuY?feature=shared.
Escamilla, K., Geisler, D., Hopewell, S., Sparrow, W. & Butvilofsky, S. (2009). Using writing to make cross-language connections from Spanish to English. In C. Rodríguez-Eagle (Ed.), *Achieving literacy success with english language learners: Insights, assessment, instruction* (pp. 141–56). Reading Recovery Council of North America.
Escamilla, K., Hopewell, S., Sparrow, W., Soltero-González, L., Ruiz-Figueroa, O. & Escamilla, M. (2014). *Literacy squared: Learning to read in a culturally and linguistically diverse world*. Caslon Publishing.
Esteve, O. (2020). Teacher agency in plurilingual learning contexts. In S. Laviosa & M. González-Davies (Eds), *The Routledge handbook of translation and education* (pp. 417–33). Routledge.
Even-Zohar, I. (1990). Polysystem theory. *Poetics Today*, 11(1), 9–26.
Fathom Events (2018). *The Sandlot: 25th anniversary - Ham homer clip* [video]. YouTube. https://www.youtube.com/watch?v=M62Kk5MvtLE.
Fenner, D. S. (2023). *California's ELA/ELD framework: Bringing it all together*. Colorín Colorado. https://www.colorincolorado.org/blog/californias-elaeld-framework-bringing-it-all-together.
Fenner, D. S. & Segota, J. (2023). *Standards that impact English language learners*. Colorín Colorado. https://www.colorincolorado.org/article/standards-impact-english-language-learners.
Fernández-Costales, A. (2021). Audiovisual translation in primary education. Students' perceptions of the didactic possibilities of subtitling and dubbing in foreign language learning. *Meta*, 66(2), 280–300. https://doi.org/10.7202/1083179ar.
Figueiredo, D. (2010). Context, register and genre: Implications for language education. *Revista Signos*, 43(1), 119–41.

Firth, A. & Wagner, J. (1997). On discourse, communication, and (some) fundamental concepts in SLA research. *The Modern Language Journal, 81*(3), 285–300.

Flores, N. (2020). From academic language to language architecture: Challenging raciolinguistic ideologies in research and practice. *Theory into Practice, 59*(1), 22–31.

Floros. G. (2021). Pedagogical translation in school curriculum design. In J. Meng & S. Laviosa (Eds), *The Oxford Handbook of translation and social practices* (pp. 281–300). Oxford University Press. https://doi.org/ 10.1093/oxfordhb/ 9780190067205.013.20.

Focus on learning: Learning intentions and success criteria. (2015). National Council for Curriculum and Assessment. Retrieved from https://ncca.ie/ media/1927/assessment-workshop-1_ en.pdf.

Fois, E. (2020). ELT and the role of translation in developing intercultural competence. *Language and Intercultural Communication, 20*(6), 561–71, https:doi.org/10.1080/14708477.2020.1800025.

Fox, D. L. & Short, K. G. (Eds). (2003). *Stories matter: The complexity of cultural authenticity in children's literature.* National Council of Teachers of English.

Fránquiz, M. E., Leija, M. G. & Salinas, C. S. (2019). Challenging damaging ideologies: Are dual language education practices addressing learners' linguistic rights? *Theory Into Practice, 58*(2), 134–44.

Frawley, W. & Lantolf, J. P. (1985). Second language discourse: A Vygotskyan perspective. *Applied Linguistics* 6(1), 19–44.

Freire, P. (1970). *Pedagogy of the oppressed.* Seabury Press.

French, M. & Armitage, J. (2020). Eroding the monolingual monolith. *Australian Journal of Applied Linguistics, 3*(1), 91–114.

Ganuza, N. & Hedman, C. (2019). The impact of mother tongue instruction on the development of biliteracy: Evidence from Somali–Swedish bilinguals. *Applied Linguistics, 40*(1), 108–31.

García, O. (2009). Emergent Bilinguals and TESOL: What's in a Name? *TESOL Quarterly, 43*(2), 322–26.

García, O. (2014). US Spanish and education: Global and local intersections. *Review of Research in Education, 38*(1), 58–80.

García, O., Aponte, G. Y. and Le, K. (2020). Primary bilingual classrooms: Translations and translanguaging. In S. Laviosa and M. González-Davies (Eds), *The Routledge handbook of translation and education* (pp. 81–94). Routledge. https://doi.org/10.4324/9781315149674.

García, O., Bartlett, L. & Kleifgren, J. (2007). From biliteracy to pluriliteracies. In P. Auer and L. Wei (Eds.), *Handbook of multilingualism and multilingual communication, 5* (pp. 207–28). De Gruyter.

García, O. & Flores, N. (2014). Multilingualism and Common Core State Standards in the United States. In S. May (Ed.). *The multilingual turn: Implications for SLA, TESOL, and bilingual education.* Routledge.

García, O., Johnson, S. I. & Seltzer, K. (2017). *The translanguaging classroom: Leveraging student bilingualism for learning.* Caslon.

García, O. & Kleifgren, J. (2019). Translanguaging and literacies. *Reading Research Quarterly, 55*(4), 553–71.

García, O., & Leiva, C. (2014). Theorizing and enacting translanguaging for social justice. In A. Blackledge & A. Creese (Eds.), *Heteroglossia as practice and pedagogy* (pp. 199–216). Springer. https://doi-org.uhd.idm.oclc.org/10.1007/978-94-007-7856-6_11

Garza, C. L. (1996). *In my family/En mi familia*. Children's Book Press.

Gasca Jiménez, L. (2017). El efecto de la traducción pedagógica en la precisión morfosintáctica: un estudio preliminar con estudiantes avanzados de ESL. *Comunicación*, 26(2), 16–28.

Gasca Jiménez, L. (2019). La práctica de la traducción no profesional y la enseñanza de español como lengua de herencia: Análisis e implicaciones pedagógicas. *Hispania*, 102(3), 335–56. https://doi.org/10.1353/hpn.2019.0071

Gasca Jiménez, L. (2022). *Traducción, competencia plurilingüe y español como lengua de herencia (ELH)*. Routledge.

Gass, S. M., Behney, J., & Plonsky, L. (2020). *Second language acquisition: An introductory course*. Routledge.

Gee., J.P. (2012). *Social linguistics and literacies: Ideology in discourses* (4th ed.). Routledge.

Genesee, F. (1994). Integrating language and content: Lessons from immersion. *Educational Practice Reports* (No. 11). Center for Applied Linguistics.

Gile, D. (2009). *Basic concepts and models for interpreter and translator training*. John Benjamins.

Gillies, A. (2005). *Note-taking for consecutive interpreting: A short course*. St. Jerome Publishing.

Global Seal Statistics. (2023). *Global seal of biliteracy*. Retrieved June 5, 2025, from https://theglobalseal.com/statistics.

Goldsmith, A. Y. & Huang, K. (2017). Why we need more translated children's books from China: Addressing the one-way street of translation in the United States. *iConference 2017 Proceedings*.

Goltsev, E., Olfert, H. & Putjata, G. (2022). Finding spaces for all languages. Teacher educators' perspectives on multilingualism. *Language and Education*, 36(5), 437–50.

González-Davies, M. (2014). *Multiple voices in the translation classroom: Activities, tasks and projects*. John Benjamins.

González-Davies, M. (2016). A collaborative pedagogy for translation. In L. Venuti (Ed.), *Teaching translation: Programs, courses, pedagogies* (pp. 71–8). Routledge. https://doi.org/10.4324/9781315623139-9.

González-Davies, M. (2017). The use of translation in an integrated plurilingual approach to language learning: Teacher strategies and best practices. *Journal of Spanish Language Teaching*, 4(2), 124–35.

González-Davies, M. (2020). Developing mediation competence. In S. Laviosa and M. González-Davies (Eds), *The Routledge handbook of translation and education* (pp. 434–50). Routledge. https://doi.org/10.4324/9781315149674.

González-Davies, M. & Soler Ortínez, D. (2021). Use of translation and plurilingual practices in language learning: A formative intervention model. *Translation and Translanguaging in Multilingual Contexts*, 7(1), 17–40.

Gonzalez, R., & Ruiz, A. (2014). *My First Book of Proverbs / Mi primer libro de dichos* (S. Cisneros, Intro.). Lee & Low Books.

Goodier, T. & Szabo, T. (2018a). *Collated representative samples of descriptors for young learners: Resource of educators (Ages 7–10)*. Council of Europe.

Goodier, T., & Szabo, T. (2018b). *Collated representative samples of descriptors for young learners: Resource for educators (Ages 11–15)*. Council of Europe.

Grahn, L. & McAlpine, D. (2017). *The keys to strategies for language instruction: Engagement, relevance, critical thinking, collaboration*. ACTFL.

Greenberg, R. D. (2004). *Language and identity in the Balkans: Serbo-Croatian and its disintegration*. Oxford University Press.

Grosjean, F. (1989). Neurolinguists, beware! The bilingual is not two monolinguals in one person. *Brain and Language*, 36(1), 3–15.

Gu, C. & Lornklang, T. (2021). The use of picture-word inductive model and readers' theater to improve Chinese EFL learners' vocabulary learning achievement. *Advances in Language and Literary Studies*, 12(3), 120–26. https://doi.org/10.7575/aiac.alls.v.12n.3.p.120.

Goundareva, S. (2011). Effective methods for vocabulary teaching in ESL classrooms. *Journal of Language Education*, 15(2), 123–35.

Gurney, L. & Demuro, E. (2022). Tracing new ground, from language to languaging, and from languaging to assemblages: Rethinking languaging through the multilingual and ontological turns. *International Journal of Multilingualism*, 19(3), 305–24.

Halley, J., Heiserman, C., Felix, V. & Eshleman, A. (2013). Students teaching students: A method for collaborative learning. *Learning Communities Research and Practice*, 1(3), 1–18. http://washingtoncenter.evergreen.edu/lcrpjournal/vol1/iss3/7.

Halliday, M. A. K. (1978). *Language as social semiotic: The social interpretation of language and meaning*. University Park Press.

Halliday, M. A. K. (1964). Some methodological guidelines for contrastive analysis and error analysis. *Language Learning*, 14(3–4), 75–83.

Hartmann, E. & Hélot, C. (2020). Pedagogical affordances of translation in bilingual education. In S. Laviosa and M. González-Davies (Eds.), *The Routledge handbook of translation and education* (pp. 95–108). Routledge.

Haywood, L., Thompson, M. and Hervey, S. (2009). *Thinking Spanish translation: A course in translation method. Spanish to English*. Routledge.

Heath, S. B. (1982). What no bedtime story means: Narrative skills at home and school. *Language in Society*, 11(1), 49–76.

Henshaw, F. G. (2015). Learning outcomes of L2-heritage learner interaction: The proof is in the posttests. *Heritage Language Journal*, 12(3), 245–70.

Hernandez, J., Campoy, F. I. & Ada, A. F. (2018). *La Matadragones: Cuentos de Latinoamérica/The dragon slayer: folktales from Latin America*. New York, TOON Books.

Hernández, M. R. (1998). La traducción pedagógica en la clase de E/LE. En *Lengua y cultura en la enseñanza del español a extranjeros: actas del VII Congreso de ASELE* (pp. 249–56). Ediciones de la Universidad de Castilla-La Mancha.

Heugh, K., Li, X. & Song, Y. (2017). Multilingualism and translanguaging in the teaching of and through English: rethinking linguistic boundaries in an Australian University. In B. Fenton-Smith, P. Humphries & I. Walkinshaw (Eds), *English medium instruction in higher education in Asia-Pacific: issues and challenges from policy to pedagogy* (pp. 259–79). Springer.

Hoch, M. L., McCarty, R., Gurvitz, D. & Sitkoski, I. (2019). Five key principles: Guided inquiry with multimodal text sets. *The Reading Teacher*, 72(6), 701–10.

Hornberger, N. H. (1989). Continua of biliteracy. *Review of educational research*, 59(3), 271–96.

Hornberger, N. H. & Link, H. (2012). Translanguaging and transnational literacies in multilingual classrooms: A biliteracy lens. *International journal of bilingual education and bilingualism, 15*(3), 261–78.

Hornberger, N. H. & Skilton-Sylvester, E. (2000). Revisiting the continua of biliteracy: International and critical perspectives. *Language and Education, 14*(2), 96–122.

House, J. (2015). *Translation quality assessment: Past and present.* Taylor & Francis Group.

House, J. (2016). *Translation as communication across languages and cultures.* Routledge.

Howatt, A. P. R. (1984). *A history of English language teaching.* Oxford University Press.

Howatt, A. P. R. & Widdowson, H. G. (2004). *A history of English language teaching.* Oxford University Press.

Huang, Q. & Chen, X. (2016). Examining the text quality of English/Chinese bilingual children's picture books. *International Journal of Bilingual Education and Bilingualism, 19*(5), 475–87. https://doi.org/10.1080/13670 050.2015.1011076.

Huong, L. P. H. (2003, July). The mediational role of language teachers in sociocultural theory. *English Teaching Forum, 41*(3), 31–5.

Hurwitz, D. R. & Kambel, E. R. (2020). Redressing language-based exclusion and punishment in education and the Language Friendly School initiative, *Global Campus Human Rights Journal, 4*(1), 5–24 http://doi.org/20.500.11825/1707.

Incalcaterra McLoughlin, L. & Lertola, J. (2014). Audiovisual translation in second language acquisition. Integrating subtitling in the foreign-language curriculum. *The Interpreter and Translator Trainer, 8*(1), 70–83.

Jidai, Y., Kultti, A. & Pramling, N. (2017). In the order of words: Teacher–children negotiation about how to translate song lyrics in bilingual early childhood education. *Research on Children and Social Interaction, 1*(2), 199–221.

Jiménez, R. T., David, S., Fagan, K., Risko, V. J., Pacheco, M., Pray, L. & Gonzales, M. (2015). Using translation to drive conceptual development for students becoming literate in English as an additional language. *Research in the Teaching of English, 49*(3), 248–71.

Kachru, B. B. (1992). World Englishes: Approaches, issues and resources. *Language Teaching, 25*(1), 1–14.

Källkvist, M. (2013). Languaging in translation tasks used in a university setting: Particular potential for student agency? *The Modern Language Journal, 97*(1), 217–38.

Kelly, D. (2014). *A handbook for translator trainers.* Routledge.

Kelly, D., Adab, B. & Schäffner, C. (2000). Text selection for developing translator competence: Why texts from the tourist sector constitute suitable material. In C. Schaffner & A. Beverly (Eds), *Developing translator competence* (Vol. 38, pp. 157–70). John Benjamins. https://doi.org/10.1075/btl.38.15kel.

Kelly, N. & Bruen, J. (2015). Translation as a pedagogical tool in the foreign language classroom: A qualitative study of attitudes and behaviours. *Language teaching research, 19*(2), 150–68.

Kenny, M. A., (2008). Discussion, cooperation, collaboration: The impact of task structure on student interaction in a web-based translation exercise module. *The Interpreter and Translator Trainer, 2*(2), 139–164.

Kern, R. (2000). *Literacy and language teaching*. Oxford University Press.

Keyes, C. S., Puzio, K. & Jiménez, R. T. (2014). Collaborative translations: Designing bilingual instructional tools. *Journal of Education*, 194(2), 17–24.

Kiraly, D. (2000). *A social constructivist approach to translator education: Empowerment from theory to practice*. Routledge.

Kiraly, D. (2012). Growing a project-based translation pedagogy: A fractal perspective. *Meta: Journal des traducteurs/Meta: Translators' Journal*, 57(1), 82–95.

Kiraly, D. (2005). Project-based learning: A case for situated translation. *Meta: Journal des traducteurs/Meta: Translators' Journal*, 50(4), 1098–1111.

Kirsten, N. (2019). Improving literacy and content learning across the curriculum? How teachers relate literacy teaching to school subjects in cross-curricular professional development, *Education Inquiry*, 10(4), 368–84. https://doi.org/10.1080/20004508.2019.1580983.

Kittle, P. (2022). *Micro mentor texts: Using short passages from great books to teach writer's craft*. Heinemann.

Kochis, M., Kamin, D., Cockrill, B. & Besche, H. (2021). Understanding and optimizing group dynamics in case-based collaborative learning. *Medical Science Educator*, 31(6), 1779–88.

Koda, K. (2007). Reading and language learning: Crosslinguistic constraints on second language reading development. *Language Learning*, 57(1). 1–44.

Koshiba, K. (2017). Mediating between discourse worlds: Developing the symbolic competence of advanced-level bilingual learners of Japanese through translation. *Language and Intercultural Communication*, 17(2), 229–43. https://doi.org/10.1080/14708477.2016.1246556.

Kramsch, C. (2008). *Language and culture*. Oxford University Press.

Kramsch, C. (2012). Authenticity and legitimacy in multilingual SLA. *Critical Multilingualism Studies*, 1(1), 107–28.

Kramsch, C. (2022). Afterword: The multilingual turn in language teacher education. *Language and Education*, 36(5), 467–71. https://doi.org/10.1080/09500782.2022.2118542.

Kramsch, C. & Nolden, T. (1994). Redefining literacy in a foreign language. *Die Unterrichtspraxis/Teaching German*, 28–35.

Kramsch, C. & Steffensen, S. V. (2008). Ecological perspectives on second language acquisition and socialization. In N. H. Hornberger (Ed.), *Encyclopedia of language and education*, 8(1), (pp. 17–28). https://doi.org/10.1007/978-0-387-30424-3_194.

Krashen, S. (1981). Second language acquisition. *Second Language Learning*, 3(7), 19–39.

Kress, G. (2010). *Multimodality: A social semiotic approach to contemporary communication*. Routledge.

Kroskrity, P. V. (2004). Language ideologies. *A companion to linguistic anthropology*, 496, 517.

Kroskrity, P. V. (2015). Language ideologies: Emergence, elaboration, and application. In N. J. Enfield, P. Kockelman & J. Sidnell (Eds), *The Routledge Handbook of Linguistic Anthropology* (pp. 95–108). Routledge.

Kultti, A. & Pramling, N. (2017). Translation activities in bilingual early childhood education: Children's perspectives and teachers' scaffolding. *Multilingua*, 36(6), 703–25.

Kultti, A. & Pramling, N. (2018). "Behind the words": Negotiating literal/figurative sense when translating the lyrics to a children's song in bilingual preschool. *Scandinavian Journal of Educational Research*, 62(2), 200–12.

Kumagai, Y., & Kono, K. (2018). Collaborative curricular initiatives: Linking language and literature courses for critical and cultural literacies. *Japanese Language and Literature*, 52(2), 247–276.

Labov, W. (1969). The logic of non-standard English. In L. Burke, T. Crowley & A. Girvin (Eds), *The Routledge Language and Cultural Theory Reader* (2000) (pp. 456–66). Routledge.

Lafond, S. (2023). *An introduction to the Common Core State Standards*. Colorín Colorado. Retrieved from https://www.colorincolorado.org/article/introduction-common-core-state-standards.

Laufer, B. & Girsai, N. (2008). Form-focused instruction in second language vocabulary learning: A case for contrastive analysis and translation. *Applied Linguistics*, 29(4), 694–716. https://doi.org/10.1093/applin/amn018.

Lave, J. & Wenger, E. (1991). *Situated learning: Legitimate peripheral participation*. Cambridge University Press.

Laviosa, S. (2020). Content-based instruction. In S. Laviosa & M. González-Davies (Eds), *The Routledge handbook of translation and education* (pp. 127–42). Routledge. https://doi.org/10.4324/9781315149674.

Laviosa, S. (2022). Language teaching in higher education within a plurilingual perspective. *L2 Journal*, 14(2), 12–31.

Laviosa, S. (2014). *Translation and language education: Pedagogic approaches explored*. Routledge.

Laviosa, S. (2019). Translanguaging and translation pedagogies. In H. V. Dam, M. N. Brøgger and K. K. Zethsen (Eds.), *Moving boundaries in translation studies* (pp. 181–199). Routledge.

Lee, L. (1994). L2 writing: Using pictures as a guided writing environment. *Rocky Mountain Modern Language Association Conference*. Educational Resources Information Center. https://files.eric.ed.gov/fulltext/ED386951.pdf

Lee, T. K. (2013). *Translating the multilingual city: Cross-lingual practices and language ideology*. Peter Lang.

Lefevere, A. (2017). *Translation, rewriting and the manipulation of literary fame*. Routledge.

Lertola, J. & Mariotti, C. (2017). Reverse dubbing and subtitling: Raising pragmatic awareness in Italian English as a second language (ESL) Learners. *The Journal of Specialised Translation*, 28(1), 103–21.

Li, W. (2010). Moment Analysis and translanguaging space: Discursive construction of identities by multilingual Chinese youth in Britain. *Journal of Pragmatics*, 43(5), 1222–35.

Li, W. (2022). Translanguaging, multimodality, southern theory, and pedagogical possibilities. *Pedagogies: An International Journal*, 17(4), 408–12. https://doi.org/10.1080/1554480X.2022.2143090.

Li, W. & García, O. (2022). Not a first language but one repertoire: Translanguaging as a decolonizing project. *RELC Journal*, 53(2), 313–24. https://doi.org/10.1177/00336882221092841.

Lichtman, K. & VanPatten, B. (2021). Was Krashen right? Forty years later. *Foreign Language Annals*, 54(2), 283–305.

Lin, A. M. (2015). Conceptualising the potential role of L1 in CLIL. *Language, Culture and Curriculum*, 28(1), 74–89.

Linares, E. (2022). The challenges and promise of classroom translation for multilingual minority students in monolingual settings. *L2 Journal*, 14(2), 51–74.

Lippi-Green, R. (2011). *English with an accent: Language, ideology and discrimination in the United States*. Taylor & Francis.

Lipski, J. M. (2008). *Varieties of Spanish in the United States*. Georgetown University Press.

Liu, Y. & Fang, F. (2022). Translanguaging theory and practice: How stakeholders perceive translanguaging as a practical theory of language. *RELC journal*, 53(2), 391–99.

Lo, S. (2023). Pedagogical translation for vocabulary learning: The parallel-text approach. *Taiwan Journal of TESOL*, 20(2), 97–135.

Los mejores libros que leí en 2018. (2018). *Linternas y bosques: Literatura infantil y juvenil*. https://linternasybosques.com/2019/01/05/los-mejores-libros-ilustrados-que-lei-en-2018/comment-page-1/.

Louie, B. & Davis-Welton, K. (2016). Family literacy project: Bilingual picture books by English learners. *The Reading Teacher*, 69(6), 597–606.

Lupo, S. M., Strong, J. Z., Lewis, W., Walpole, S. & McKenna, M. C. (2018). Building background knowledge through reading: Rethinking text sets. *Journal of adolescent & adult literacy*, 61(4), 433–44. https://doi.org/10.1002/jaal.701.

MacGregor-Mendoza, P. (2000). Aquí no se habla español: Stories of linguistic repression in Southwest schools. *Bilingual Research Journal*, 24(4), 355–67.

MacSwan, J. (2017). A multilingual perspective on translanguaging. *American Educational Research Journal*, 54(1), 167–201. https://doi.org/10.3102/0002831216683935

Makalela, L. (2013). Translanguaging in kasi-taal: Rethinking old language boundaries for new language planning. *Stellenbosch Papers in Linguistics Plus*, 42, 111–25.

Makoni, S. & Pennycook, A. (2005). Disinventing and (re)constituting languages. *Critical Inquiry in Language Studies: An International Journal*, 2(3), 137–56.

Malova, I., Bengochea, A, Massey, S. R. & Ávalos, M. A. (2019). Exploring multimodal representations of words in a fourth-grade English language arts teacher guide to support emergent bilinguals' vocabulary instruction. In L. C. De Oliveira & B. E. Smith (Eds.), *Expanding literacy practices across multiple modes and languages for multilingual students* (pp. 21–37). Information Age Publishing.

Manyak, P. C. (2004). "What did she say?": Translation in a primary-grade English immersion class. *Multicultural Perspectives*, 6(1), 12–18.

Manyak, P. C. (2008). What's your news? Portraits of a rich language and literacy activity for English-language learners. *The Reading Teacher*, 61(6), 450–458. https://doi.org/10.1598/RT.61.6.4.

Marrero-Colón, M. (2021). Translanguaging: Theory, concept, practice, stance … or all of the above? *Center for Applied Linguistics*. Retrieved from https://www.cal.org/publications/translanguaging/.

Martínez-Roldán, C. M. (2013). The representation of Latinos and the use of Spanish: A critical content analysis of *Skippyjon Jones*. *Journal of Children's Literature*, 39(1), 5–14.

Martínez, R. A., Orellana, M. F., Pacheco, M. & Carbone, P. (2008). Found in translation: Connecting translating experiences to academic writing. *Language Arts*, 85(6), 421–31.

Marx, N., Gill, C. & Brosowski, T. (2021). Are migrant students closing the gap?: Reading progression in the first years of mainstream education. *Studies in Second Language Acquisition*, 43(4), 813–37.

Mattheoudakis, M., Chatzidaki, A. & Maligkoudi, C. (2020). Heritage language classes and bilingual competence: The case of Albanian immigrant children in Greece. *International Journal of Bilingual Education and Bilingualism*, 23(8), 1019–35. Retrieved from https://doi.org/10.1080/13670050.2017.1384447

May, S. (Ed.). (2013). *The multilingual turn: Implications for SLA, TESOL, and bilingual education*. Routledge.

May, S. (2019). Negotiating the multilingual turn in SLA. *The Modern Language Journal*, 103, 122–9.

Mazak, C. M. & Carroll, K. S. (Eds.). (2017). *Translanguaging in higher education: Beyond monolingual ideologies* (Vol. 104). Multilingual Matters.

McCarty, T. L. & Nicholas, S. E. (2014). Reclaiming indigenous languages: A reconsideration of the roles and responsibilities of schools. *Review of Research in Education*, 38, 106–36. https://doi.org/10.3102/0091732X13507894.

McConachy, T. (2019). L2 pragmatics as 'intercultural pragmatics': Probing sociopragmatic aspects of pragmatic awareness. *Journal of Pragmatics*, 151, 151–76.

McLaughlin, M., Laviosa, S., Linares, E., Pintado-Gutiérrez, L., Postlewate, L. Roesler, L. & Thow, D. (2022). Reflections. *L2 Journal*, 14(2), 107–14.

Mellinger, C. D. (2021). Preparing informed users of language services in public service interpreting courses: Differentiated learning outcomes for a diverse student population. In R. Moratto and D. Li (Eds.), *Global Insights into Public Service Interpreting* (pp. 171–84). Routledge.

Mellinger, C. D. (2017). Translation, interpreting, and language studies: Confluence and divergence. *Hispania*, 100(5), 241–6.

Mellinger, C. & Gasca-Jimenez, L. (2019). Challenges and opportunities for heritage language learners in interpreting courses in the U.S. context. *Revista Signos*, 52(101), 950–74.

Mendoza, A. (2020). Negotiating the multilingual turn in SLA: Response to Stephen May. *The Modern Language Journal*, 104(1), 304–8.

Mitchell, R., & Miles, F. (1998). *Second Language Learning Theories*. Edward Arnold.

Moll, L. C., Amanti, C., Neff, D. & González, N. (1992). Funds of knowledge for teaching: Using a qualitative approach to connect homes and classrooms. *Theory into Practice*, 31(2), 132–41. https://doi.org/10.1080/00405849209543534.

Munday, J., Pinto, S. R. & Blakesley, J. (2022). *Introducing translation studies: Theories and applications*. Routledge.

Muñoz-Basols, J. (2019). Going beyond the comfort zone: Multilingualism, translation and mediation to foster plurilingual competence. *Language, Culture and Curriculum*, 32(3), 299–321.

Nagy, W. (2007). Metalinguistic awareness and the vocabulary–comprehension connection. In R. K. Wagner, A. E. Muse & K. R. Tannenbaum (Eds.), *Vocabulary acquisition: Implications for reading comprehension* (pp. 52–77). Guilford.

National Governors Association Center for Best Practices & Council of Chief State School Officers. (2010). *Common Core State Standards for English language arts and literacy in history/social studies, science, and technical subjects.* Authors.

New London Group. (1996). A pedagogy of multiliteracies: Designing social futures. *Harvard Educational Review* 66(1), 60–92.

Nikolajeva, M. (2011). Translation and cross-cultural reception. In S. A. Wolf, K. Coats, P. A. Enciso & C. Jenkins (Eds), *Handbook of research on children's and young adult literature* (pp. 404–16). Routledge.

Niranjana, T. (1992). *Siting translation: History, post-structuralism, and the colonial context.* University of California Press.

Noorashid, N. & McLellan, J. (2018). Teaching and learning an ethnic minority language at university level: The case of Dusun in Brunei. *GEMA Online Journal of Language Studies*, 18(1), 217–33. https://doi.org/10.3102/00917 32X13507894.

Nord, C. (2018). Translating as a purposeful activity: A prospective approach. *The Journal of Specialised Translation*, 29, 25–39.

Norton, B. (2013). *Identity and language learning: Extending the conversation* (2nd ed.). Multilingual Matters & Channel View Publications. https://doi.org/10.2307/jj.18799909

Norton, B. (1997). Language and identity. *TESOL Quarterly*, 31(3), 409–429.

Nuñez, I. (2023). Toward border-crossing biliteracies: Pláticas of midwest transnational Latinx families reading and (re)writing the world. *Reading Research Quarterly*, 58(4), 475–94.

Omidire, M. F. & Ayob, S. (2020). Exploring the role of language in the multilingual education of students in South Africa. *Perspectives in Education*, 38(2), 54–67. Retrieved from https://doi.org/10.18820/2519593X/pie.v38i2.4.

Oprica, D. (2016). Examples of practice: an intercultural approach to translate Romanian children's folklore into Spanish. *Intercultural Education*, 27(1), 111–16. https://doi.org/10.1080/14675986.2016.1141600.

Orlando, M. (2019). Training and educating interpreter and translator trainers as practioners-researchers-teachers. *The Interpreter and Translator Trainer*, 13(3), 216-232.

Orr, R. B., Csikari, M. M., Freeman, S. & Rodriguez, M. C. (2022). Writing and using learning objectives. *CBE Life Sciences Education*, 21(3), fe3–fe3. Retrieved from https://doi.org/10.1187/cbe.22-04-0073.

Orellana, M. F., Dorner, L. & Pulido, L. (2003). Accessing assets: Immigrant youth's work as family translators or "para-phrasers." *Social Problems*, 50(4), 505–24. Retrieved from https://doi.org/10.1525/sp.2003.50.4.505.

Ortega, F. (2020). *The rhetoric of lowriding: A misunderstood cultural movement in the public realm* [Master's Thesis, The California State University]. Scholar Works.

Ortega, L. (2013). SLA for the 21st century: Disciplinary progress, transdisciplinary relevance, and the bi/multilingual turn. *Language Learning*, 63, 1–24.

Ortega, S. V. (1996). *Fundamentos de morfología.* Editorial Síntesis.

Pacheco, M. B., David, S. S. & Jiménez, R. T. (2015). Translating pedagogies. *Middle Grades Research Journal*, 10(1), 49–63.
Panau, D. (2013). Equivalence in translation theories: A critical evaluation. *Theory & Practice in Language Studies*, 3(1), 1–6.
Park, J. Y., Simpson, L., Bicknell, J. & Michaels, S. (2015). 'When it rains, a puddle is made': Fostering academic literacy in English learners through poetry and translation. *The English Journal*, 4(104), 50–8.
Parmegiani, A. (2014). Bridging literacy practices through storytelling, translanguaging, and an ethnographic partnership: A case study of Dominican students at Bronx Community College. *Journal of Basic Writing*, 33(1), 23–51.
Pavan, E. (2013). The Simpsons: Translation and language teaching in an EFL class. *Studies in Second Language Learning and Teaching*, 3(1), 131–45.
Pavlenko, A. (Ed.). (2006). *Bilingual minds: Emotional experience, expression and representation*. Multilingual Matters.
Phipps, A. & Gonzalez, M. (2004). *Modern languages: Learning and teaching in an intercultural field*. Sage.
Piccardo, E. (2017). Plurilingualism as a catalyst for creativity in superdiverse societies: A systemic analysis. *Frontiers in Psychology*, 8, 1–13, https://doi.org/10.3389/fpsyg.2017.02169.
Pintado-Gutiérrez, L. (2021). Translation in language teaching, pedagogical translation, and code-switching: Restructuring the boundaries. *The Language Learning Journal*, 49(2), 219–39. https://doi.org/10.1080/09571736.2018.1534260.
Postlewate, L. & Roesler, L. (2022). Tandem and translation: A bilingual telecollaboration course in social science translation. *L2 Journal*, 14(2).
Prieto-Velasco, J. A. & Fuentes-Luque, A. (2016). A collaborative multimodal working environment for the development of instrumental and professional competences of student translators: An innovative teaching experience. *The Interpreter and Translator Trainer*, 10(1), 76–91.
Prilutskaya, Marina. (2021). Examining pedagogical translanguaging: A systematic review of the literature. *Languages*, 6(180). Retrieved from https://doi.org/10.3390/languages6040180.
Pulinx, R., Van Avermaet, P. & Agirdag, O. (2017). Silencing linguistic diversity: the extent, the determinants and consequences of the monolingual beliefs of Flemish teachers. *International Journal of Bilingual Education and Bilingualism*, 20(5), 542–56. Retrieved from https://doi.org/10.1080/13670050.2015.1102860.
Puzio, K., Keyes, C. S., Cole, M. W. & Jiménez, R. T. (2013). Language differentiation: Collaborative translation to support bilingual reading. *Bilingual Research Journal*, 36(3), 329–49.
Pym, A. (2004). *The moving text: Localization, translation, and distribution*. John Benjamins.
Pym, A. (2010). *Exploring translation theories* (1st ed.). Routledge.
Pym, A. (2015). *Exploring Translation Theories* (2nd ed.). Routledge.
Pym, A. (2023). *Exploring translation theories* (3rd ed.). Routledge.
Pym, A. (2012). *On translator ethics: Principles for mediations between cultures*. John Benjamins Publishing Company.
Pym, A. (2018). Where translation studies lost the plot - Relations with language teaching. *Translation and Translanguaging in Multilingual Contexts*, 4(2), 203–222.

Pym, A. & Ayvazyan, N. (2018). Linguistics, translation and interpreting in foreign-language teaching contexts. In K. Malmkjaer (Ed.), *The Routledge handbook of translation studies and linguistics* (pp. 393–407). Routledge.

Qian, D. (1999). Assessing the roles of depth and breadth of vocabulary knowledge in reading comprehension. *Canadian Modern Language Review, 56*(2), 282–308.

Qian, D. D. & Schedl, M. (2004). Evaluation of an in-depth vocabulary knowledge measure for assessing reading performance. *Language Testing, 21*(1), 28–52.

Rajendram, S. (2015). Potentials of the multiliteracies pedagogy for teaching English language learners (ELLs): A review of the literature. *Critical Intersections in Education, 3*, 1–18.

Read the standards (2021). Common Core State Standards Initiative. Retrieved from https://www.thecorestandards.org/read-the-standards/.

Reiss, K., Nord, C. & Vermeer, H. J. (2014). *Towards a general theory of translational action: Skopos theory explained*. Routledge.

Reyes, I., Kenner, C., Moll, L. C. & Orellana, M. F. (2012). Biliteracy among children and youths. *Reading Research Quarterly, 47*(3), 307–27.

Reyhner, J. (2018). American Indian boarding schools: What went wrong? What is going right? *Journal of American Indian Education, 57*(1), 58–78.

Richards, J. C. (2013). Curriculum approaches in language teaching: Forward, central, and backward design. *RELC journal, 44*(1), 5–33. Retrieved from https://doi-org.uhd.idm.oclc.org/10.1177/0033688212473293.

Richards, J.C. & Rodgers, T.S. (2001). *Approaches and methods in language teaching*. Cambridge University Press.

Rivera-Ashford, R. C. (2015), *My Tata's Remedie/Los remedios de mi tata*. Cinco Puntos Press.

Rogoff, B. (1990). *Apprenticeship in thinking: Cognitive development in social context*. Oxford University Press.

Rosenblatt, L. (1978). *The reader, the text and the poem*. Southern Illinois University Press.

Rossato de Almeida, C. (2019). Translanguaging writing practices and implications for multilingual students. In L. C. De Oliveira & B. E. Smith (Eds.), *Expanding literacy practices across multiple modes and languages for multilingual students* (pp. 73–81). Information Age Publishing.

Rowe, D. & Fain, J. G. (2013). The family backpack project: Responding to dual-language texts through family journals. *Language Arts, 90*(6), 402–16.

Rowe, L. W. (2019). Emergent bilingual students' translation practices during eBook composing. *Bilingual Research Journal, 42*(3), 324–42.

Rowe, L. W. (2018). Say it in your language: Supporting translanguaging in multilingual classes. *The Reading Teacher, 72*(1), 31–8, https://www.jstor.org/stable/26632656

Rowling, J. K. (1998). *Harry Potter and the sorcerer's stone*. Arthur A. Levine Books.

Rydland, V., Aukrust, V. G. & Fulland, H. (2010). How word decoding, vocabulary and prior topic knowledge predict reading comprehension. A study of language-minority students in Norwegian fifth grade classrooms. *Reading and Writing, 25*(2), 465–82.

Savski, K. (2020). Local problems and a global solution: Examining the recontextualization of CEFR in Thai and Malaysian language policies.

Language Policy, 19, 527–47. Retrieved from https://doi.org/10.1007/s10 993-019-09539-8.

Schmidt, R. (1990). The role of consciousness in second language learning. *Applied Linguistics*, 11, 129–158.

Schulte, R. (n.d.). *Translation and reading*. Center for Translation Studies. https://translation.utdallas.edu/what-is-translation-studies/translation-and-reading/.

Sembiante, S. (2016). Translanguaging and the multilingual turn: Epistemological reconceptualization in the fields of language and implications for reframing language in curriculum studies. *Curriculum Inquiry*, 46(1), 45–61.

Sembiante, S. F., Ramírez, J. A. & de Oliveira, L. C. (2019). Using multimodal practices to support students' access to academic language and content in Spanish and English. In L. C. De Oliveira & B. E. Smith (Eds), *Expanding literacy practices across multiple modes and languages for multilingual students* (pp. 39–55). Information Age Publishing.

Sentence frames and sentence starters. (n.d.). Colorín Colorado. https://www.colorincolorado.org/sentence-frames.

Shohamy, E. (2006). *Language policy: Hidden agendas and new approaches*. Routledge.

Short, K. G. (1996). *Creating classrooms for authors and inquirers*. Heinemann.

Short, K. (2024). *Resources from Professor Kathy Short*. The University of Arizona College of Education. https://coe.arizona.edu/resources-professor-kathy-short.

Short, K. G. & Cueto, D. W. (2023). *Essentials of children's literature* (10th ed.). Pearson.

Short, K. G., Lynch-Brown, C., & Tomlinson, C. M. (2014). *Essentials of children's literature*. Pearson.

Sikes, C. L. & Villanueva, C. K. (2021). Creating a more bilingual Texas: A closer look at bilingual education in the Lone Star State. *Every Texan*.

Skutnabb-Kangas, T. (2017). Beyond named languages. In O. García, A.M.Y. Lin & S. May (Eds), *Bilingual and Multicultural Education, Third Edition* (pp. 117–31). Springer.

Skutnabb-Kangas, T. (1988). Multilingualism and the education of minority children. In T. Skutnabb-Kangas & J. Cummins (Eds), *Minority education: From shame to struggle* (pp. 9–44). Multilingual Matters.

Smith, B. E., Pacheco, M. B. & Khorosheva, M. (2020). Emergent bilingual students and digital multimodal composition: A systematic review of research in secondary classrooms. *Reading Research Quarterly*, 56(1), 33–52.

Smith, S. L. (2019). Teaching multimodal practices to multilingual elementary students through picture books. In L. C. De Oliveira & B. E. Smith (Eds.), *Expanding literacy practices across multiple modes and languages for multilingual students* (pp. 1–19). Information Age Publishing.

Sneddon, R. (2009). *Bilingual books, bilingual children*. Multilingual Matters.

Sneddon, R. (2012). Telling the story of the computer geek: Children becoming authors and translators. *Language and Education*, 26(5), 435–450.

Son, Y. A. (2017). Toward useful assessment and evaluation of heritage language learning. *Foreign Language Annals*, 50(2), 367–386.

Spangenberg, M. (2022, October 8). Introduction to translating children's literature [Webinar]. CERCLL. https://nci.arizona.edu/workshop/introduction-translating-childrens-literature

Stachl-Peier, U. (2020). Language mediation, translation/interpreting and the CEFR. In A. Schmidhofer & A. Wussler (Eds), *Bausteine Translationsorientierter Sprachkompetenz und translatorischer Basiskompetenzen* (pp. 34–77). Innsbruck University Press.

Stoof, A., Martens, R. L., Van Merrienboer, J. J. & Bastiaens, T. J. (2002). The boundary approach of competence: A constructivist aid for understanding and using the concept of competence. *Human Resource Development Review, 1*, 345–65.

Street, B. V. (1984). *Literacy in theory and practice* (Vol. 9). Cambridge University Press.

Street, B. (2006). Autonomous and ideological models of literacy: Approaches from New Literacy Studies. *Media Anthropology Network, 17*, 1–15.

Stromberg, G. (Ed.). (2018). *Tonelhuayo uan totlahtoltzin/La raíz y la voz*. Secretaria de Cultura.

Swain, M. (1996). Integrating language and content in immersion classrooms: Research perspectives. *The Canadian Modern Language Review, 52*(4), 529–548.

Swain, M. (2005). The output hypothesis: Theory and research. In E. Hinkel (Ed.), *Handbook of research in second language teaching and learning*. (pp. 471–83). Routledge.

Swain, M. & Lapkin, S. (1995). Problems in output and the cognitive processes they generate: A step towards second language learning. *Applied linguistics, 16*(3), 371–91.

Talaván, N., Ibáñez, A. & Bárcena, E. (2016). Exploring collaborative reverse subtitling for the enhancement of written production activities in English as a second language. *ReCALL, 29*(1), 39–58. https://doi.org/10.1017/S0958344016000197.

Talaván, N. & Lertola, J. (2022). Audiovisual translation as a didactic resource in foreign language education. A methodological proposal. *Encuentro, 30*, 23–39.

Tardy, C. M. (2011). The history and future of genre in second language writing. *Journal of Second Language Writing, 1*(20), 1–5.

Tardy, C. M., Sommer-Farias, B. & Gevers, J. (2020). Teaching and researching genre knowledge: Toward an enhanced theoretical framework. *Written Communication, 37*(3), 287–321.

The National Standards Collaborative Board. (2015). *World-readiness standards for learning languages*. 4th ed. ACTFL.

Toury, G. (2012). *Descriptive translation studies – And beyond*. John Benjamins.

Turnbull, B. (2018). Reframing foreign language learning as bilingual education: Epistemological changes towards the emergent bilingual. *International Journal of Bilingual Education and Bilingualism, 21*(8), 1041–8.

Troyan, F. J. (2012). Standards for foreign language learning: Defining the constructs and researching learner outcomes. *Foreign Language Annals, 45*(1), 118–40.

Tschida, C. M. & Buchanan, L. B. (2015). Tackling controversial topics: Developing thematic text sets for elementary social studies. *Social Studies Research and Practice, 10*(3), 40–56.

Tymoczko, M. (2002). Translation in a postcolonial context: Early Irish literature in English translation, in M. Tymoczko, & E. Gentzler (Eds.), *Translation and Power* (pp. 19–40). University of Massachusetts Press.

Tymoczko, M. (2007). *Enlarging translation, empowering translators*. Routledge.
Ulanoff, S. & Pucci, S. (1993, April 14). *Is concurrent-translation or preview-review more effective in promoting second language vocabulary acquisition?* [Presentation]. American Education Research Association 1993 Conference, Atlanta, GA.
Valdés, G. (2001). Heritage languages students: Profiles and possibilities. In J. K. Peyton, D. A. Ranard & S. McGinnis (Eds.), *Heritage languages in America: Preserving a national resource* (pp. 37–77). Center for Applied Linguistics/Delta Systems.
Venuti, L. (2018). *The translator's invisibility: A history of translation*. Routledge.
Velásquez, E. (2020). The effect of discipline-related knowledge on heritage language learners' reading comprehension. *Athens Journal of Education*, 7(1), 31–48.
Voevoda, E. (2020, March). Teaching minority languages: Social and cultural problems. In *4th International Conference on Culture, Education and Economic Development of Modern Society* (ICCESE 2020) (pp. 664–7). Atlantis Press.
Vygotsky, L. S. (1978). *Mind in society: The development of higher psychological processes*. Harvard University Press.
Waddington, C. (2001). Different methods of evaluating student translations: The question of validity. *Meta: Journal des traducteurs*, 46(2), 311–25
Walton, P., Baca, L. & Escamilla, K. (2002). *A national study of teacher education: Preparation for diverse student populations*. Center for Research on Education, Diversity, and Excellence (CREDE).
Warner, C. & Dupuy, B. (2018). Moving toward multiliteracies in foreign language teaching: Past and present perspectives … and beyond. *Foreign Language Annals*, 51(1), 116–28.
Washbourne, K. (2010). *Manual of Spanish–English translation*. Prentice-Hall.
Washbourne, K. (2012a). Active, strategic reading for translation trainees: Foundations for transactional methods. *The International Journal of Translation and Interpreting Research*, 4(1), 38–55.
Washbourne, K. (2012b). Load-managed problem formats: Scaffolding and modeling the translation task to improve transfer. *Target. International Journal of Translation Studies*, 24(2), 338–54.
wa Thiong'o, N. (2023). *The language of languages: Reflections on translation*. Seagull Books.
Welch, I. (2015). Building interactional space in an ESL classroom to foster bilingual identity and linguistic repertoires. *Journal of Language and Identity*, 14(2), 80–95.
Widdowson, H. (2003). *Defining issues in English language teaching*. Oxford University Press.
Widdowson, H. (1978). *Teaching language as communication*. Oxford University Press.
Wilson, J. & González-Davies, M. G. (2017). Tackling the plurilingual student/monolingual classroom phenomenon. *TESOL Quarterly*, 51(1), 207–19.
Wolsey, T. D., Wood, K. & Lapp, D. (August 2014). Conversation, collaboration, and the Common Core: Strategies for learning together. *IRA E-ssentials Series*. International Reading Association. https://doi.org/10.1598/e-ssentials.8061.
Woolard, K. A. & Schieffelin, B. B. (1994). Language ideology. *Annual review of anthropology*, 23(1), 55–82.

Yang, M., Cooc, N. & Sheng, L. (2017). An investigation of cross-linguistic transfer between Chinese and English: A meta-analysis. *Asian-Pacific Journal of Second and Foreign Language Education*, 2(15), 1–21. https://doi.org/10.1186/s40 862-017-0036-9.

Yang, X., Li, J., Guo, X. & Li, X. (2015). Group interactive network and behavioral patterns in online English-to-Chinese cooperative translation activity. *The Internet and Higher Education*, 25, 28–36.

Yao, J. & Turner, M. (2024). Exploring the waning interest in Nuosu Yi education in Liangshan, China. *International Journal of Bilingual Education and Bilingualism*, 27(3), 374–88. https://doi.org/10.1080/13670050.2023.2174373.

Yeganeh, H. (2022). Orality, literacy and the "great divide" in cultural values. *The International Journal of Sociology and Social Policy*, 42(5), 564–82. Retrieved from https://doi.org/10.1108/IJSSP-04-2021-0088.

Zapata, G.C. (2018). The role of digital learning by design instructional materials in the development of Spanish heritage learners' literacy skills. In G. C. Zapata & M. Lacorte (Eds.), *Multiliteracies pedagogy and language learning: Teaching Spanish to heritage speakers*, (pp. 67–106). Palgrave MacMillan.

Zengin, B. (2019). Use of film scripts and their translations in teaching English as a foreign language. *International Online Journal of Education and Teaching (IOJET)*, 6(4). 944–58, http://iojet.org/index.php/IOJET/article/view/718.

Zhang, D., Koda, K., Leong, C. K. & Pang, E. (2019). Cross-lagged panel analysis of reciprocal effects of morphological processing and reading in Chinese in a multilingual context. *Journal of Research in Reading*, 42(1), 58–79.

INDEX

academic language 61, 159, 198
academic literacy 64, 78
ACTFL *see* American Council on the Teaching of Foreign Languages
ACTFL Proficiency Guidelines 180
ACTFL Proficiency Scale 172
ACTFL World-Readiness Standards 74, 98, 100, 171, 172, 180–2, 174, 176
 five C's 180
 heritage languages 182–3
 proficiency 180–1
additive bilingualism 46, 114
affect, student 28, 29, 61, 62, 68, 84, 153, 158, 165
affective filter 61
after-school language programs 11, 135, 211
alignment of standards and/or objectives, translation activities, and assessment 89, 171, 173, 181, 185, 187–9
American Council on the Teaching of Foreign Languages 60 (*see also* ACTFL)
 collaboration 155–6
Argueta, J. 85, 117, 126, 130
así se dice 54, 78, 84, 105, 137, 158
assessment 154, 171, 172
 bilingual writing 171
 defined 174
 differentiation (*see* differentiation of assessment)
 through biliteracy lens 174–7
 translation 173–4, 175, 176, 177, 178, 179–82
assessment, alignment with standards, objectives and translation activities (*see* alignment of standards and/

or objectives, translation activities, and assessment)
assessment, formative/informal 161, 174, 177, 185–6
assessment of translation quality, framework 177–8
 rubric design 178
assessment, summative/formal 173, 174
 backward design of 185, 188
asset perspective 4, 27, 52, 70
assimilation 94, 104, 115
asynchronous instruction 132, 154, 162
audience awareness 30, 53, 55, 56, 57, 58, 59, 70, 78, 83, 99, 100, 104–5, 112, 123, 126, 135, 141, 161, 178, 181, 190
audiovisual translation 86, 139–40, 139, 143–6
authentic texts 113–15, 119, 123, 138, 181, 199, 200, 213
author intent 30, 53, 203
AVT (*see* audiovisual translation)
background knowledge
 reading comprehension 78–9, 123–4, 199

Baker, M. 6, 53
Bassnett, S. 52, 53, 126
Beaudrie, S. 25, 185
Benjamin, W. 51
Bialystok, E. 80
bilingual
 defined 2
 emergent (*see* emergent bilingual)
 identity (*see* Identity, bilingual)
bilingual education 5, 20, 25, 57, 61, 98, 177, 194
bilingual learners 68, 97, 98, 102, 198

pedagogical translation 98, 102, 132, 173
bilingual practices 30, 52, 57, 60, 78, 113, 117, 136, 172
bilingual teaching 9, 21, 25, 31, 105, 198
bilingual teaching strategies 21, 105, 134–5
  pedagogical translation 6, 9, 21, 57, 205
bilingual texts (see texts, bilingual)
bilingualism
  additive (see additive bilingualism)
  biliteracy 45
  defined 26
  dynamic 23
  receptive 4
  productive 4
  and translation 9
  sequential 18, 21, 199
  simultaneous (18
  subtractive (see subtractive bilingualism)
  symbolic capital 45
bilingualization 3, 4, 7, 20, 88, 114, 198, 199, 212
biliteracy 7, 8, 25, 32, 44–9, 59, 78, 113, 114, 117, 127, 134, 164, 171, 174–7, 199, 212, 213
  context 47, 53, 113 (see also continua of biliteracy)
  continua of biliteracy (see continua of biliteracy)
  defined 8, 44
  educational programs (45–6)
  oracy 176
  pedagogical translation 7, 78, 127, 174–7, 199
  pluriliteracy 44–5
Bishop, R. 121
Block, D. 3, 4, 8, 19, 22, 33, 35, 52, 59, 93, 104
Blommaert, J. 34
Bourdieu, P. 23, 25, 26, 27, 45, 116
Botelho, M. 121, 134
bottom-up teaching 28
  pedagogical translation 206

Bowles, D. 50, 53, 56, 117, 122, 125, 130, 199
Butzkamm, J. A. 30, 57, 79, 87, 143, 174
Byram, M. 93, 94, 96, 97, 98, 101, 102, 179, 212

Caldwell, J. A. 30, 57, 79, 87, 143, 174
Canagarajah, A. S. 206
Can-Do Statements 156, 181, 189
Carreira, M. 67, 72, 154, 184–5, 199, 206
Carreres, A. 24, 29, 31, 32, 51, 206, 212
CCSS (see Common Core State Standards)
CEFR (see Common European Frame of Reference)
cheng-yu stories and pedagogical translation 126
choral reading 126–7
Cisneros, S. 125, 130
CLI (see Communicative language instruction)
code switching in texts 113, 117, 122
cognates 71, 84, 131
Colina, S. 1, 7, 9, 10, 15, 28, 29, 30, 31, 51, 56, 59, 63, 67, 77, 78, 79, 90, 105, 106, 107, 111, 116, 129, 143, 171, 177, 178, 180, 184, 186, 195, 196
colonialism
  culture 94, 95, 98
  language 21, 34, 35, 94, 118
  translation 49, 95, 98
collaboration 28, 65, 66, 69, 143, 153
  distributed expertise 155
  mediation 156
  purposes of 153–7
collaboration, home-school 161, 163–4, 212
collaboration, instructor-student 156, 199
collaboration, peer-to-peer 157–61, 212
  Setting up (162, 206)
collaborative group structures 155, 160–1, 212
collaborative translation 43, 53, 55, 59, 71, 73, 74, 80, 83, 84, 87, 99, 104, 106, 139–40, 157, 196, 212

INDEX

collocations 83, 84, 102, 131, 139, 167, 186
Collation of Descriptors for Young Learners 88
Cook, G. 4, 6, 7, 8, 9, 13, 15, 17, 21, 23, 26, 27, 29, 32, 33, 51, 53, 54, 55, 56, 58, 59, 73, 99, 168
Common Core State Standards 60, 74, 89, 165, 172, 180
   assessment 171, 183
   bilingual lens 74, 85, 172, 173
   bilingual strategies 60, 155, 156
   collaboration 155, 160
   objectives 171
Common European Frame of Reference 9, 10, 48, 63, 65, 74, 88, 99–100, 172
   assessment 179, 180
   collaboration 153, 155, 156, 157, 162, 165
   heritage languages 176
   intercultural competence 93, 96
   mediation 22
   minoritized languages 176
   objectives 172, 173
   proficiency 178–9, 180
Common European Frame of Reference Companion Volume 180
communicative approach 17
communicative competence 15, 22, 48, 61, 95–9
communicative language instruction 17, 18, 64, 179
   pedagogical translation 64, 206
concurrent translation 8, 29, 159
connotation 56, 57, 83, 86, 96, 98, 103, 182
CBLI (*see* Content-based language instruction)
content-based language instruction 89, 165, 183
context clues 83, 102, 131, 132
continua of biliteracy 46–9, 59, 117
   critical continua of biliteracy 45, 47, 48, 49, 59, 117
contrastive analysis 62, 64, 65
critical thinking 10, 30, 31, 39, 43, 69, 114, 143, 158, 173, 189

cross-linguistic connections 78, 80, 81, 184
   pedagogical translation 37, 82, 175
cultural authenticity 51, 113, 122, 200
cultural comparison 96, 98, 105, 107–9, 131, 182
cultural difference 41, 52, 57, 58, 85, 120, 122, 136, 190, 202, 203
cultural eradication 26
cultural insiders 54, 83, 105, 119
cultural outsiders 54, 83, 119, 121
cultural products, practices and perspectives 93, 100–2, 142, 207
culturally relevant pedagogy 42
culturally sustaining pedagogy 73, 95
culture
   defined 93–4
   defined for language teachers 93
   dominant (*see* dominant culture)
   high culture 50, 95
   language 3, 6, 7, 9, 10, 21, 22, 23, 26, 27, 30, 36, 39, 40, 41, 43, 49, 52, 60, 65, 66, 70, 71, 94, 95, 96, 98–102, 113, 115, 134, 194, 204
   translation 43, 50, 52, 55, 58, 60, 65, 71, 72, 80, 85, 86–7, 94, 95, 96, 97, 98, 100, 102–5, 120, 124, 134, 153, 164, 186
culture, Big C and Little c 101
Cummins, J. 30, 46, 61, 71, 73, 94, 95, 159, 197
   BICS and CALP 61
   common underlying proficiency (CUP) 61
   linguistic interdependence hypothesis 61

Daly, N. 112, 118, 120
decolonization 63, 66, 67, 68, 70, 72, 73, 115, 118, 205–6
deficit perspective 20, 45
denotation 83
design of meaning framework (*see also* multiliteracies) 42–4
dialect 10, 22, 34, 35, 66, 199–200
   within texts 27, 86, 205
dictionary use in pedagogical translation 71, 83, 139, 195

differentiated instruction 9, 67, 72, 159, 160, 183–5, 194, 195, 199
  of assessment 183, 185, 189
digital media 136, 140
  pedagogical translation 139
digital storytelling and pedagogical translation 140, 167
Direct Method 15, 17–18, 19, 29
direct translation 88
discourse 7, 35, 39, 40–1, 42, 48, 49, 54, 57, 68, 77, 198, 202, 206, 212
domestication 52, 55, 58, 104, 119, 203
dominant culture 23, 27, 54, 58, 104, 121, 140, 204
dominant language 4, 25, 45, 46, 47, 55, 94, 121, 182, 205, 211
  assessment in 175–6
  translation 55, 58, 104, 116
dual edition texts (*see* texts, dual edition)
dubbing 86, 139, 143
Duolingo 17

EBs (*see* emergent bilinguals)
EFL (*see* English as a Foreign Language)
ELD (*see* English language development)
ELPS (*see* English Language Proficiency Standards)
emergent bilinguals 4, 36, 45, 46, 64, 73, 79, 82, 84, 85, 101, 104, 137, 158, 159, 175, 184, 200, 203, 211
En mi familia/In My Family 90, 91, 100, 104, 120, 130
engagement, learner 60, 78, 121, 141, 154, 155
English as a Foreign Language 126, 138, 139, 156, 157
English as a Second Language 20, 32, 46, 64, 62, 83
English dominance 26, 94, 95, 115, 116, 117
English language development 173
English language proficiency standards 60, 172
equivalence 29, 30, 31, 82, 85, 181
  defined 53, 77
  pragmatics 77, 105

pedagogical translation 55, 56, 57, 64, 79, 80, 84, 85, 87, 101, 105, 108, 138, 149, 158, 164, 182, 186, 202
  role of (52–9)
  translation studies 52
Escamilla, K. 8, 9, 18, 37, 54, 57, 58, 78, 80, 82, 84, 87, 91, 101, 115, 134, 137, 158, 176, 177, 183, 203
ESL (*see* English as a second language)
evaluation, defined 174
Even-Zohar 55
expertise, student 64, 155, 158
expertise, teacher 194–7, 198
explication 53, 55, 57, 100, 105, 105

figurative language 176, 183, 203 (*see also* Literary devices)
first language acquisition 18, 19, 35
first language use (*see* Home language use)
Firth, A. 22
Flores, N. 4, 5, 27, 34, 44, 74, 156, 157, 172, 173, 194, 198, 205
foreign language learning 2, 3 (*see also* world language learning)
foreign language teaching 16, 96, 197 (*see also* world language teaching)
foreignization 52, 100, 203
form 17, 49, 62, 75, 80, 85, 87, 113, 160, 178, 179, 182
  function 49, 179
Frawley, W. 155
Freire, P. 7, 39, 42, 58
  functional translation 54, 57, 62, 82, 84, 85, 87, 91, 99, 100, 106, 110, 114, 116, 122, 131–2, 176, 178, 181
  assessment of 178, 179
functionalism 52

García, O. 3, 4, 5, 6, 18, 20, 22, 23, 24, 25, 34, 44, 45, 50, 63, 66, 68, 69, 70, 71, 72, 73, 74, 94, 97, 117, 137, 172, 173, 194, 204
Garza, C. L. 90, 100, 104, 120, 130
Gasca Jiménez, L. 7, 9, 20, 45, 51, 67, 80, 184
Gass, S. M. 59

INDEX

Gee, J. P. 7, 23, 27, 35, 37, 38, 40
genre 30, 40, 42, 43, 87, 175, 202
   defined 53
   pedagogical translation 53, 83, 201, 203
Gillies, A. 145, 146
globalization 9, 34, 38, 41
González-Davies, M. 8, 9, 10, 17, 18, 20, 30, 32, 43, 52, 61, 65, 66, 77, 84, 88, 100, 154, 157, 158, 184, 193, 212
grammar, teaching of 179, 200, 206
Grammar Translation 8, 16–17, 178, 179, 211
Grosjean, F. 3, 25
guided writing 83, 84, 89–93, 129, 177

Halliday, M. A. K. 5, 55
Heath, S. B. 38, 39, 40
hegemony 21, 38, 39
   English 25, 68
   language 38, 55
   literacy 39
heritage language learners 4, 29, 43, 45, 54, 67, 102, 122, 175, 183, 199
   assessment 184–5
   reading comprehension 67, 84, 102
heritage language standards 182–3
heritage language teaching 72, 83, 182, 185, 206, 211
   pedagogical translation 67, 97, 102, 206
   reading comprehension 83, 84, 102
HLLs (*see* Heritage language learners)
home language 4, 20–1
home language use 20–1, 28, 30, 60, 62, 71, 73, 177, 197
   suppression of 19, 193
Hornberger, N. 8, 20, 25, 32, 36, 39, 43, 45, 46, 47, 48, 59, 68, 97, 101, 117, 127, 212
House, J. 28, 79, 178
Howatt, A. P. R. 16, 19

identity
   bilingual 62, 67, 198
   culture 94, 95, 96, 98, 104, 124, 125, 130–2, 142, 183, 207–9
   language 101, 122, 164, 198

   learner 60, 66, 68, 69, 135, 136, 183, 198
   teacher 200
ideological clarity 27–9
idiomatic expressions 56, 71, 82–3, 84, 101, 164, 196
In My Family/En mi familia 89, 100, 104, 120, 130
indigenous language 26
inequity
   educational 68, 205, 211
   social 211
   sociolinguistic 21
   systemic 211
inference 38, 54, 56, 129–33, 174, 183, 196
input-interaction-output model (IIO) 22
input hypothesis 22
integrated plurilingual approach 65, 197
   mediation 66
   pedagogical translation 65–7
   skill transfer 66
intercultural action 65–6
intercultural being 36, 57, 59, 95–9, 114, 124, 139
   pedagogical translation 99, 114, 139, 212
intercultural competence 18, 36, 43, 66, 93, 95–9, 174
   pedagogical translation 43, 64, 65, 97, 99, 104, 212
intercultural communicative competence 94–9
   Byram's *savoirs* 98
   pedagogical translation 97, 98
interference, first language 17, 25, 60, 177
interpretation vs. translation 7, 9
interpretation notes and AVT 145–6
inverse translation 88
IPA (*see* Integrated plurilingual approach)

Jakobson, R. 57
Jiménez, R. 31, 56–7, 71, 72, 77, 79, 80, 82, 84, 85, 87, 115, 125, 141, 155

Kachru, B. B. 24
Kagan, O. 74, 154, 184–5

Kern, R. 7, 8, 31, 37, 38, 40, 41, 44, 48, 49, 79, 82, 83, 113, 114, 133, 174, 175, 178, 179, 185, 194, 195, 202, 212
Kiraly, D. 9, 153
Kramsch, C. 7, 15, 19, 20, 30, 33, 38, 39, 40, 49, 59, 82, 85, 94, 95, 101, 114, 205, 206
Krashen, S. 2, 22, 35, 61, 62
Kress, G. 133, 147
Kroskrity, P. V. 15, 23

language
  additional language 4, 71
  architecture 27, 44, 198
  boundaries 68, 69
  defined 33–4
  foreign language 4, 25
  heritage language 4
  home language 4, 30
  integrated systems 46 (*see also* language, Invention of)
  invention of 34, 35
  maintenance (*see* language maintenance)
  national language 23, 24
  nationalism 23, 24, 25, 69
  new language 4
  non-standard 27
  second language 4
  separation 29, 94
  standard 26–7
  vernacular (*see* language, vernacular)
  world language (4)
  written (47
language and content, intersection of 194
language brokers (*see* language mediators)
language education policy (LEP) 24, 28
  monolingual language ideology 24
language for specific purposes 5
language hierarchy 20, 58, 68, 71, 117, 120, 205 (*see also* power imbalance)
language ideologies 23, 68, 118
  defined 23
  institutional 15, 21, 23, 24, 29, 35, 50, 59, 70, 197, 200, 205, 213
  individual 15, 23, 27, 197, 213
  power (23, 24, 33, 47, 50, 118)
  monolingual (*see* monolingual language ideology)
  societal 15, 23, 24, 25, 27, 205
  standard (*see* standard language ideology)
  translanguaging as 68
language learning
  bilingual 9, 171
  cognitive process 49
  defined 35–7
  languaging (5, 35, 36)
  literacy-based (*see* literacy-based language learning)
  multiliteracies (8)
  social justice 5
  socially situated 49, 85
  translanguaging 5
  translation 30, 35
  utilitarian 5
language loss 25, 175, 182
  cultural eradication 22
language maintenance 8, 175
language mediators 67, 73
language mixing (*see* languages in contact; *see also* Spanglish)
language objectives (*see* objectives)
language orientations
  language as problem 197
  language as resource 20, 27, 52, 70, 197
language policy 94, 182, 197, 211
language proficiency
  assessment 179–83
  defined 178–9
  objectives 179
language standards
  CEFR (*see* Common European Frame of Reference)
  ELD (*see* English Language Development)
  ELPS (*see* English Language Proficiency Standards)
  proficiency 178–9
  World Readiness (*see* ACTFL World-Readiness Standards)
language teachers
  defined 193–4

preparation 197
role 199, 200
language teaching
  foreign language (*see* foreign language teaching)
  literacy-based (*see* literacy-based language teaching)
  monolingual 50, 70, 104, 198
  top-down 10, 206
language, vernacular 50, 118, 119 (*see also* dialect)
languages in contact 34, 115, 154, 198 (*see also* Spanglish)
languaging 5, 32, 35, 36, 42, 59
Lantolf, J. P. 155
Laviosa, S. 9, 60, 66, 67, 68, 136
learner agency 27, 42, 44, 70, 136, 141, 198, 212
learner motivation 59, 86, 124, 141, 153, 156, 212
learning objectives (*see* objectives)
Lee, T. K. 6, 23, 25, 55, 59, 87, 115, 117, 118, 122
Lefevere 58, 59, 203
Li, W. 68, 69, 136, 141
Lin, A. M. Y. 21, 29
linguistic authenticity 65, 115, 118, 119, 122, 199, 200, 201, 211
linguistic capital 6, 116
linguistic landscape 120–1
linguistic repertoire 3, 4, 21, 23, 25, 28, 65, 66, 67, 68, 69, 81, 141, 154, 172, 198, 199, 203
  defined 20
Lippi-Green, R. 26, 34, 45, 200
Lipski, J. M. 23, 33
literacy
  autonomous view 7, 37–8, 47, 50, 172
  defined 7, 37–48
  home language literacy 37, 62
  ideological view 7, 38–9, 47
  monolingual 45, 47, 48
  multiliteracies (*see* multiliteracies)
  oral-literate divide 40
  socially situated (*see* socially situated literacy; *see* also *new literacy studies*)
  traditional (*see* autonomous view)

literacy-based language teaching 7, 49, 183, 194, 202–4
  pedagogical translation 85–6, 202–5
literacy, digital (*see* digital literacy)
literacy events 49, 212
literacy teachers, defined 193, 194
literal translation 31, 57, 82, 84, 85, 86, 91, 131, 138
literary devices and pedagogical translation 30–1, 176, 183
literary texts 158, 159
literary translation 25, 55, 58, 59, 116, 158, 159, 201, 202
Makoni, S. 34, 46
maximum exposure 95
May, S. 15, 20, 21, 30, 60
Me dicen Güero/They Call Me Güero 117, 122, 125, 130, 199
meaning
  co-construction of 66, 155, 156, 176
  loss of in translation 55–6
  meaning making 38, 42, 43, 45, 49, 68, 70, 71–4, 137, 139, 145, 185, 204, 209
  meaning making and illustration 115, 116
  meaning making and translation 62, 80, 110, 139, 154, 157, 158, 176, 184, 196
  negotiation of 31, 36, 43, 52, 55, 57, 83, 84, 131, 140, 154, 156, 158, 159, 176, 183–4, 212
mechanical translator use 170
mediation 6, 7, 9, 18, 22, 38, 57, 59, 60, 95–6, 103, 104, 136, 154, 194, 200, 204
  CEFR 22, 57, 66, 154, 156
  defined 9, 52
  pedagogical translation 9, 10, 52, 57, 63, 65, 75, 77–8, 97, 103, 110, 115, 153
Mellinger, C. D. 51, 67, 75, 204
metalinguistic awareness 43, 56, 69, 71, 80, 82, 84, 153, 156, 173, 174, 181, 199
reading comprehension 80, 174, 201
teacher preparation 201–2
minoritized speakers 45, 68, 173

mirrors, windows and doors 121, 123, 124
mixed classrooms 9, 72, 73, 98, 102, 199–200, 211
  assessment 183
  collaboration 157, 159, 160
  differentiation 160, 183
modes 140, 143
Moll, L. 161
monolingual language ideology 5, 21, 23–5, 27, 45, 60, 69, 95, 115, 120, 197, 200, 205, 211 (*see also* Language ideologies)
monolingualism 17–18, 21, 23
  language teaching 66
  power 47, 59
  SLA 21
morphemes 81–2
morphological awareness 81
morphology 81–2
  vocabulary knowledge 84
multilingual
  competence 7
  defined 2
  stance 22
multilingual turn 19–22, 60, 101, 178–9, 205
  pedagogical translation 30, 32, 204
multilingualism 21
  defined 19
  multiliteracies 41
  traditional literacy 38
  Vs. plurilingualism 65
multimedia 133
multimodal
  communication 136
  defined 133–4
  design 137–41
  pedagogy, and pedagogical translation 134–40
  text sets 140–2, 212
  texts 134, 143–4
multimodality 133, 134, 206
  multiliteracies 41, 43, 135–7
  pedagogical translation 137, 138, 164
  reading comprehension 138
  social-situatedness 135
  multilingualism as 136

scaffolding in language learning 135, 137
multiliteracies 7, 8, 41–4, 60, 85, 118, 135
  digital literacy 140
  language learning 8
  pedagogical translation (*see* Pedagogical translation and multiliteracies)
  available designs 79, 127, 194, 202
  defined 8
  design of meaning framework 42–4, 127
  designing 127
  redesign 79, 127
Munday, J. 54, 57, 58, 77, 115, 116, 117, 120, 134, 135, 143

named languages 62
nation state 34, 45
  culture 94
  language 45, 50
native-speakerism 18, 20, 49, 66, 97
negotiation of meaning (*see* meaning, negotiation of)
new literacy studies 39–40, 47, 172, 212
New London Group 8, 38, 41, 43, 85, 119, 135
Niranjana, T. 34, 49, 50, 95, 115, 118, 204
non-dominant language 24, 25, 45, 46, 47, 55, 94, 140, 209
  translation 55
Nord, C. 53, 55, 56

objectives 154, 200
  biliteracy 175
  content 128
  differentiation of 183, 184–5
  language 124, 128, 137
  learning 49, 124, 171–2, 183
  literacy 18, 187
  proficiency 179
  writing 176–7
objectives, designing for translation 186–9
oracy 176
  objectives 176

oral language development 126, 134, 185
   pedagogical translation 185
   reading comprehension 185
oral texts (*see* texts, oral)
oral tradition 140, 142
oral translation 155
Ortega, L. 15, 19, 20, 21

parallel texts 71, 123, 139, 162
pedagogical translation (*see* translation, pedagogical)
pedagogical translation
   and cultural learning 212
   and linguistic learning 212
   and literacy learning (212)
Pennycook, A. 34, 46
Phipps, A. 3, 5, 6, 18, 30, 31, 33–4, 35, 36, 40, 42, 45, 47, 93, 94, 99, 101, 104, 114, 115, 119, 124, 134, 139, 155, 174, 212
phonological awareness 80–1
pluricultural competence 60, 63, 99, 100
pluriliteracy and translanguaging 44–5
plurilingual·
   competence 60–3
   defined 2
   language learning 20
plurilingualism 65, 182
polysystems theory 55
post-colonialism 50, 58, 116, 204
power
   critical continua of biliteracy (*see* continua of biliteracy)
   dominant power norms 32, 37, 48, 49, 50, 59, 212
   imbalance 19, 20, 23, 55, 63, 71, 115, 118, 201 (*see also* Language hierarchy)
   symbolic (*see* symbolic power)
   translanguaging 73
   translation 43, 49, 115, 117
pragmatic awareness 86
pragmatic competence 85, 158, 178
pragmatics 61, 85–6, 103
   defined 54, 83
   equivalence 57, 62

pedagogical translation 54, 57, 62, 79, 117, 195
   subtitling 86
professional development 201, 204
proficiency (*see* language proficiency)
proverbs
   cultural comparison 105, 181–2
   translation of 105, 181–2
publisher, ideological role of 120
Pym, A. 5, 17, 19, 20, 33, 43, 62, 80, 94, 212

Qian, D. 83

raciolinguistic ideology 21, 198
reader response 1231, 202–3
reading as translation 103
reading, choral (*see* choral reading)
reading comprehension 45, 54, 82
   authentic texts 114
   bilingual strategies 42, 154
   heritage language learners (*see* heritage language learners)
   multimodality 138
   pedagogical translation 30, 56, 57, 58, 72, 74, 87, 102, 126, 158, 174, 184, 200
   translanguaging 69
   vocabulary knowledge 83, 84
register 40, 43, 87
   pedagogical translation 87, 103, 195, 199
Reiss, K. 53, 55, 56
repertoire, linguistic see *linguistic repertoire*) Rosenblatt, L. 123, 202

scaffolding 154, 158, 194
   language learning 155, 201
   mediation 154–5
   pedagogical translation activities 195
schema 79, 195, 204
Schieffelin, B. B. 15, 23, 27
second language acquisition 2, 4, 18–19
   cognitive models 22, 59
   monolingualism 19, 21, 24, 46
   multilingual turn (*see* multilingual turn)
   social turn (see social turn)
   theory 55, 59–60, 61, 62, 178–9

translation 60–1
second language learning 35, 36, 74, 80, 183, 211
second language learners 5, 7, 40, 101, 165, 175, 180, 198, 211
semantics 79, 82, 98
  equivalence 57, 158
  pedagogical translation 31, 44, 56, 84, 156, 183, 195
  semi-bilingual texts (*see* texts, semi-bilingual)
Short, K. G. 115, 118, 119, 120, 126, 167, 203
skopos theory 56
Skutnabb-Kangas, T. 18, 19, 68, 94
Sneddon, R. 30, 71, 140, 141, 159, 161, 164, 165, 168, 195
social constructivism 38–9, 154
social turn 22, 29, 30, 101, 176–7, 205
  pedagogical translation 30, 204, 212
socially situated literacy 7, 39, 40, 41, 45, 48, 49, 101, 102, 109, 133, 164, 194, 211
  biliteracy 44, 103
  collaboration 157
  language proficiency standards 178–9
  pedagogical translation 50, 211, 212
sociocultural theory 52, 59, 154
  defined 9
  pedagogical translation 59
sociocultural views of literacy (*see* socially situated literacy)
source audience 83, 100, 104, 181
source culture 58, 119–20, 204
source language 58, 71, 86, 120, 179
source text 54, 56, 79, 80, 87, 114, 157, 199, 202
Spanglish 23, 34 (*see also* languages in contact and language mixing)
standard language (26–8, 34, 41, 48, 58, 94, 116, 117, 119, 124
standard language ideology 26, 34, 115, 120, 121, 198, 200, 205, 213
  defined 26
  resistance to 27, 205
standardized tests 48, 61, 174, 175, 177
standards
  ACTFL World Readiness (*see* ACTFL World Readiness Standards)

CCSS (*see* Common Core State Standards)
CEFR (*see* Common European Frame of Reference)
content 183
defined 171–2
framework 172, 177
Native Language Arts 172
stereotypes 117, 123, 134
  illustration 134
  cultural 123, 124
  linguistic 123
Street, B. V. 7, 37, 38, 39, 154
style 40, 41, 43, 79, 119
subtitling 86, 139, 143
  creative 143
  interlingual 144
  intralingual 143–4
  notetaking for 145–6
  reverse 139, 143, 145
  selection for 143
subtractive bilingualism 45
Swain, M. 62
symbolic capital 40, 45, 46, 115, 206
symbolic power 26, 27, 55, 94, 116, 117
synchronous instruction 139, 154
synonyms 56, 83, 137, 183, 195
syntax 84–5
  assessment of 179
  equivalence 57
  pedagogical translation 57, 71, 83, 84, 183, 195
systemic functional linguistics 55

Tardy, C. M. 40, 55
target audience 53, 55, 57, 58, 59, 83, 99, 112, 181
target culture 43, 58, 62, 65, 97, 99, 100, 119, 194, 204
target language 4, 35, 54, 58, 64, 71, 78, 88, 90, 91, 99, 101, 105, 106, 108–9, 110–12, 114, 115, 118, 120, 127, 129, 136, 139, 164, 167, 179, 194, 195, 196, 198, 203
target text 79, 114, 115, 118, 119, 123, 162
task-based language teaching 17, 62
  translation 62, 206

TBLT see *task-based language teaching*
teacher preparation for pedagogical translation 193, 194–7, 200–6, 213
text selection for translation 27, 55, 79, 82, 92, 104, 114, 116–18, 184, 199, 200, 203, 212
   bilingual children's books 115–16
   cultural relevance 118, 121–2, 123, 124
   language ideologies 116, 117
   linguistic relevance 118, 121–2, 123, 124
   power differentials 116, 118, 120
   student and parent involvement in 121
text sets 114, 118, 122–7, 200, 213
   guidelines for selection 123–7, 200
   multimodal (*see* multimodal text sets)
   pedagogical translation 124–6, 212
   reading comprehension 124
texts
   availability of translated 55, 58, 95, 214
   defined 7, 8, 133
   digital 133, 140–1
   hybrid 27, 71, 137, 167
   literary (*see* literary texts)
   multimodal 7, 8, 134, 137
   oral 50, 114, 119, 134, 135
   parallel (*see* parallel texts)
   source (*see* source text)
texts, authentic (*see* authentic texts)
texts, bilingual 90, 112, 113, 115, 117–20, 125, 127, 129, 203
texts, dual edition 59, 113, 115, 117–20, 122, 125, 127, 129
texts, role of 113–15
texts, semi-bilingual 112
They Call Me Güero/Me dicen Güero 117, 122, 125, 130, 199
Toury, G. 52
translanguaging 5, 20, 23, 28, 34, 35, 46, 50, 68, 136, 137
   defined 20, 47
   decolonial perspective 68, 72, 73
   ESL 20
   literacy 50, 69
   multimodality 136
   pluriliteracy 45

plurilingual approach to pedagogical translation 63, 66, 67, 173
social justice 68, 70, 172
socially situated literacy 136
translanguaging and vocabulary instruction 71
translanguaging approach to pedagogical translation 67–74, 70, 71, 212
translanguaging pedagogy 50, 68, 70
   heritage language learning and teaching 71, 102
   professional development 70, 74
translanguaging practice 68, 70
translanguaging space 69, 78, 139, 157
translanguaging stance 20, 70, 154, 205
TRANSLATE protocol 73, 156, 184
translation
   concurrent 8
   definition 6, 10, 29, 52
   directionality of 25, 55
   editor's role 115
   explication 55
   interlingual 9
   intralingual 9, 199–200
   intersemiotic 10
   literary 58
   loss of meaning (*see* meaning, loss of in translation)
   natural 8, 32, 78
   orofessional 8, 10
translation as end 183 (*see also* translation, pedagogical as fifth skill)
translation as literacy 137
translation as means 183
translation as literacy practice 78–87
translation as rewriting 58, 59, 78, 203
translation, collaborative (*see* collaborative translation)
translation, concurrent (*see* concurrent translation)
translation for other learning contexts (TOLC) 9
translation in language teaching (TILT) 9
translation, pedagogical
   barriers to 22–9
   benefits of 30

compared to grammar translation 30
cross-linguistic connections 82
definition 9
end 31, 183 (*see also* fifth skill)
fifth skill 10, 31, 67, 183
functionalism 53, 62
means 32
multilingual turn in SLA 30, 32, 212
multiliteracies 8, 43–4, 202
planning and implementation 194–9, 200–1
plurilingual approach to 65–7, 212
reading comprehension (*see* reading comprehension)
social turn in SLA (*see* social turn)
translanguaging 30, 63
traditional approach to 63, 64–5, 212
translanguaging approach to 67–74
translation quality assessment framework 181
translation, role of 6, 51–2, 95
mediator/mediation 6, 52, 63, 79–80
translation spotlights
described 88–9
designing language and content translation assessments to align with standards and objectives 186–91
dual-language family story writing activity 161–9
guided writing 88, 89–92
sample thematic unit 207–9
translation of an advertisement 110–12
translation of bilingual/dual editions of children's books 127–32
translation of proverbs 106–8
video subtitling 146, 148–9
translation studies 20, 51, 61, 75, 138, 177–8, 202
equivalence (*see* equivalence)
functionalism (*see* functionalism)
language teaching 28, 51, 136, 160, 160–2, 186
translator
negotiation of meaning 52
ideologies 120
invisibility of 58
role of 52, 98, 119, 120

training 71
writer 78
translingual competence 60, 136
translingual pedagogy and pedagogical translation 73, 136
translingual practices 205
TS (*see* translation studies)
Turnbull, B. 3, 4, 20, 171
Tymoczko, M. 43, 58

Valdés, G. 4
variation
cultural 67, 97, 126
language 86, 105, 121, 125, 126, 199
(*see also* dialect)
Venuti, L. 58, 95, 103, 115, 119, 203, 204
Vermeer, H. J. 55, 56
vocabulary knowledge
breadth of 83, 84, 167
depth of 83, 84, 167, 184
vocabulary learning and pedagogical translation 64, 84, 126, 160, 167, 183
Vygotsky, L. 9, 38, 52, 154

Washbourne, K. 78, 83, 84, 87, 88, 103, 104, 105, 115, 123, 153, 160
wa Thiong'o, N. 6, 19, 23, 52, 58, 59, 94, 95, 101, 101
Widdowson, H. G. 3, 16, 19, 20, 24, 25, 28, 197, 199, 212
Woolard, K. A. 15, 23, 27
world language learners 54, 101, 102
cultural perspectives 101
world language learning 3, 70, 201
assessment of 175
world language teaching 70, 104, 198, 206, 211
writing checklist 166, 169, 190, 209
writing, dual language 30, 74, 140, 161, 164, 165, 166, 176, 187, 208–9, 213
writing, guided (*see* guided writing)
writing, narrative (*see* narrative writing, dual language)
writing skills
bilingual teaching strategies 154, 159

pedagogical translation 27, 59, 71, 78–9, 83, 84, 85, 87–88, 89–92, 126, 127, 137, 139, 140, 141, 157, 159, 163–5, 166–69, 175, 176, 178, 185, 188, 190–1

YouTube 139, 144, 168

ZPD (*see* zone of proximal development)
zone of proximal development 154–5